Contents

Preface

Structured finance transactions and environmental, social and governance factors would have been, years ago, the two irreconcilably opposite poles not only of law but also of the social sciences more generally. By contrast, nowadays, the agendas of lawmakers, as well as the commentaries of scholars, seem to converge, inexorably, towards new models and theories where bankers and businesses are required to partly give up their ruthlessness, whereas the "social," summarised in the controversial acronym "ESG," appears to aspire, all of a sudden, to profit.

Although the "cooperative" purpose of enterprise and financial transactions has been part of many communities across the world for centuries, it is remarkable that, now, capitalistic entities are pushed towards this way of carrying out entrepreneurial activity, fundamentally altering common ways of thinking.

Against this background, the work discusses and analyses, from a legal perspective, the evolution of structured finance transactions, or securitisations, particularly from the STS "label" (the simple, transparent and standardised concept) to the more recent legislation of the EU. In the latter statute, due to the pandemic, the ESG factors have started making their unceremonious debut in law, also in connection with securitisations, with financial transactions under the spotlight of this piece of work.

In this ever-changing scenario, where Brexit may play a further complex and unpredictable role, the new horizons of technology, particularly digitalisation, constitute fertile terrain for discussion, particularly in connection with the SPV and its possible characterisation as "drone." Ultimately, from the old Mesopotamian era, where the first forms of financial transactions were "manufactured," to the most recent frontiers of the capital markets, securitisations are still the way finance finds its way to progress and to succeed. ESG factors, in this future, should represent, hopefully, the "new compass" to the benefit of both business and the whole society.

In conclusion, the *fil-rouge* of this research book is the idea that finance, i.e. financial transactions, is strictly tied to human evolution. There is not such a great distance to travel from the plants' securitisations to personal data securitisations via QR codes. The future scenario where securitisations can become successful is the smart city: the city next to come, in which all human activities can become technological and digital. Hence, the real challenge and fight lies in the protection of the human being. As a result, both financial issues and philosophical conundrums tend to blend with each other so that to recognise their original nature becomes an impossible task.

List of Abbreviations

ABCP	Asset-Backed Commercial Paper
ABS	Asset-Backed Securities
ADIs	Authorised Deposit-Taking Institution
AIFM	Alternative Investment Fund Manager
AV	Autonomous Vehicle
BCBS or BCBS-IOSCO	Basel Committee on Banking Supervision
CBC	Cover Bond Company
CDO	Collateralised Debt Obligation
CDS	Credit Default Swap
CMBS	Commercial Mortgage-Backed Securities
CMU	Capital Markets Union
CNS	Continuous Net Settlement
CRR	Capital Requirements Regulation
EBA	European Banking Authority
ECB	European Central Bank
EIOPA	European Insurance and Occupational Pensions Authority
ESA	Exchange Settlement Account
ESG	Environmental, Social and Governance
ESMA	European Securities and Markets Authority
ESRB	European System Risk Board
ESRB	European Systemic Risk Board
EU	European Union
EuGB	European Green Bond
EUWA	the European Union (Withdrawal) Act
FCA	Financial Conduct Authority
FSB	Financial Stability Board
GDPR	General Data Protection Regulation
GTAG	Green Technical Advisor Group
IOSCO	International Organization of Securities Commissions
LO	Legal Opinion
M&A	Mergers and Acquisitions

MiFID	Market in Financial Instruments Directive
NCA	National Crime Agency
OJEU	Official Journal of the European Union
PRA	Prudential Regulation Authority
RMBS	Residential Mortgage-Backed Securities
SECR	Securitisation Regulation (EU) 2017/2402
SFDR	Sustainable Finance Disclosure Regulation
SME	Small and Medium-sized Enterprise
SPV	Special Purpose Vehicle
SSPE	Securitisation Special Purpose Entity
STS	Simple, Transparent and Standardised securitisations
TEU	Treaty on the European Union
TFEU	Treaty on the Functioning of the European Union
TPV	Third-Party Verification
TTP	Temporary Transitional Power
UAV	Unmanned Aerial Vehicle
UCITS	Undertaking Collective Investment in Transferable Securities
UK SR	United Kingdom Securitisation Regulation

1 Introduction

1.1 Securitisations: an overview

Securitisations[1] fall within the realm of structured finance transactions. They constitute a "sea-change" from a traditional bank model hinged upon the collection of savings and the granting of loans to a more complex one. In the latter, on the one hand the credit institution aims at seeking alternative forms of funding, and on the other it reaches out to a more diversified and multifarious range of advisory activities of a financial nature.

1 They have been defined in different ways: "virtually every asset with a payment stream and a long-term payment history is an eventual candidate for securitisation" (L. Sloane, *New Securities Tied to Assets*, New York Times, 20 July 1985, online). Additionally, "securitization, a dirty word these days, must play a greater role. This whole business has a tarnished brand, post-crisis, but efforts are under way to address this" (J. Authers, *Banks Can't Lend if They Can't Find Borrowers*, Financial Times, 23 April 2003, online). Finally, securitisation is referred to as the "modern alchemy of financial engineering" (P. Volcker, *Restoring the Economy: Strategies for Short-term and Long-Term Change, Joint Economic Committee*,Washington DC, 27 February 2009, online). Further definitions are: "securitisation is the process of transforming otherwise illiquid financial assets (such as residential mortgages, auto loans, and credit card receivables), which have typically been the bread and butter of banking institutions, into marketable capital market securities" (F.S. Mishkin, *The Economics of Money, Banking and Financial Markets*, Pearson, Boston, 2007). From a legal perspective, "securitisation is the process by which a range of cash receivables or similar assets are grouped together and offered to investors in the form of a security in return for a capital payment from the investors" (A. Hudson, *The Law of Finance*, Sweet & Maxwell, London, 2013, 1294). The latter expression is a definition that takes up the one offered by a different school of thought: "the carefully structured process whereby loans and other receivables are packaged, underwritten, and sold in the form of securities (instruments commonly known as asset-backed securities)" (A. Rosenthal, J.M. Ocampo, *Securitization of Credit: Inside the New Technology of Finance*, John Wiley, New York, 1988). Finally, even from a legal standpoint, a further definition emphasises the final stage of the securitisation transaction: "securitisation is a technique which can be used by either a company or a lender to transfer the credit risk of receivables (either (in the case of a company) trade receivables or (in the case of a lender) loan receivables or even bonds) and/or to receive immediate finance from rights to payment in the future" (L. Gullifer, J. Payne, *Corporate Finance Law: Principles and Policy*, 2nd ed., Hart Publishing, Oxford, 2015, 467). See also L. Gullifer, J. Payne, *Corporate Finance Law: Principles and Policy*, 3rd ed., Hart Publishing, Oxford, *passim*.

DOI: 10.4324/9780429293436-1

Within this context, securitisation transactions engender the development of a parallel investment market in which both savings and investments are first solicited and, at a later stage, collected via thinly capitalised companies, the vehicles. In the financial and legal jargon, they are commonly defined as "Special Purpose Vehicles," or more frequently with the acronym "SPVs."[2] SPVs operate in an area of finance which is alternative to traditional financial markets: the demarcation line between the two (the innovative finance and the traditional one) is dependent on the circumstance that the issuer of a traditional debt capital market is usually a multiple purpose company rather than a special purpose company with a traditional high capitalisation.[3]

Although research on securitisations has only "blossomed" in the last three decades, and its focus has mainly been the mortgage securitisation market, such transactions are not a new phenomenon. Some primordial, albeit raw, forms of structured financial agreements can be traced back to the Genoese Republic, one of the four Italian Maritime Republics. In the twelfth century, the sale of tax credits by that sovereign State is reminiscent of contemporary securitisation.[4]

Furthermore, the ancestor of the modern concept of mortgage securitisation would be the sale of loans linked with plantations and related crops in the eighteenth century.[5] Thus, it can be affirmed that financial innovation should be interpreted as a process of evolution, growth and improvement. These phenomena coincide with the establishment of the relevant markets.

From a historical point of observation, though, it can be recalled that the first derivatives were negotiated at the time of the Mesopotamian civilisation as a support for the swap of agricultural goods and to assure against the risk of disasters that otherwise would have caused populations to starve. Added to this is the circumstance that the first futures on wheat were the subject of exchange at the Temple. The members of the clergy acted as guarantors for purposes of the successful finalisation of the operation.

2 In this work, reference will be made to either "Special Purpose Vehicles" or SPVs.

3 About the concept of capital and its functions, from a common law perspective, see P.L. Davies, S. Worthington, C. Hare, *Gower: Principles of Modern Company Law*, Thomson Reuters/Sweet & Maxell, London, 2021, 595–596. Although the word "capital" is tainted with a number of meanings, in company law, including in the UK, it "connotes the value of the assets contributed to the company by those who subscribe for its shares" (*ibidem*) and its importance for the creditors dates back to the entrenched *dictum* of *Re Exchange Banking Co (Flitcroft's Case)* (1882) 21 Ch. D. 519 at 533–534. "The creditor, therefore, I may say gives credit to that capital, gives credit to the company on the faith of the representation that the capital shall be applied only for the purposes of the business, and he has therefore a right to say that the corporation shall keep its capital and not return to the shareholders" (Jassel Master of Rolls).

4 This is the credit market during the medieval period; the purchase was based on the expected tax revenues.

5 J. Riley, *International Government Finance and the Amsterdam Capital Market 1740–1815*, Cambridge University Press, Cambridge, 1980. K.G. Rouwenhorst, *The Origins of Mutual Funds*, in W.N. Goetzmann, K. Geert Rouwenhorst, (eds), *Origins of Value*, Yale University Press, Yale, 2005.

Later on, in 1695, a structured, negotiated and secured credit instrument was conceived on the West Indies assets and pegged to plantation revenues, with these plantations consisting of either coffee or sugar. However, such a market was not sustainable because all the risks that were borne were reflected on the return on the investment itself.[6]

In order to find the first successful securitised market of loans, it is necessary to move to Germany and France, a few decades later.[7] The German mortgage-backed bond market was a response to the financial crisis following the Seven Years' War. Known as *Pfandbriefe* or guarantee bonds, these instruments became a pillar of the European market in those years. In the United States, in contrast, three attempts were made, all of which were unsuccessful, to convert loans into negotiable securities, which took place in the 1870s, 1880s and 1920s.[8] The first US securitisation market was, at least initially, privately funded. However, probably due to its unregulated nature, it came to an end in an unceremonious way. It caused serious defaults and this experience may provide an incorrect and misleading reconstruction of the European experience.[9]

Within the modern securitisation literature, three phases of the development of these transactions are usually outlined.[10] At the end of the 1960s, mortgage securitisations were seen and perceived as an effective response to the risk of both early repayment of the loans and variation of their interest rates. In this respect, other scholars[11] refer to securitisations as a delayed response to "monetarism." More specifically, this phenomenon may have started from savings and lending institutions. Since many financial institutions sought additional revenues by turning their attention to fees and commissions, this made the practice of securitisations increasingly popular and widespread.[12]

In the late 1980s, because of the savings and loans crisis, the Resolution Trust Corporation used securitisation transactions in order to undertake this procedure

6 It should be pointed out that there was an important gap between borrowers and investors, making the loans increasingly opaque and subject to fraudulent valuation.

7 K. Wandschneider, *Lending to Lemons: Landschafts Credit in the 18th Century Prussia*, Working Paper No. 19159, National Bureau of Economic Research, Cambridge (MA), 2013; D.M. Frederiksen, 'Mortgage Banking in Germany' (1894) *Quarterly Journal of Economics* 9, 47–76.

8 K.A. Snowden, *Mortgage Securitization in the US; Twentieth Century Developments in Historical Perspective*, in M.D. Bordo, R. Sylla, (eds), *Anglo-American Financial Systems: Institutions and Markets in the Twentieth Century*, Burr Ridge, Irwin, 1995, 261–298.

9 *Ibidem*.

10 M. Zandi, *Financial Shock*, FT Press, Upper Saddle River (NJ), 2009.

11 H.P. Minsky, L.R. Wray, *Securitization*, Economics Policy Note Archive, Levy Economics Institute, February 2008.

12 The US Department of Housing and Urban Development (HUD) promoted securitisation through government-sponsored entities (GSE). During the 1970s, the securitisation market was characterised by public securitisation for loans that were compliant in terms of loan size and the ratio of loan to value. Therefore, it can be affirmed that, until the financial crisis of 2007–2008 occurred, securitisation transactions were a very profitable activity for the GSE. See A. Mian, A. Sufi, 'The Consequences of Mortgage Credit Expansion: Evidence from the US Mortgage Default Crisis' (2009) *Quarterly Journal of Economics* 124, 1449–1496.

as much as possible, from commercial mortgages to automotive loans. In 1992, the SEC acknowledged that securitisation was becoming one of the most dominant means of funding in the US.[13]

Between 2002 and 2004, the market switched to non-regulated securitisations,[14] typically managed by investment banks. In this new securitisation scenario, all global institutions benefited from this. The time was no longer favourable to a business model where banks carried out their activities merely to the benefit of the local securities markets.[15] By contrast, with these transactions, banks began to rely on the possibility of passing on credit risks to both international investors and hedge funds; therefore the coverage was no longer limited to the local context.

The legal central role of securitisations is not played exclusively by the documentation, the *papel*, which is issued by the "vehicle,"[16] and in which the metamorphosis of the receivable (from credit to debt) materialises as a consequence of

13 S. Schwarcz, *Securitization and Structured Finance*, in G. Caprio (ed.), *Handbook of Key Global Financial Markets, Institutions, and Infrastructure*, Elsevier Academic Press, Amsterdam, 2012, Chapter 51.

14 They have been defined as "the new world wealth machine" (J.C. Edmunds, 'Securities: The New World Wealth Machine' (1996) *Foreign Policy*, 118–134). The first research paper dealing with the topic of securitisations dates back to the late 1990s, namely L.M. LoPucki, 'The Death of Liability' (1999) *Yale Law Journal* 106(1) 23–30. Two fundamental pieces of research on securitisation were later published. One of them claimed that securitisation was not able to pursue the objective of isolating the securitised assets from a possible bankruptcy of the originator. See D.G. Carlson, 'The Rotten Foundations of Securitization' (1998) *William & Mary Law Review* 39, 1055 ff. Another school of thought has addressed the different issues of securitisation, whilst starting from the question of whether these transactions can be efficient from an economic point of view. Hence, the ultimate question – to which a negative response was given – is whether they increase the net well-being of all individuals. Further concerns relate to the weaknesses of the theoretical legal framework of securitisations, where it is highlighted how they are likely to be invalidated if the seller of the receivables (the originator) were to be subject to bankruptcy proceedings. See L.R. Lupica, 'Asset Securitization: The Unsecured Creditor's Perspective' (1998) *Texas Law Review* 76, 595 ff.; L.R. Lupica, 'Revised Article 9, The Proposed Bankruptcy Code Amendments and Securitizing Debtors and their Creditors' (2002) *Fordham Journal of Corporate & Finance Law* 7, 321 ff.; L.R. Lupica, 'Circumvention of the Bankruptcy Process: The Statutory Institutionalization of Securitization' (2000) *Connecticut Law Review* 33, 199 ff. Admittedly, even the legal systems with the highest presence of legal concepts inconsistent with securitisations have meanwhile put in place tools which make these transactions, fundamentally, immune from a theoretical invalidity.

15 Via the issuance of bonds placed among the local investors, where the issuing bank operated with its branches.

16 The necessary caveat is that, thanks to the development of technology, the paper at stake is not materially issued, rather it becomes electronically available via a centralised system to which the contemporary circulation of securities is informed.

the assignment.[17] Rather, it is the definitive transfer of credit risk[18] and the ensuing segmentation of securities – either protected or backed by the transferred assets – in different risk classes: in the end, these two features combined allow for the placement of securities in the market at different rates; without this conversion, the placement would not occur successfully.

The transfer, or broadly speaking the sale, from which the securitisation stems describes only a part of the phenomenon, the initial part, in which the originator, as a result of the true character of the sale – the true sale – is protected from the risk of insolvency of the debtors of the assigned claims or the insolvency of the SPV.

The remaining – albeit preponderant from a quantitative point of view – part of the securitisation lies in both the issuance of securities and the fragmentation of investors' risk according to classes, which shall be at least two. Credit segmentation, therefore, seems to be the term that describes securitisations better, since their distinctive and quintessential connotation is the creation of classes of securities. By contrast, the mere sale of the assets, which in itself defines a financing transaction, is not tantamount to an investment transaction.[19]

In the development of the financial markets of the United States and the United Kingdom, securitisation transactions[20] pursue different objectives. They prop up public policy objectives, such as supporting the development of financial

17 Dissenting opinion could be that of other scholars (M. Zaccheo, entry *Cartolarizzazione*, in www.treccani.it). The Author affirms: "The separation of the relations, either formal or non-formal, [...] makes the former autonomous with respect to the latter by virtue of the title, which becomes virtual, and the incorporation of the right in the document. The neologism of securitisation understates precisely this decisive profile, namely the transformation of an intangible asset into a tangible one capable of becoming the subject matter of both ownership and custody" (our translation, albeit not literal, from Italian).

18 "Securitisation was traditionally meant to transfer risks from the banking sector to outside investors and thereby disperse financial risks across the economy. Because the risks were meant to be transferred, securitisations allowed banks to reduce regulatory capital, a practice that eventually contributed to the largest banking crisis since the Great Depression." In this paper, the analysis is focused on one form of securitisation, namely asset-backed commercial paper (ABCP) conduits, as an example of how banks exposed themselves to such risks. See Viral V. Acharya, P. Schnabl, G. Suarez, 'Securitization without Risk Transfer' (2013) *Journal of Financial Economics* 107, 515–516.

19 Again, in relation to the meaning of the securitisation, it has been pointed out that "the term 'securitisation' is thus a misnomer insofar as it suggests that the issuance of securities is the heart of the matter. The debt instruments issued to the financiers in a securitisation transaction might be securities issued into the capital markets, although this is not a necessary requirement: "they might just as well be loan obligations owed to a syndicate of banks, involving no securities at all." See K.C. Kettering, *Securitization and Its Discontents: The Dynamics of Financial Product Development* (2008) *Cardozo Law Review*, 29(4), 1557.

20 See V.L.S. Ranieri, *The Origins of Securitization, Source of its Growth, and its Future Potential*, in, T. Kendall, M.J. Fishman (eds), *A Primer on Securitization*, The MIT Press, Cambridge, 1996, 31 ff.; K. Engel, P. Mccoy, *The Subprime Virus*, Oxford University Press, Oxford, 2010; D.C. Bonsall, *Securitization*, Butterworths, Oxford, 1990.

markets, with particular regard to capital and loan markets.[21] Second, they help comply with regulatory requirements for financial institutions, in particular as regards capital adequacy and lending limits applicable to banks.[22] Finally, they carry out risk transfer transactions in the context of impaired assets and portfolio diversification.[23]

The usefulness and practical help provided by these financial transactions has led both operators and relevant legal systems around the world to seek the development of similar practices and contractual/legislative frameworks in their own financial markets. The most successful examples have taken place within the European Union, whose regulation, alongside that of the UK, constitutes the focus of this work.

This trend, however, shall be contextualised within a broader reflection: asset securitisation is a structured finance transaction which takes place in a complex capital market. Moreover, it is based on a complexity of financial – but also legal – features, "sewn" via a thin, yet powerful, thread of legal elements.

It follows from this that traditional asset securitisation structures cannot be nonchalantly transferred to different financial markets, especially emerging countries whose economies may be too different. Additionally, the transplant of securitisations may be problematic in financial markets whose legal system is based on a civil law tradition. In these cases, although the financial transactions at stake need to cater to the same functions for which they were initially designed in the financial markets and legal systems of origin, the US and the UK, the different legal systems and heterogeneous principles of the law of the markets where they are expected to be translated may be quite different and inconsistent.[24]

It is well-known that the consolidated pillars of legal systems based on a civil law tradition may drive a coach and horses through some "obsessions" of the traditional legal systems of the "Old Continent." However, although it is true that some theories such as the "essential reason" of the contract may be a "scarecrow,"[25] in reality a more evolutionary approach from scholars may help achieve more reassuring outcomes. In borrowing this method of interpretation,

21 D. Barbour, J. Norton, T. Slover, 'Asset Securitization in Emerging Market Economies: Fundamental Considerations' (1998) *London Institute of International Banking, Fin. & Dev. L., Essays in International Financial & Economic Law* 13, 8–11.

22 According to the Basel Committee on Banking Supervision, banks that securitise assets are able to accomplish several objectives: "1) reduce regulatory capital requirements; 2) obtain an additional source of funding, generally at lower cost; 3) enhance financial ratios; [...] 4) manage portfolio risk; and 5) diversify their portfolios" (Basel Committee on Banking Supervision, Standards. Minimum Capital Requirements for Market Risk, January 2019, online).

23 D. Barbour, J. Norton, T. Slover, 'Asset Securitization in Emerging Market Economies' (n. 21), *passim*.

24 A. Douglas, 'Emerging Market Economics and Government Promotion of Securitization' (2002) *Duke Journal of Comparative & International Law* 12(2), 505 ff.

25 This theory is also known as the "*causa del contratto*," the essential element of the contract, for instance in Italy.

hinged upon the economic theory of the essential reason of the contract,[26] one may look at the essential reason of the contract as the essential reason for the whole combination of transactions rather than each transaction. Ultimately, the broad picture of securitisations, with the different contracts which make it up (namely, the sale of receivables; the servicing agreements; the issuance of bonds), would corroborate the view that this is a lawful transaction, worthy of being acknowledged by the relevant legal system where it is deployed, because it is aimed at achieving interests worthy of being recognised: the need of banks, quintessential players of contemporary society, for liquidity, coupled with the investors' need for access to global markets.

1.2 Regulatory developments

An operational conundrum that both banks and financial intermediaries need to deal with is that, fundamentally, they are exposed to the risk of regulatory constraints.[27] Starting from this premise, regulatory limits have been introduced to safeguard not only public savings but also the stability of the financial system, both nationally and internationally.

In this respect, a brief digression is necessary.

It is well-known that the Basel Committee on Banking Supervision was founded at the end of 1974 by the governors of the central banks of the G10 countries on the initiative of the ministers of finance and the central banks of their countries, with a leading role played particularly by the Bank of England.[28] The main aim of Basel I (1988) was to improve banking supervision by establishing a system for both minimum capital requirements and the measurement of credit risks.[29] The agreements that were signed within that context (usually referred to as the Basel Accords, also including the further two versions) were the starting point from which credit transfer instruments began developing.[30] Therefore, it was not before the banking crises of the late 1980s that minimum capital requirements for both banks' balance sheets and the provision of increased capital protection for risky

26 The theory, developed in Spanish and Italian, is conceived by Professor Enrico Gabrielli, in some of his works. See E. Gabrielli, *Operazione economica*, in G. D'Amico (ed), *Enciclopedia del diritto. I. Contratto*, Giuffré Frances Lefebvre, Milano, 2021; E. Gabrielli, *El contrato. Del tipo contractual a la operacion economica*, Ediciones Olejnik, Santiago de Chile, 2020.

27 It is undeniable too that regulation increases the costs for financial players.

28 M. Andenas, I.H.Y. Chiu, *The Foundations of and Future of Financial Regulation: Governance for Responsibility*, Routledge, London and New York, 2013.

29 G. Hertig, 'Basel II and Fostering the Disclosure of Banks' Internal Credit Ratings' (2006) *European Business Organization Law Review* 7, 625–646.

30 Z. Pozsar, 'The Rise and Fall of the Shadow Banking System' (2008) *Regional Financial Review*, 13–82.

activities were applied. Again, this new scenario unfolded, bearing in mind the – then – novelty of Basel I.[31]

Before Basel I, the regulation of the equity of financial intermediaries only consisted of minimum levels of capital required for banks, although no attention was fundamentally paid to the risk profile, accordingly ignoring their off-balance-sheet positions.

In summary, the Basel Accords, in their first version, Basel I, are based on four principles. First, banks must have a procedure in place to assess the adequacy of their assets to the risk profile and a strategy for maintaining the level of capital. Second, Supervisory Authorities must examine and assess the internal mechanisms to evaluate the level of bank assets and the strategy of banks in this regard and ensure compliance with capital ratios. Third, banks may retain their assets in a proportion above the regulatory ratio and must be able to demonstrate that they hold more than the minimum amount of assets. The Authorities must endeavour to intervene quickly in the event that the assets of the banks do not comply with the regulatory coefficient.

Since 1987, the Basel Committee has proposed the adoption of a system for establishing a minimum level of capital, this being based on credit exposure. The ultimate purpose is twofold: strengthening the solvency and soundness of the banking system and decreasing the regulatory arbitrage between banks.[32] In other words, the ultimate objective which was pursued as a result of this further initiative was to avoid the risk[33] of a banking crisis without, at the same time, undermining the conditions of international competition by consequently ensuring the maintenance of a relationship of trust in banking.[34]

The system, as outlined above, was transposed by the various Authorities of the Member States with the Capital Agreement of 1988, which, in turn, contained

31 B. Colmant, C. Samson, *2008 L'année du Krach*, De Boeck & Larcier, Bruxelles, 2009.

32 M. Ianno, 'New Horizons for the Italian Securitisation Market further to the Newly Implemented Legislation' (2019) *Journal of International Banking Law and Regulation* 34(8), 287–294; J. Wagner, C. Sullivan, 'NPE Servicers Prepare to Retain Risk under EU Securitisation Regulation' (2022) *Butterworths Journal of International Banking & Financial Law* 37(1), 50; D.K. Roussis, 'The Autonomous Application of the Securitisation Law within the Sale of the NPEs Loans in Greece' (2018) *Journal of International Banking Law and Regulation* 33(11), 429–433; M. Huertas, 'Tackling Non-Performance: Does the Banking Union Need a Pillar IV in the Form of a Single Asset Management Company – Could COVID-19 Now Be the Catalyst for Change?' (2020) *Journal of International Banking Law and Regulation* 35(11), 433–443; M. Huertas, 'Tackling Non-Performance: Does the Banking Union need a Pillar IV in the Form of a Single Asset Management Company for the Management of Illiquid, Non-Performing Assets and Exposures?' (2017) *Journal of International Banking Law and Regulation* 32(3), 113–120; A. Miglionico, 'Asset Quality of Banks: The Resolution Regimes of Non-Performing Loans' (2020) *Journal of International Banking Law and Regulation* 35(1), 23–28.

33 It is recalled that credit risk is one of the most significant *bête noire* that banks can be exposed to, even if the current development of the market for derivative financial instruments offers credit institutions a whole series of new possibilities to face this peril.

34 F. Masera, G. Mazzoni, *Basilea III: Il nuovo sistema di regole bancarie dopo la grande crisi*, Franco Angeli, Milan, 2012, 17.

two conditions. The first was concerned with the minimum capital ratio: namely, banks were required to maintain a minimum capital *ratio* in relation to risk-weighted assets of 8%.[35] Furthermore, the second is related to the application of capital requirements, specifically connected with market risk. The latter is construed as "the risk that a bank suffers a loss of positions on or off the balance sheet as a result of unfavourable changes in market factors."[36]

Basel II is the second of the Basel Accords, partly extended but also partially overturned by Basel III. Initially published in June 2004, it aimed at changing the international banking standards pertaining to the control of the quality of the capital that banks are required to hold in order to protect themselves against both financial and operational risks. Ultimately, the aim of Basel II was to improve banking supervision by incorporating some changes in risk management practices, allowing banks to make greater use of their internal models in order to assess the required assets on which the credit risk is usually calculated.[37]

Specifically, the objectives of Basel II were to: a) ensure that the capital absorption of banks was more risk-sensitive; b) introduce capital requirements for operational risk; c) improve the level of convergence between economic and supervisory capital; d) encourage banks to use internal risk calculation systems.

The entities which the agreement is addressed to are credit institutions with international operations since it is required that all banking and financing activities carried out within a group should be included in the scope of consolidation, so long as that bank belongs to that group.

35 Bank for International Settlements. As far as the international literature relating to the BRI is concerned, see N. Courtis, 'Behind the Scenes in Basel' (2002) *Central Banking* 13(1), 114–117; A. Cornford, 'BIS Banking Statistics Amid the Financial Turmoil' (2008/2009) *Financial Regulation International*, Dec/Jan, 12–14; P. Yeoh, 'Basel IV: International Bank Capital Regulation Solution or the Beginnings of a Solution?' (2018) *Business Law Review* 39(5), 176–183; L. Zhang, 'Comparative Law and the Enhancement of Financial Regulation' (2020) *Business Law Review* 41(4), 139–145; C. Borio, 'The Great Financial Crisis: Setting Priorities for New Statistics' (2013) *Journal of Banking Regulation* 14(3/4), 306–317; R. Ivory, T. Soreide, 'The International Endorsement of Corporate Settlements in Foreign Bribery Cases' (2020) *International & Comparative Law Quarterly* 69(4), 945–978; R. Sappideen, 'Cross-border Electronic Funds Transfers through Large Value Transfer Systems, and the Persistence of Risk' (2003) *Journal of Business Law*, Nov, 584–602; G. Heinrich, 'International Initiatives Regarding the Harmonisation of Rules Having an Effect on Payment, Funds Transfers and Bankruptcy' (1991) *International Business Law Journal* 2, 315–327; M.S. Barr, G.P. Miller, 'Global Administrative Law: The View from Basel' (2006) *European Journal of International Law* 17(1), 15–46; G.G. Kounadis, 'Striking the Correct Balance between Imposing a Suspension of Close-out Netting Rights while Preserving Legal Certainty and Market Integrity in View of the Bank Recovery and Resolution Directive 2014/59/EU: Part A' (2015) *Journal of International Banking Law and Regulation* 30(4), 228–235; C.M. Friesen, 'Bank Corporate Governance, Compliance and Reputation Risk: A Pro-Active Approach for International Banks with Cross-Border Operations' (2006) *Journal of International Banking Law and Regulation* 21(5), 238–242.

36 F. Masera, G. Mazzoni, *Basilea III: Il nuovo sistema di regole bancarie dopo la grande crisi* (n. 34), 28.

37 G. Hertig, 'Basel II and Fostering the Disclosure of Banks' Internal Credit Ratings' (n. 29), *ibidem*.

Basel II is based on three pillars: minimum capital requirements; supervisory review; market discipline. With regard to the first pillar, the Basel Committee envisages the introduction of more sophisticated rules for the estimation of credit risk for banking books based on the use of credit ratings and the introduction of a minimum capital requirement for operational risks.

Specifically, banks are provided with two options in order to measure their credit risk, the choice being between the standard method or the internal ratings-based approach, which in turn can be either basic or advanced.[38]

The second pillar introduces the prudential control process whereby banks can determine their capital needs and cover the risks undertaken by planning any necessary action to maintain a level of adequate capitalisation. Using this process, the Supervisory Authorities are in a position to verify the adequacy of the process itself, by implementing prudential and timely interventions if required.[39]

Finally, the third pillar is focused on information sharing: the starting point is that credit markets are characterised by incomplete information. From this, the Committee proposed a set of disclosure requirements to enable market participants to be properly informed about the risks to which a bank is exposed and the capital adequacy that it can claim against those risks. They plan to publish information tables relating to many aspects such as the accounting policies adopted, corporate governance and economic performance.

The economic and financial crisis that occurred in 2007–2008 signalled the existence of gaps in standards on key issues.[40] Firstly, the quantity and quality of

38 The main difference between the two methods relates to the different way of calculating input parameters for the determination of credit risk.

39 These processes will be referred to as the Internal Capital Adequacy Assessment Process and Supervisory Review and Evaluation Process.

40 C. Fernandes, J. Farinha, F. Vitorino, M.C. Mateus, 'Determinants of European Banks' Bailouts Following the 2007–2008 Financial Crisis' (2016) *Journal of International Economic Law* 19(3), 707–747; A. Nolan, 'Not Fit for Purpose? Human Rights in Times of Financial and Economic Crisis' (2015) *European Human Rights Law Review* 4, 360–371; I. MacNeil, 'The Trajectory of Regulatory Reform in the UK in the Wake of the Financial Crisis' (2010) *European Business Organization Law Review* 11(4), 483–526; J. Zhao, 'Promoting More Socially Responsible Corporations through UK Company Law after the 2008 Financial Crisis: The Turning of the Crisis Compass' (2011) *International Company and Commercial Law Review* 22(9), 275–284; A. Suetin, 'Post-Crisis Developments in International Financial Markets' (2011) *International Journal of Law and Management* 53(1), 51–61; O. Akseli, 'Securitisation, the Financial Crisis and the Need for Effective Risk Retention' (2013) *European Business Organization Law Review* 14(1), 1–27; N. Moleney, 'The European Securities and Markets Authority and Institutional Design for the EU Financial Market – A Tale of Two Competences: Part 1: Rule-Making' (2011) *European Business Organization Law Review* 12(1), 41–86; A. Segura-Serrano, 'International Economic Law at a Crossroads: Global Governance and Normative Coherence' (2014) *Leiden Journal of International Law* 27(3), 677–700; H. Marjosola, 'Regulating Financial Markets under Uncertainty: The EU Approach' (2014) *European Law Review* 39(3), 338–361; J. Tortuero Ortiz, T.J. Acosta Alvarez, 'Corporate Governance in Financial Institutions: Recent Developments in the European Union' (2011) *Journal of International Banking Law and Regulation* 26(8), 398–404; E. Ferran, 'After the Crisis: The Regulation of Hedge Funds and Private Equity in the EU' (2011) *European Business Organization Law Review* 12(3), 379–414; S. Wen, 'The Magnitude of Share-

capital requirements proved to be insufficient: during the crisis, it became clear that some liabilities included in the regulatory definition of capital, such as hybrid instruments, were able to absorb the losses only in the event of a full-blown disaster and could give rise to contagion phenomena. The second shortcoming was concerned with the imbalance in the prudential treatment of credit and financial risks.

Starting from the experience of the economic and financial crisis, the Committee published the first Basel III draft, the essential elements of which relate to some fundamental aspects: a) more capital with the provision of additional buffers which are themselves diversified in relation to the systemic relevance of the bank, and in such a way that macro-prudential risks can be addressed; b) better quality capital, i.e. financial instruments capable of effectively absorbing unexpected losses in the absence of default; c) new requirements for previously overlooked risks, such as credit valuation adjustment; 4) liquidity requirements; 5) limits on leverage. The Basel III recommendations were published in December 2010, revised in 2011, and they have been in their full-blown form since 1 January 2022.

Turning our attention to the Securitisation Regulation, it is necessary to make reference to certain subordinate pieces of legislation. Specifically, on 3 September 2020, two technical standards on disclosure requirements under the Securitisation Regulation were published in the *Official Journal of the European Union*:

holder Value as the Overriding Objective in the UK: The Post-Crisis Perspective' (2011) *Journal of International Banking Law and Regulation* 26(7), 325–337; K. Alexander, 'Principles v. Rules in Financial Regulation: Re-Assessing the Balance in the Credit Crisis: Symposium at Cambridge University, 10–11 April 2008' (2009) *European Business Organization Law Review* 10(2), 169–173; M. Aloui, A. Jarboui, 'The Effects of Corporate Governance on the Stock Return Volatility: During the Financial Crisis' (2018) *International Journal of Law and Management* 60(2), 478–495; N. Alam, 'Does Banking Regulation Affect Banking Efficiency? A Survey of Dual Banking Systems' (2012) *Journal of International Banking Law and Regulation* 27(6), 231–238; N. Alam, K.S. Ngo, 'Regulatory Compliance and Cost of Banking Operation: A Survey of US Banking Sector' (2014) *Journal of International Banking Law and Regulation* 29(11), 657–664; A. Weitbrecht, 'A Well-Watered Plateau: EU Merger Control 2011–2013' (2014) *European Competition Law Review* 35(6), 282–291; M. Salib, 'The Bank of England's Statutory Immunity from Damage: Its Logic and Limits' (2018) *Journal of Business Law* 7, 606–632; D. Gibbs, 'Ex Ante Governance Controls on Non-Executive Director Self-Interest: Empirical Evidence on Multiple Directorships 2006–2010 in the UK' (2016) *International Company and Commercial Law Review* 27(9), 287–298; E.Z. Geva, 'Convergence and Persistence in Corporate Insolvency Law: Employee Participation in Corporate Insolvency Restructuring' (2011) *European Business Organization Law Review* 12(2), 315–352; E. Wymeersch, 'The Structure of Financial Supervision in Europe: About Single Financial Supervisors, Twin Peaks and Multiple Financial Supervisors' (2007) *European Business Organization Law Review* 8(2), 237–306; L-J. White, 'Credit-Rating Agencies and the Financial Crisis: Less Regulation of CRAs is a Better Response' (2010) *Journal of International Banking Law and Regulation* 25(4), 170–179; T. Buck, 'External Provider Social Loans: Joining up Financial Inclusion and Social Fund Reform' (2010) *Journal of Social Security Law* 17(1), 39–57; E. Cabrol, W. Ben Hamida, F. Horchani, Y. Elkabas, A. Bettaieb, R. Ben Khalifa, 'International Investments – Law and Practice' (2009) *International Business Law Journal* 2, 239–254.

- Commission delegated regulation supplementing Regulation (EU) 2017/2402 with regard to regulatory technical standards specifying the information and the details of a securitisation to be made available by the originator, sponsor and SSPE (hereinafter: the disclosure RTS)[41]; and
- Commission implementing regulation laying down implementing technical standards with regard to the format and standardised templates for making available the information and details of a securitisation by the originator, sponsor and SSPE (hereinafter: the disclosure ITS).[42]

These technical standards entered into force on 23 September 2020. As of that date, the transitional provision allowing for the use of the so-called "CRA 3" reporting templates ceased to apply (see Article 43(8) of the Securitisation Regulation). The disclosure technical standards include 15 reporting templates.

However, the most significant regulatory development of the Securitisation Regulation is given by Regulation 2021/558, a piece of legislation which better clarifies and adapts the STS criteria to the new COVID scenario,[43] while aiming at introducing a new parallel, rather than alternative, market of sustainable securitisations.[44]

1.3 The osmosis among securitisations, *shadow* banking and technology

Shadow banking, as a term, was conceived in 2008 to identify a peculiar *modus operandi* that financial intermediaries had been adopting for a while.[45] In this new scenario, the investor, in subscribing securities, in turn issued by a vehicle, does not enjoy, in the event of insolvency, the form of protection traditionally provided to the depositor, the latter being the traditional counterparty of a bank.

41 Commission Delegated Regulation (EU) 2020/1224 of 16 October 2019 supplementing Regulation (EU) 2017/2402 of the European Parliament and of the Council with regard to regulatory technical standards specifying the information and the details of a securitisation to be made available by the originator, sponsor and SSPE.

42 Commission Implementing Regulation (EU) 2020/1225 of 29 October 2019 laying down implementing technical standards with regard to the format and standardised templates for making available the information and details of a securitisation by the originator, sponsor and SSPE.

43 This is discussed in more detail in Chapter 3 below.

44 The details of this prospective market are introduced in Chapter 2 below.

45 See E. Rogge, *Economic Regulation: Regulating Multinational Banks*, in P.T. Muchlinski (ed), *Multinational Enterprises and the Law*, 3rd ed., Oxford University Press, Oxford, 2021, 386. It is highlighted as follows: "Banks are not the only finance providers; there is also market-based financing. Often called 'shadow banking,' this term has a more negative connotation referring to credit intermediation outside the regular banking sector. However, it helps support the real economy and provides competition for the banking sector. A non-exhaustive list of shadow banking examples includes: money market funds (MMFs), which have deposit-like characteristics of maturity transformation; repurchase agreements (repos) and securities lending, which are forms of secured financing; securitisation vehicles, for example, asset-backed securities; or hedge funds using leverage to finance their positions" (*ibidem*).

More specifically, in shadow banking, the activity is carried out by specific specialised institutions, the conduits, whose task is to carry out functions of transformation of both the credits and the relevant expiry. This transformation materialises through the issuance of securities, albeit without granting, again, the traditional depositor's protection, the public safety net.[46]

Internationally, scholars have questioned the exact definition of banking activity in a new era of shadow banking.[47] The legal ground of this analysis shall be necessarily connected with the traditional area of the banking business and the need to define it. The perimeter of the latter, under the aegis of credit intermediaries carrying out a reserved activity, is hinged upon the collection of savings from depositors and other creditors (such as bondholders) on the one hand and the simultaneous lending of long-term loans to borrowers on the other. This lending is accompanied by the ability to provide liquidity to customers through payment facilitation. However, a problem arises in connection with the practice of taking out short-term deposits and providing long-term financing: this activity can potentially become risky in circumstances where banks fail to manage their risk in a practical and effective way.[48] By contrast, within the realm of shadow banking, this mismatching is neutralised or, at least, its risk is minimised, since the assets transferred to the SPV and the bonds issued by the latter tend to coincide with each other, as far as their maturity is concerned.

Another element that helps to draw a demarcation line between shadow banking and traditional banking[49] is that the latter receives direct support from the public sector while the former does not appear to be subjected to the copious prudential rules to which public banks are subjected.[50] Should a credit institution fail, depositors, or at least a large majority of them, will be protected via a specific depositors' protection scheme, which is mandatory in major jurisdictions. By contrast, shadow banking activities turn out to be only indirectly or implicitly

46 As a result, the transaction described above does not provide investors with a guarantee of repayment in relation to their own investments, which is the typical protection afforded to depositors.

47 "While the transferring of credit risk off banks' balance sheets is not a new phenomenon, the recent wave of securitisation differs from previous ones for the widespread use of sophisticated techniques, facilitating banks to transfer credit risk of more opaque assets to other market participants [...] information associated with structured securities are much more opaque than traditional securities." G. Guo, H-M. Wu, 'A Study on Risk Retention Regulation in Asset Securitization Process' (2014) *Journal of Banking & Finance* 45, 61.

48 K. Alexander, *Principles of Banking Regulation*, Cambridge University Press, Cambridge, 2019, 295.

49 It has been carefully observed that unregulated shadow banks fund themselves through uninsured forms of funding which, in turn, may – or may not – be protected by liquidity facilities from real banks. P.A. McCulley, *The Shadow Banking System and Hyman Minsky's Economy Journey*, PIMCO, Global Central Bank Focus, 2009.

50 E. Avgouleas, *Regulation Financial Innovation*, in N. Moloney, E. Ferran, J. Payne (eds), *The Oxford Handbook of Financial Regulation*, Oxford University Press, Oxford, 2015, 666 ff.; V. Lemma, *The Shadow Banking System*, Palgrave Macmillan, London, 2016.

supported.[51] As regards securitisation activities, the credit institutions from which they originate are allocated off their relevant balance sheet.[52]

Ultimately, it is possible to affirm that securitisations constitute the result of a process of globalisation of finance, where the bank is vested with a new role.[53] Before the 1970s, banks kept loans on their books and, in order to grow, they needed to go through either mergers and/or a deposit (and credit) boost.

Securitisation transactions have stepped up to the plate, in this field, in a way that the paradigm hinted above has completely changed.[54] The new economic structure, therefore, results in being "blessed" by two fundamental features: it speeds up the lending activity; i.e. it increases the pace at which both banking fees and income are generated.

Securitisation has been a popular method of financing for a while,[55] not only in the mortgage market but also within the consumer credit market.[56] At the same time, securitisations have been lauded as one of the greatest financial innovations of the last century,[57] but also, on the negative side, an example of a credit boom that typically precedes a financial crisis.[58]

51 J. Gallin, *Shadow Banking and the Founding of the Nonfinancial Sector*, Federal Reserve Board, Washington DC, Finance and Economy Discussion Series, Divisions of Research & Statistics and Monetary Affairs, 2013.

52 X. Kong, 'Is It the Right Time for Chinese Banking to Run a Mixed Business?' (2004) *Journal of International Banking Law and Regulation*, 348–355.

53 In this regard, there are those who have argued that this is, *de facto*, the demise of the bank in favour of managed money. H. Minsky, L.R. Wray, *Securitization: Levy Economics Institute of Bard College*, Policy Note, 2008, no. 2.

54 G.H. Sellon, D. Van Nahmen, 'The Securitization of Housing Finance' (1988) *Economic Review* (July/August), 3–20. There is no doubt that securitisations have altered the role of transformation of the liquidity of bank loans. Historically, the common bank financing model was known as the "originate-to-hold" model. More specifically, banks usually kept loans on their books and had to grow through mergers and deposit activities. In this system, credit, income and guarantees were the criteria that were mainly used for credit activity. With the advent of securitisation operations, the model described above has become "originate-to-distribute". D.W. Diamond, 'Financial Intermediation and Delegated Monitoring' (1984) *Review of Economic Studies* 51, 393–414.

55 B.G. Buchanan, 'The Way We Live Now: Financialization and Securitization' (2017) *Research and International Business and Finance* 39, 663–677.

56 Before the financial crisis of 2007–2008, two-thirds of US real estate loans were securitised, and between 30% and 70% of consumer loans were securitised. In 2007, more than half of the loans and credit cards were securitised in the US. See: T. Arnold, B. Buchanan, J.F. Robertson, 'The Economics of Sallie Mae' (2012) *Journal of Structured Finance* 18, 65–76. M. Aalbers, 'The Sociology and Geography of Mortgage Markets: Reflections of the Financial Crisis' (2019) *International Journal of Urban and Regional Res*earch 33, 281–290; M. Aalbers, 'The Globalization and Europeanization of Mortgage Markets' (2009) *International Journal of Urban and Regional Research* 33, 389–410.

57 G. Gorton, A. Metrik, *Securitization*, *NBER Working Paper*, No. 18611, 2012; J. McConnell, S. Buser, 'The Origins and Evolution of the Market for Mortgage Backed Securities' (2011) *Annual Review Financial Economics* 3, 173–192.

58 T. Donaldson, 'Three Ethical Roots of the Economic Crisis' (2012) *Journal Business Ethics* 106, 5–8; K. Eggert, 'The Great Collapse: How Securitization Caused the Subprime Meltdown,' (2009) *Connecticut Law Review* 41, 1257–1312.

In the run-up to the financial crisis, securitisation had already embodied the phenomenon of the "financialisation" of the mortgage market, the outcome of which was an unsustainable increase in lending activity. Since the financial crisis of 2007–2008, many sections of the securitisation market, such as loans, mortgages, and covered debt obligations, have been decimated.

The decentralisation of the activity of issuing securities – *ergo* the shift from the bank that shapes them to the vehicle – brings benefits to the investor. Firstly, this decentralisation can increase consumer welfare by expanding the variety of funds and financial products that are made available to individual investors.[59] Secondly, decentralisation can be useful to strengthen the financial system. It may be stronger against negative market shocks by distributing losses between different and smaller financial institutions, thus reducing the risk of "too-big-to-fail."[60]

For the sake of completeness, it is also necessary to point out that there are also disadvantages to this parallel financial market: scholars have affirmed that market failures are more likely to occur in shadow banking than in a traditional banking system.[61] The crucial point concerns the fact that decentralisation has consequences including market fragmentation as well as interconnectivity and opacity. Therefore, it is not unproblematic for the participants themselves to process the information producing a progressive accumulation of risk.[62]

Another critical aspect has to do with the market failures originating from shadow banking. Such failures can be classified and divided into information failures, rationality failures, principal-agent failures and incentive failures. As for the first, the fact the shadow banking system is a very complex phenomenon can affect disclosure,[63] which represents an information failure.[64] In relation

59 K. Alexander, *Principles of Banking Regulation* (n. 44), 302.

60 *Ibidem.*

61 *Ibidem.*

62 *Ibidem.* For the sake of completeness, see 'Securitisation (Editorial): The Financial Crisis and the Need for Effective Risk Retention' (2015) *European Business Organization Law Review* 1–27; C.C. Ajibo, 'Shadow Banking, MMF runs a Risk Regulation, and a Case for Regulatory Harmonisation' (2015) *International Company and Commercial Law Review*, 395–404.

63 It has been pointed out that even a possible protection of creditors passing through mandatory disclosure does not appear to be risk-free, given that empirical experience, unlike economic and legal experience, demonstrates the many limitations of the concept, as well as the issues related to its effectiveness. It is possible to articulate the reasoning on four levels. First, the major investors who negotiate financial clauses and thereby ensure the solvency of the company act as *de facto* trustees of small creditors thus limiting the need for additional disclosure. Second, the communication of small enterprises suffers from limitations on the expectation of solvency and reliability. Third, the current mandatory corporate disclosure regime does not sufficiently require soft disclosure about the company's prospective solvency. Finally, it seems necessary to reform the comprehensibility, timeliness and activation of the communication in order to protect the creditors of the company effectively. See H. Merkt, 'Creditor Protection through Mandatory Disclosure' (2006) *European Business Organization Law Review*, 95–122.

64 A solution to this problem could be simplification or standardisation, even though it may create a paradoxical effect. In other words, the standardisation of derivatives transactions could indirectly increase systemic risk by concentrating exposure on derivatives. P. de Gioia Carabellese, *Car-*

to rationality failures, it is well-known that human beings do not always make rational choices and this would explain why, despite the complexity of the shadow banking phenomenon, market participants can act without a proper and complete understanding of it. These hypotheses of rationality failure can include investment choices based on models that are not understandable because they are too technical. Hence, investors should refrain from investing in situations of partial or total lack of understanding of the financial transaction they are about to undertake.

A principal-agent failure relates to conflicts of interest that may arise between managers and owners of banks and investment firms: managers are in fact risk takers, since they are paid according to short-term compensation mechanisms which are in turn based on variable compensations: hence the interest and incentive to conclude high-risk contracts.[65] The last element concerns incentive failures: this is

tolarizzazioni semplici, trasparenti e standardizzate. Dallo shadow banking al techno banking, Cacucci, Bari, 2020, 34.

65 D. Arsalidou, 'The Regulation of Executive Pay and Economic Theory' (2011) *Journal of Business Law* 5, 431–456; S. Letza, J. Kirkbride, X. Sun, C. Smallman, 'Corporate Governance Theorising: Limits, Critics and Alternatives' (2008) *International Journal of Law and Management* 50(1), 17–32; A. Keay, 'Stewardship Theory: Is Board Accountability Necessary?' (2017) *International Journal of Law and Management* 59(6), 1292–1314; I. Omotayo Bolodeoku, 'Economic Theories of the Corporation and Corporate Governance: A Critique' (2002) *Journal of Business Law*, Jul, 411–438; J.E.O. Abugu, 'Directors' Duties and the Frontiers of Corporate Governance' (2011) *International Company and Commercial Law Review* 22(10), 322–340; I.H-Y. Chiu, D. Katelouzou, 'Making a Case for Regulating Institutional Shareholders' Corporate Governance Roles' (2018) *Journal of Business Law* 1, 67–99; A. Kokkinis, 'Rethinking Banking Prudential Regulation: Why Corporate Governance Rules Matter' (2012) *Journal of Business Law* 7, 611–628; A. Pacy Sifuna, 'Disclose or Abstain: The Prohibition of Insider Trading on Trial' (2012) *Journal of International Banking Law and Regulation* 27(9), 340–352; M. Yan, 'Agency Theory Re-Examined: An Agency Relationship and Residual Claimant Perspective' (2015) *International Company and Commercial Law Review* 26(4), 139–144; M. Domina, 'The Role of Corporate Governance in the Protection of the Alternative Investment Fund's Investors' (2021) *Journal of International Banking Law and Regulation* 36(5), 220–223; J. Green, L. Johnston, B. Williams, 'Corporate Governance in Financial Institutions' (2017) *Compliance Officer Bulletin* 146(May), 1–30; I. Ofoeda, 'Corporate Governance and Non-Bank Financial Institutions Profitability' (2017) *International Journal of Law and Management* 59(6), 854–875; A. Griffiths, 'The Economic Implications of Validating Unauthorised Contracts Made by Corporate Agents' (2003) *European Business Organization Law Review* 4(1), 51–81; D. Chekroun, Q. Moreau, Pa. Hubert-Petit, 'Relations between Shareholders and Issuers of Securities: From Cooperation to Distrust' (2018) *International Business Law Journal* 4, 327–345; S. Sheikh, 'Introduction to the Corporate Governance Themed Issue' (1998) *International Company and Commercial Law Review* 9(10), 267–274; J. Holland, 'Self -Regulation and the Financial Aspects of Corporate Governance' (1996) *Journal of Business Law*, Mar, 127–164; J. Green, L. Johnston, B. Williams, 'Corporate Governance in Financial Institutions' (2020) *Compliance Officer Bulletin* 180(Oct), 1–42; M.M. Blair, L.A. Stout, 'Specific Investment and Corporate Law' (2006) *European Business Organization Law Review* 7(2), 473–500; E. Mujih, 'Corporate Governance Reform and Corporate Failure in the UK' (2021) *Company Lawyer* 42(4), 109–119; A. Schiavone, 'Debt as a Device for Corporate Control – The Case of Countries in Transition' (2001) *Journal of International Banking Law* 16(2), 48–56; A. Young, 'Frameworks in Regulating Company Directors: Rethinking the Philosophical Foundations to Enhance Accountability' (2009) *Company Lawyer* 30(12), 355–361; C. Nyombi, T. Mortimer, R. Lewis, G. Zouridakis, 'Shareholder Primacy and Stakeholders' Interests in the Aftermath

a problem that arises when, given the technological developments, investors can diversify the exposure to the risk of their portfolio.[66] This is based on an erroneous perception, i.e. *ex ante* minimisation of the risk, and therefore the lack of *ex post* supervision of the same, thus giving rise to a mechanism that can lead to the pulverisation of the investment value.

Overall, the definition of the relationship between securitisation and shadow banking appears to be tautological, since shadow banking is a less regulated banking activity than banking, which, in turn, is strictly regulated by definition. In addition, the lack of regulation at the origin of the shadow banking phenomenon has encouraged its development and growth.[67]

1.4 Securitisations and capital markets

Following the adoption of Regulation (EU) 2017/2402,[68] in force since 1 January 2019,[69] structured transactions such as securitisations are regulated by a single

---

of a Takeover: A Review of Empirical Evidence' (2015) *International Business Law Journal* 2, 161–186; R. Sappideen, 'Fiduciary Obligations to Corporate Creditors' (1991) *Journal of Business Law*, Jul, 365–397; M. Zubair Abbasi, 'Legal Analysis of Agency Theory: An Inquiry into the Nature of Corporation' (2009) *International Journal of Law and Management* 51(6), 401–420; J. Paterson, 'Corporate Governance in India in the Context of the Companies Bill 2009: Part 2: Evaluation' (2010) *International Company and Commercial Law Review* 21(3), 83–95; M. Yavasi, 'A Socio-Legal and Economic Introduction to Corporate Governance Problems in the EU' (2001) *Company Lawyer* 22(6), 162–170.

66 As regards the possibility of diversification, it was observed that "the theoretical result regarding the dark side of diversification is based on linear diversification strategies. That is, financial institutions diversify asset holdings by exchanging shares in their projects. Although this result has several important applications, it does not apply unconditionally to securitisation. This is because securities on loan portfolios are usually sliced into tranches with different seniority levels. The payoff of those tranches is nonlinear in the return of the underlying loan portfolio. Diversification through securitisation is therefore not the same as linear diversification. Interestingly, taking tranching into account proves to have a substantial impact from both a microprudential and macroprudential point of view. From a microprudential perspective, tranching facilitates a decrease in the probability of individual failures beyond the minimum level that could be achieved by linear diversification strategies. From a macroprudential viewpoint, diversification through securitisation may help avoid the dark side of diversification. In contrast to the result on linear diversification in the literature, we find that diversification through securitisation does not necessarily increase the probability of systemic failures" (M.R.C van Oordt, 'Securitization and the Dark Side of Diversification' (2014) *Journal of Financial Intermediation* 23, 215).

67 K. Alexander, *Principles of Banking Regulation* (n. 44), 301.

68 Henceforth also the "STS EU Regulation" or "Securitisation Regulation." This piece of statute was preceded by the Proposal of the EU Commission of September 2015, whose purpose is to ensure that the European Parliament and the Council establish common rules on securitisation in order to outline a European framework for simple, transparent and standardised securitisations by making amendments to Directives 2009/65/EC, 2009/148/EC and 2011/61/EU and Regulations (EC) No 1060/2009 and (EU) No. 648/2012, COM(2015)472, 30 September 2015. See S. Graziadei, 'The "New" European Regulatory Framework on Securitisations of the Regulation (EU) 2017–2402' (2018) *Banking Law*, online.

69 Regulation (EU) 2017/2402 of the European Parliament and of the Council of 12 September 2017 defines a general framework for securitisation by establishing specific rules for simple, transpar-

regulatory framework, applicable to all countries belonging to the European Economic Area (EEA),[70] so long as the relevant securities may benefit from a future, which is also a brand, called "STS."

The most important aspect embedded with the EU legislation is the definition of a "typical" securitisation transaction: this takes place when there are specific parameters of transparency, simplicity, and standardisation, i.e. the "STS" features. In this way, the EU legislature apparently draws an ideal demarcation line between "good" and "bad" securitisations.[71]

In addition to this, due diligence is required to avoid the risks that led to the 2007–2008 financial crisis: according to this requirement, the institutional entity – even before investing in securitised securities – must produce a comprehensive assessment, including from a legal point of view, of the investment it is about to make.

Additionally, there is a retention requirement explicitly imposed by the new regulations with regard to securities issued by the vehicle. The only aspect left out of the regulatory set relates to the issue of the credit rating agency, whose role is strictly connected with the arrangement of structured finance transactions.[72]

Furthermore, Regulations No. 557 and No. 558/2021,[73] which entered into force on 9 April 2021, are aimed at extending the legislative framework of STS securitisations to synthetic on-balance-sheet securitisations. Additionally, their purpose is to remove the regulatory hurdles previously existing between STS securitisations and those of non-performing exposures.

The objective pursued by the adoption of these regulations is to provide support to both credit institutions and financial intermediaries to remove non-performing exposures from their balance sheets in order to be able to continue to

---

ent and standardised securitisations. At the same time, Directives 2009/65/EC, 2009/138/EC and 2011/61/EC and Regulations (EC) No. 1060/2009 and (EU) No. 648/2012 are amended. Pursuant to Art. 48 of the Regulation the entry into force is scheduled for the twentieth day following publication in the CJEU, while paragraph n. 2 of the same article states that the starting date should be from 1 January 2019.

70 It is worth mentioning that the United Kingdom, still a Member State at the time of the promulgation of the STS Regulation, continues to retain, despite Brexit, the corresponding British STS Regulation as its own domestic legislation. See Chapter 3 below.

71 In this sense, scholars have hinted at the "patent of originality underpinning securitisation transactions" (our literal translation from Italian). P. de Gioia Carabellese, *Cartolarizzazioni semplici, trasparenti e standardizzate. Dallo shadow banking al techno banking*, Cacucci, Bari, 2020, 29.

72 It should be noted that the same has been the subject of copious and effective regulatory interventions, hence the reasonable choice of the legislature to keep them subject to their own framework (the *sedes materiae*). On the topic of credit rating agencies, see J. De Haan, F. Amtenbrink, 'Taming the Beast? New European Regulation for Credit Rating Agencies' (2012) *Journal for Comparative Government and European Policy*, 433 ff.; J. De Bruyne, 'Liability of Credit Rating Agencies: Regulatory Changes and Tendencies in Case Law Following the Financial Crisis' (2016) *International Company and Commercial Law Review* 27(3), 87 ff.

73 This new European securitisation regime entered into force in January 2019 and was subject to a comprehensive review in January 2022. See the EBA Report, *Developing a Framework for Sustainable Securitisation*, EBA/REP/2022/06, online.

provide credit to enterprises necessary for managing the economic crisis caused by COVID-19.[74]

The idea behind this new approach is that the credit institution can continue to lend funds to the real economy: from this perspective, securitisations can play a key role in transforming loans into actionable securities. The European Commission is currently preparing a proposal for a Council Directive on the approximation of the laws of the Member States.

The above-mentioned regulations introduce changes to the previous European regulations in force. Precisely, EU Regulation No. 2021/557 contains legal provisions aimed at amending EU Regulation No. 2017/2402 by establishing specific rules regarding simple, transparent and standardised securitisations which are necessary to support the recovery from the COVID-19 crisis. This regulation introduced, for the first time, the category of securitisations of non-performing exposures. This "genre" is the securitisation hedged by an aggregate of non-performing exposures whose nominal value represents not less than 90% of the entire nominal value of the portfolio at the time of creation and at any subsequent point in time when assets are added to the portfolio underlying or withdrawn from it because of a reconstitution, restructuring or any other relevant reason.

In other words, they refer to transactions with exposures that qualify as "defaulting" in accordance with industry regulations and to an extent of not less than 90%. Another new element, compared to the discipline contained in the Securitisation Regulation, relates to the legal provision that the obligation to maintain the relevant economic interest at 5% should be calculated on the net value of the underlying exposure rather than on the gross value. Thirdly, in the logic of the new European intervention, it did not seem appropriate that net economic interest could be held exclusively by the originator, promoter or original lender in relation to transactions in which the originator and original lender are often extraneous.

In light of this, and especially based on the consideration that the rationale for holding the economic interest is to create an alignment of interests between investors and other parties involved in the transaction, the European body of law in this area has extended the possibility to possess 5% to the servicer of the operation of securitisation. Finally, EU lawmakers have introduced a derogation concerning the originator's obligation to securitise original claims because of solid, predetermined and pre-defined criteria. This requirement did not appear to have any usefulness for the affected securitisations and, consequently, a different principle is now in place, requiring the adoption of sound rules for the selection and setting of the sale price of affected exposures.

74 On post-coronavirus crisis management, see M. Palmieri, 'La Ricapitalizzazione Pubblica delle Imprese nel Decreto Rilancio. Luci ed Ombre di un New Deal post Covid-19' (2020) *Analisi Giuridica dell'Economia*, 441.

The most recent development in the EU legislation on securitisations is Regulation No. 2021/558, concentrated on Regulation No. 2013/575. The latter relates to the adaptation of the securitisation framework to support the post-COVID-19 economic recovery. This regulation contains a treatment defined as prudential as far as affected exposure securitisations are concerned. The ultimate purpose, in this specific scenario, is to ensure that the legislation does not turn out to be an obstacle to market developments for this particular type of transaction.

The innovative aspect relates to the approach of the 2021 EU regulation. In the previous statute, in fact, the prudential criterion was required for the different classes of securitisation securities. It varied according to the specific transaction, and it was closely related to the intrinsic characteristics of the securities themselves, requiring disproportionate capital requirements in the case of non-performing credit securitisations. The new regulatory approach, given the consideration that the market for non-performing exposures following the crisis is likely to grow from COVID-19, adapted the risk weight for the securitisation positions of non-performing exposures. In this context, a 100% weighting factor has been provided for senior NPE securitisations, which may be reduced by applying a lower risk-weighting event and subject to a minimum threshold of 50% (Art. 269-bis, par. 6).

Against this background, one of the main objectives of this work is to verify whether shadow banking is still possible within the context of the actions wielded by the EU legislator, particularly in view of an STS securitisation. Also, one further goal is to verify whether shadow banking, at the present time, still retains its own *raison d'être* in the light of the complex set of rules. More generally, STS securitisations are assessed and analysed from a broader perspective: sustainability, particularly the ESG factors. These constitute the new mantra of the financial business, although it is not clear yet how it interacts with the STS framework.

The European securitisation, focused on the figure of STS securities, seems to accentuate the integration of the European capital market. There are new rules imposed on institutional investors in the purchase of STS securities. In fact, these legal provisions should go in the direction of avoiding, since the beginning, the shocks to the financial system of 2007–2008, caused precisely by "slogans" that could just be the antithesis of simple, transparent, standardised: difficult, opaque, complex.

Securitisation seems to move more and more from a legal and economic model based on traditional credit to a technological and virtual paradigm, in which credit expands from the "bare claim" to an ordinary flow, necessary, yet sufficient, for the transfer of risk to the vehicle. In this scenario, the flow has transcended and overcome the same materiality of traditional credit.

There is no doubt that this allows the operator to avoid any uncertainty about the subject matter of the transfer. While the legal structure of the transfer may enjoy a higher degree of flexibility, some legal systems, such as those with Roman roots, are faced with new challenges: the credit, its "crisis" and the creditor in search of a lost identity.[75] Added to this – and in fact consequentially – is the need to develop new categories, which may go beyond the traditional perimeter of credit.

75 The blows inflicted on the creditor, in the latest developments in the European Union, are manifold. Most remarkably, the BRRD and the conversion and/or write-off of the claims that may be inflicted by the Supervisory Authority, in cases of a failing bank, are probably the pinnacle of the "debacle," or at least, the struggles, of the creditor. See P. de Gioia Carabellese, *Banking Resolution Tools, Bail-In and Fundamental Rights*, Wolters Kluwer International, Madrid, 2019.

2 Structured finance transactions: STS and sustainability

2.1 The economic structure of securitisations

Securitisations are usually private law transactions. In this "epiphany" of contracts, strictly connected with each other, one of the major steps is given by the transfer of assets from one seller (the originator), that is usually – but not necessarily – a bank, to another entity, the vehicle (SPV). Differently from other forms of banking contracts, such as factoring, the vehicle pays receivables not with its own money[1] but with what it collects through the placement – in the relevant capital market – of the securities issued alongside the purchase of the assets.[2]

Security-holders, in subscribing to these financial instruments, do not invest according to the traditional criteria that normally guide depositors or investors in either banking products or non-securitised securities.[3] Securitisation-investors, in subscribing securities, make a double assessment.[4] First, they carry out a financial

1 In fact, the vehicle is a thinly capitalised company, without assets.

2 The special nature of the Anglo-American model, namely the British legislation and English law, means that the vehicle must not be necessarily incorporated in an *ad hoc* corporate fashion. Very often, the SPV is a limited company with minimal capitalisation. In one jurisdiction, Italy, on the contrary, a specific corporate structure has been created by law, including a very peculiar concept of separate assets. This approach has a number of legal and financial implications. From a "philosophical" point of view, though, one demarcation line between the two approaches appears to be nearly self-explanatory. The choice of the British legal system, informed by a *laissez-faire* attitude, refrains from choosing a model that can be defined as a "legal segregation," therefore a segregation based on legislation. The separation is of a contractual nature, whereas in Italy this separation seems to be the outcome of a legislative choice. Despite the different legal and philosophical approaches, in the end, the objectives pursued by the two legal systems converge towards the same direction. For an analysis of the securitisations from the standpoint of Ireland, see M. Zambelli, 'Securitisation Special Purpose Vehicles in Ireland: Regulatory Nature and Central Bank of Ireland Supervision' (2019) *Journal of International Business and Law* 19(1), 24–47.

3 The criteria that could be defined as "traditional," especially for the purpose of repayment, are based on the assessment of the solvency of the counterparty, that is, the bank or the issuing company.

4 The description can be found in Recital No. 2 of the EU Regulation (EU) 2017/2402, which reads as follows: "Securitisation involves transactions that enable a lender or a creditor – typically a credit institution or a corporation – to refinance a set of loans, exposures or receivables, such as residential loans, auto loans or leases, consumer loans, credit cards or trade receivables, by transforming them into tradable securities. The lender pools and repackages a portfolio of its loans, and organises them

DOI: 10.4324/9780429293436-2

analysis of the transferred claims rather than of the assets of the vehicle (which in reality are negligible), since the subject matter of the sale – its object – will ensure investors' claims are duly honoured. Second, the assessment relates to all the contractual relationships pertaining to the securitisation transaction.

Entailed in these two assessments is a contractual artificial tool. Since the claims are transferred to a vehicle that is not multi-purpose but rather one with a specific and very limited corporate object, investors in securitised products seemingly are the only creditors of the vehicle. Consequently, there is a very limited risk for investors to face other creditors. On such grounds, the securities issued should be very attractive, for the reason that investors may simply rely on the credit rating of receivables, certified by a special agency. By contrast, the creditworthiness of the vehicle, which is the usual criterion leading to the decision of lending money to a corporate entity, fades away and becomes totally irrelevant.[5]

From a non-legal perspective, the underpinning objectives of a securitisation transaction are different and multifarious. They may vary according to the needs of the different parties involved. According to this line of reasoning, if an investor's perspective is taken into account, securitisation enables such "players" to invest, albeit indirectly, in assets such as land credits and credit card loans in which investing would otherwise prove to be extremely difficult, even because they are geographically distant from the investors' area of business or residence. In essence, securitised financial instruments are quoted in a regulated market, this meaning that the investor, wherever they might be located, may have access to remote markets. In addition to this, investors may be attracted to buying bonds issued by an SPV, since these securities mirror assets with a relatively low credit risk, *ergo* with a high rating and a relatively high profit.

For the originator, the purposes may be both financial and regulatory.

First, the originator may want an off-balance treatment of receivables and a "leverage ratio."[6] This is a goal that can be pursued by originators because they

into different risk categories for different investors, thus giving investors access to investments in loans and other exposures to which they normally would not have direct access. Returns to investors are generated from the cash flows of the underlying loans."

5 The creditworthiness at stake is not the traditional one, where a bank evaluates the consumer's reliability, but rather a reverse one, where an investor evaluates the bank and/or vehicle. Regarding traditional creditworthiness, see A. van 't Hof, 'The First Years of the Creditworthiness Assessment under the Mortgage Credit Directive: Is It Enough?' (2021) *Journal of European Consumer and Market Law* 10(1), 4–13; C. Adams, 'Credit Where It's Due, Banker' (2008) *Banker*, Oct Supp (Quantum), 45–49; L. Mason, 'Personal Data and Credit Reference Agencies: UK Statutory Obligations Owed to Consumers and the Means of Redress' (2014) *Journal of International Banking Law and Regulation* 29(7), 411–416; M. Munir, 'Creditworthiness Isn't Enough' (1995) *Euromoney*, Nov, 91–92.

6 M.J. Raines, 'Off-Balance Sheet Treatment for Securitised Assets: The New UK and Irish Accounting Standard' (1994) *Journal of International Banking Law* 9(7), 281–284; M.J. Raines, 'Off-Balance Sheet Treatment for Securitised Assets: New UK Accounting Proposals' (1993)

no longer hold the credit risk of the receivables, duly transferred to a different party, for which they receive immediate cash. The latter is the consideration that the SPV pays for receivables. The advantage of this structure is obvious: the originator receives an upfront payment, without having to wait for the expiry of the receivables or credits. In doing so, and thanks to cash payment, the originator is in a position to relieve the outstanding liability in order to obtain a better "leverage ratio." Therefore, a better balance between equity and debt is achieved.[7]

Additionally, the second reason why the originator may decide to securitise its assets is that a transaction of this kind may represent value-for-money funding, in comparison with what the originator may obtain in a traditional fashion: the issuance of bonds. The cost of funding a securitisation – the money that the originator receives from the SPV – turns out to be relatively low (particularly if compared with the funding of bonds). The reason for this is that the rating of the bonds issued by the SPV is usually higher than the one at which the underlying assets would have been valued in the absence of a securitisation transaction.[8] From this perspective, securitisations may represent a less expensive alternative

---

Journal of International Banking Law 8(5), 200–204; M.J. Raines, 'Off-Balance Sheet Treatment for Securitisation in the United Kingdom' (1992) *Journal of International Banking Law* 7(6), 230–237; A. Haynes, 'Commercial Lending, Whole of Business Securitisation and Synthetic Securitisation' (2020) *Company Lawyer* 41(1), 1–3; M. Yagci, J.Y. Cheng Cheah, 'Should Reverse Payment Settlements be Subject to Competition Law Scrutiny? – A Discussion on the Economics and the Anti-Competitive Effects of Pharmaceutical Patent Settlements' (2018) *European Competition Law Review* 39(7), 306–324; J-C. Papeians, 'Asset Securitization: A Comparative Study between the United States and Belgium' (1996) *International Business Law Journal* 3, 341–369; Journal of International Banking Law (editorial), 'Proposal for a European Parliament and Council Directive on Cross-border Credit Transfers, (1995) *Journal of International Banking Law* 10(1), Supp, i–iv; J. Hitchins, 'The Accounting Treatment of Securitisations' (1993) *Journal of International Banking Law* 8(2), 45–47; V. Bavoso, 'Financial Innovation and Structured Finance: The Case of Securitisation' (2013) *Company Lawyer*, 34(1), 3–12; P.A. Perinetto, 'The Complexities of the EU Competition Law Assessment of Pharmaceutical Pay-for-Delay Agreements' (2018) *European Competition Law Review* 39(2), 70–76; I. Bell, 'Securitisation of Credit Card Receivables: New Bank of England Rules' (1992) *Journal of International Banking Law* 7(8), 297–299; M. Autio, 'Finland: Transactions – Cross-Border Credit Transfers' (1999) *International Company and Commercial Law Review* 10(9), n. 65; J.G.J. Rinkes, 'European Union: EC Directive on Cross-Border Credit Transfers' (1997) *International Banking and Financial Law* 15(12), 141–144; C. Reis-Roy, 'Rating Securitisation Structures' (1998) *Journal of International Banking Law* 13(9), 298–304; M. Raines, J. Cresswell, 'European Securitisation Undergoes Transition' (2002) *European Lawyer* 22, 46–48; H. Stakheyeva, 'Competition Law v Patent Settlement Agreements in Pharmaceutical Sector' (2014) *Global Competition Litigation Review* 7(3), 173–179; R. Budge, L. Davis, 'Securitisation in the Property Market' (1998) *International Banking and Financial Law* 16(10), 106–108.

7 In synthetic securitisations, off-balance sheet treatment is not possible by definition, since assets are not transferred to the SPV.

8 This more generous rating may be also due to the fact that, as already emphasised, the SPV, differently from a multiple purpose company, does not incur the risks of arranging an unfettered range of deals, with the ensuing problem of unleashing a huge variety of creditors.

to other funding methods, such as, for example, a syndicated loan or the issuance of corporate bonds.[9]

A third motive which may justify the arrangement and finalisation of a securitisation transaction is that this "economic contractual package" allows the originator to offer its assets to a wider audience than the ordinary issuance of bonds. In essence, securities issued by an SPV are easier to trade than the underlying assets, given the role played by a regulated market where they are expected to be offered.

A fourth reason for opting for a structured finance transaction relates to the regulatory capital relief that can be achieved through the transfer of the receivables from the originator to the SPV. The credit risk that the originator bears on its claims impacts on the regulatory capital of a bank. At a time when credit risk is not borne by the books, the originators release regulatory capital which, in the opposite case, they would be required to keep.[10]

Finally (the fifth reason), a bank may opt for securitising its portfolio because the European Central Bank accepts some bonds issued by the SPV as collateral.[11]

9 S. Brodie, 'Bonds and Restructurings: Corporate Bond Considerations in the Design of Debt Restructuring Frameworks in Emerging Market Economies' (2017) *Law & Financial Markets Review* 11(2/3), 117–125; M. Tell, 'Corporate Bonds in Denmark' (2015) *Intertax* 43(8/9), 531–539; D. Lenzi, 'Corporate Social Bonds: A Legal Analysis' (2021) *European Company and Financial Law Review* 18(2), 291–319; Norton Rose Fulbright, 'Qualifying Corporate Bonds: Redenomination in Euros' (2014) *PLC Magazine* 25(11), 88–89; G. de Bondt, J.-D. Lichtenberger, 'The Euro Area Corporate Bond Market: Where Do We Stand since the Introduction of the Euro?' (2003) *European Business Organization Law Review* 4(4), 517–539; Z. Zhang, 'Enhancing Retail Investors' Access to the Corporate Bond Market: The Latest Development in Singapore' (2015) *Company Lawyer* 36(10), 319–324; Shearman & Sterling, 'United Kingdom: Tax – Qualifying Corporate Bonds' (2015) *Journal of International Banking Law and Regulation* 31(8), n. 109–n. 111; K. Tully, 'Dicing with the Bond Bubble' (2003) *Euromoney*, May, 38–41; A. McGregor, 'Case of the Week: Banking and Finance' (2012) *Lawyer* 26(38), 13; S. Edwards, 'The Name is Bond' (2000) *Taxline* 3, 10–11; S. Bain, 'Hello, Mr Bond' (2001) *Chartered Accountant Magazine* 105(1140), 18–19; S. Armitage, 'The Choice between Banks and Bonds' (1993) *Banking World* 11(11), 38–41; Norton Rose, 'Qualifying Corporate Bonds' (2008) *PLC Magazine* 19(3), 100–101; Norton Rose, 'Qualifying Corporate Bonds' (2003) *PLC Magazine* 14(10), 86; Norton Rose Fulbright, 'Qualifying Corporate Bonds: Euro Conversion Provisions' (2018) *PLC Magazine* 29(2), online.

10 K. Alexander, *Principles of Banking Regulation*, Cambridge University Press, Cambridge, 2019, 85–126.

11 P. Pahapill, 'Amendments for Financial Collateral Arrangements Regulation' (2011) *Corporate Rescue and Insolvency* 4(1), 16–17; Capital Markets Law Journal (editorial), 'Financial Collateral Regulations: Floating Charges and Meaning of "Control,"' (2010) *Capital Markets Law Journal* 5(4), 513; D. Wilde Sapte, 'Floating Charges and Financial Collateral Arrangements' (2010) *PLC Magazine* 21(8), 86; G. Davies, 'Using Intermediated Securities as Collateral: Equitable Interests with Inequitable Results?' (2007) *Butterworths Journal of International Banking & Financial Law* 22(2), 70–73, G. Nunez, J. Martin Perrotto, 'Collateral Becomes More Lender Friendly in Spain' (2005) *International Financial Law Review* 24(6), 41–42; E. White, 'Security: Financial Collateral Arrangements' (2008) *Journal of International Banking Law and Regulation* 23(11), n. 113–114; A. Fawcett, 'The Financial Collateral Directive: An Examination of Some Practical Problems Following Its Implementation in the UK' (2005) *Journal of International Banking Law and Regulation* 20(6), 295–299; Shearman & Sterling (editorial), 'EU Law: Financial Collateral

In this case, credit is provided to the banks: otherwise, the ECB would not accept a security interest on the receivable underlying assets. Needless to say, the last two circumstances are applicable exclusively to a scenario in which the originator is a bank rather than a merely commercial entity.

In general, securitisations do not entice managers to engage in excessively high levels of risk. In other words, the fact that banks are able to offload risk onto less-informed third parties (those who invest in securities issued by the SPV) is not likely to affect the required prudence standards a bank must comply with. From a practical perspective, the contractual partner is usually informed about securitisation, with the riskiest pool of loans being generally left with the lender.

Instead, managerial behavioural biases are identified as the most influential factors instrumental to excessively risk-taking decisions. The reforms so far implemented by regulators have put more weight on the issue of asymmetric information in securitisations and do not sufficiently deal with the issue of behavioural biases. The due diligence required for STS securitisations should solve this operational conundrum. Consequently, capital adequacy relief should not be afforded automatically to banks that transfer credit risk away from their books to non-authorised deposit-taking institutions (ADIs), as SPVs usually are. Instead, capital relief should only be afforded to banks if the party which has accepted the credit risk holds a sufficient amount of capital to protect itself from possible future losses. This means that, in cases in which the risk has been transferred

---

Obligations' (2017) *Journal of International Banking Law and Regulation* 32(3), n. 24–n. 25; B. James, W. Nevin, 'Banks Welcome Changes to Collateral Law' (2004) *International Financial Law Review* 23(3), 37–38; Shearman & Sterling LLP (editorial), 'United Kingdom: Security – Financial Collateral Arrangements' (2013) *Journal of International Banking Law and Regulation* 28(3), n. 34–n. 35; T. Carter, A. Dodds, L. Walker, 'Financial Collateral Arrangements: Tricky Issues and Practical Considerations' (2018) *Butterworths Journal of International Banking & Financial Law* 2018, 33(11), 684–686; A. Kennedy, C. Parrott, M. Kappler, A. Alfreahat, 'Financial Collateral and Brexit: A Comparative Perspective' (2021) *Butterworths Journal of International Banking & Financial Law* 36(6), 409–410, A. Sharp, 'The Collateral Directive – A New Way of Thinking about Security' (2004) *Insolvency Intelligence* 17(10), 145–148; Freshfields Bruckhaus Deringer, 'Financial Collateral: Appropriation' (2009) *PLC Magazine* 20(6), 52–53; M. Hughes, 'The Financial Collateral Regulations' (2006) *Butterworths Journal of International Banking & Financial Law* 21(2), 64–69; Commercial Law Practitioner (editorial), 'EU Financial Collateral Directive' (2004) *Commercial Law Practitioner* 11(4), 101–102; M. Lantelme, 'The Implementation in Italy of the Financial Collateral Directive May Solve a Number of Issues' (2004) *Journal of International Banking Law and Regulation* 19(12), 510–512; G. Yeowart, 'Validity of the Financial Collateral Regulations' (2008) *Law & Financial Markets Review* 2(6), 493–494; D. Turing, K. Lester, 'Implementation of the EU Directive on Financial Collateral Arrangements in the United Kingdom' (2005) *Journal of International Banking Law and Regulation* 20(2), 65–71; S. Salzedo, D. Heaton, 'Validation of the Financial Collateral Arrangements Regulations Post-Brexit: Legal Considerations' (2021) *Butterworths Journal of International Banking & Financial Law* 36(4), 250–252; G.L. Gretton, 'Financial Collateral and the Fundamentals of Secured Transactions' (2006) *Edinburgh Law Review* 10(2), 209–238; R. Parsons, M. Dening, 'Financial Collateral – an Opportunity Missed' (2011) *Law & Financial Markets Review* 5(3), 164–175; N. McGrath, 'The Financial Collateral Directive: Perfection Perspectives' (2010) *Commercial Law Practitioner* 17(4), 72–77.

to non-ADIs, a margining system should be put in place. Such a requirement would ensure that a sufficient amount of capital is held in the economy for the aggregate level of credit risk created by the banks. Perhaps more importantly, the requirement would ensure that bank managers refrain from excessive lending practices (through making capital relief more burdensome) while investors put more efforts into exploring the quality of mortgage-backed securities. This recommendation has in mind the long-term stability of the credit market through prudent lending practices. In essence, there should be a disincentive to excessive lending, generally speaking. The Securitisation Regulation seems to take on board this matter within one of its legal provisions, more specifically Recital No. 29:

> A strong reliance on the repayment of securitisation positions on the sale of assets securing the underlying assets creates vulnerabilities, as illustrated by the poor performance of parts of the market for commercial mortgage-backed securities (CMBS) during the financial crisis. Therefore, CMBS should not be considered to be STS securitisations.

Nevertheless, as a result of the 2007–2008 financial crisis, securitisations were heavily criticised and regarded[12] by some practitioners, as well as scholars, as being illegal should the originator be a bank.[13] Currently, despite these concerns, the EU legislators view them positively.[14] Specifically, Recital No. 4 of the Securitisation Regulation highlights its advantages. It is stipulated as follows:

> Securitisation is an important element of well-functioning financial markets. Soundly structured securitisation is an important channel for diversifying funding sources and allocating risk more widely within the Union financial system. It allows for a broader distribution of financial-sector risk and can help free up originators' balance sheets to allow for further lending to the economy. Overall, it can improve efficiencies in the financial system and provide additional investment opportunities. Securitisation can create a

12 The EU Securitisation Regulation highlights: "The Union aims to strengthen the legislative framework implemented after the financial crisis to address the risks inherent in highly complex, opaque and risky securitisation. It is essential to ensure that rules are adopted to better differentiate simple, transparent and standardised products from complex, opaque and risky instruments and to apply a more risk-sensitive prudential framework" (Recital No. 3).

13 The theory of an implicit legal prohibition to transfer of assets from a bank to an SPV is not so popular, albeit hinted in a very authoritative way, in one jurisdiction, Italy. See F. Merusi, 'Per un Divieto di Cartolarizzazione del Rischio di Credito' (2009) *Banca Borsa Titoli di Credito*, 253 ff. Theoretically, these stances could not be confuted, in the light of the fact that the banking activity, as a reserved activity, could not permit the sale of assets. Having said that from a theoretical point of view, the need for liquidity of the banking sectors eventually overcomes any observation to the contrary.

14 For a post-financial crisis regulation and its contours, see G. Penn, T. Papadogiannis, 'Regulating Securitisation in the Aftermath of the Global Financial Crisis: Lessons from Europe' (2021) *Journal of International Banking Law and Regulation* 36(6), 225–248.

> bridge between credit institutions and capital markets with an indirect benefit for businesses and citizens (through, for example, less expensive loans and business financing and credits for immovable property and credit cards). Nevertheless, this regulation recognises the risks of increased interconnectedness and of excessive leverage that securitisation raises. It also enhances the micro-prudential supervision by competent Authorities of a financial institution taking part in the securitisation market. Ultimately, the macroprudential oversight of that market by the European Systemic Risk Board (ESRB) results in being improved. The latter has been established by Regulation (EU) No. 1092/2010 of the European Parliament and of the Council and by the national competent and designated authorities for macroprudential instruments.[15]

Scholars, in examining the securitisation economic-legal issues through the lenses of the banking business and bankers, place particular emphasis on the fact that the regulation of this sector should aim at maximising efficiencies and minimising risk. In fact, while this area of finance is adjacent to shadow banking, a limitation of the latter is not realistic.

To this end, two possible types of regulation have been identified. The first one maintains that a certain degree of resiliency is quintessential and generally resilient "by forcing investors or institutions to hold certain funds in reserve out of a booming market."[16] To elaborate, it would be desirable to force investors or institutions, who have invested in securitised instruments, to hold certain funds in reserves. This would be a safe harbour approach, in cases of an "explosive" market where SPVs were not in a position to pay bond-holders. A second method would be even more peculiar: it is based on the idea that investors can be instantly protected through the provision of funds, the ultimate purpose of which is to protect depositors.

All these points of view, not always corroborated, may warrant an irrefutable thesis. Securitisation is the most sensitive area to be regulated.[17] Indeed, the

15 This principle is consistent with the additional Recital No. 5: "Establishing a more risk-sensitive prudential framework for simple, transparent and standardised ('STS') securitisations requires that the Union clearly define what an STS securitisation is, since otherwise the more risk-sensitive regulatory treatment for credit institutions and insurance companies would be available for different types of securitisations in different Member States. This would lead to an unlevel playing field and to regulatory arbitrage, whereas it is important to ensure that the Union functions as a single market for STS securitisations and that it facilitates cross-border transactions."

16 E.F. Gerding, 'Laws against Bubbles: An Experimental-Asset-Market Approach to Analyzing Financial Regulation' (2007) *Wisconsin Law Review*, 1038.

17 In this way, Recital No. 6 of the Securitisation Regulation prescribes: "In line with the existing definitions in Union sectoral legislation, it is appropriate to provide definitions of all the key concepts of securitisation. In particular, a clear and encompassing definition of securitisation is needed to capture any transaction or scheme whereby the credit risk associated with an exposure or pool of exposures is tranched. An exposure that creates a direct payment obligation for a transaction

intervention of lawmakers should not be unbalanced[18] or unduly influenced by previous crises.

On this point, the need for a "discipline" on the matter has been both felt "ideologically" and implemented practically by the EU. The European Union, in essence, stepped up to the plate with the adoption of a piece of EU legislation whose goal is to establish STS securitisations. Linguistically, 'STS' simply is an acronym: Simple, Transparent, Standardised. However, as clarified in this work, something more definite lies in these adjectives.[19]

Specifically, it is possible to mention the fact that the aims of the EU Securitisation Regulation are manifold: a) restart markets on a more sustainable basis so that simple, transparent and standardised securitisations can act as an effective "collection channel" for the economy; b) facilitate a more efficient and effective transfer of risk to a range of institutional investors, including banks;[20] c) protect investors and manage systemic risk to avoid using an erroneous model of mere generation and distribution.[21]

Following the Securitisation Regulation, it is possible to contend that there has been a resurgence of securitisations, which, in turn, are part of a larger project aimed at building a pan-European capital market within the Capital Markets Union.[22]

The Union's rules on securitisations, in the latest fashion, are not intended to replace the national private law of each Member State. By contrast, they are supposed to engender a regulatory framework applicable to circumstances where institutional operators play a role, either as originators, sponsors or investors in such securities.

---

or scheme used to finance or operate physical assets should not be considered an exposure to a securitisation, even if the transaction or scheme has payment obligations of different seniority."

18 L. Enriques, 'Regulators' Response to the Current Crisis and the Upcoming Regulation of Financial Markets: One Reluctant Regulator's View' (2009) *University of Pennsylvania Journal of International Law*, 1147; E.F. Gerding, *Law, Bubbles, and Financial Regulation*, Routledge, London and New York, 2013, 2.

19 As regards the requirements of STS securitisation, the Regulation, at Recital 37, stipulates as follows: "The requirements for using the designation 'simple, transparent and standardised' (STS) securitisation are new and will be further specified by EBA guidelines and supervisory practice over time. In order to avoid discouraging market participants from using that designation, competent authorities should have the ability to grant the originator, sponsor and SSPE a grace period of three months to rectify any erroneous use of the designation that they have used in good faith. Good faith should be presumed where the originator, sponsor and SSPE could not know that a securitisation did not meet all the STS criteria to be designated as STS. During that grace period, the securitisation in question should continue to be considered STS-compliant and should not be deleted from the list drawn up by ESMA in accordance with this Regulation."

20 The idea is that they are tempted to invest in STS-branded securitised securities.

21 The reference is to the "originate-to-distribute" model.

22 V. Bavoso, *Regulating Complex Financial Products Post-Crisis: Between the STS Regulation and ESAM Products Intervention Powers*, in D. Cash, R. Goddard (eds), *Regulation and the Global Financial Crisis: Impact, Responses, and Beyond*, Routledge, London and New York, 2021, 10.

It should be pointed out that the STS "label," which is investigated in more depth in Chapter 3 below, is not a European Union exclusive. Similar initiatives have been taken by IOSCO:[23] initially the creation of STC securitisation (simple, transparent and comparable – a wording that, even *prima facie*, is not very distant from the simple, transparent and standardised eventually embraced by the Brussels lawmakers). In short, the STS and STC "brands" help describe a structure of negotiations with transparent underlying assets, with a better chance of predicting the risks of performance for the benefit of investors. In doing so, the interests of the originator and the investors turn out to be convergent,[24] in stark contrast with the divergence of interests existing in the securitisation era preceding the 2008 financial crisis.

2.2 Alternative forms of structured finance

The pay-through mechanism is the form of securitisation usually defined as "traditional."[25] A special feature of this kind of securitisation is that the vehicle acquires full ownership of the portfolio and undertakes to repay the financing exclusively with the cash flows resulting from the collection of the portfolio. The "pay-through" terminology seems to be evocative of the fact that the only security for the holders of the financial instruments is represented by the flows generated by the receivables sold. The holders of the notes do not have the possibility, *de facto*, to see their credit repaid though the liquidation of the capital of the issuer, should the debtor (the SPV) fail to honour its debts. Since the issuer is a *nummo uno* company,[26] they would not have any interest in enforcing their credits against the SPV: both the share capital and, more generally, the assets of the company are of a negligible amount.

23 It should be noted that after the financial crisis of 2007–2008, the structured finance market has become devoid of vitality for both a technical and "psychological" reason. With regard to the former, reference is made to the new liquidity forecasts provided for by Basel II, the LCR and the NSFR, while the latter refers to the risk aversion of investors in this type of product. In relation to IOSCO, see Recital No. 19: "It is essential to establish a general and cross-sectorally applicable definition of STS securitisation based on the existing criteria, as well as on the criteria adopted by the Basel Committee on Banking Supervision (BCBS) and the International Organisation of Securities Commissions (IOSCO) on 23 July 2015 for identifying simple, transparent and comparable securitisations in the framework of capital sufficiency for securitisations, and in particular based on the opinion on a European framework for qualifying securitisation published on 7 July 2015 by the European Supervisory Authority (European Banking Authority) (EBA), established by Regulation (EU) No 1093/2010 of the European Parliament and of the Council."

24 V. Bavoso, *Regulating Complex Financial Products Post-Crisis* (n. 22), 10.

25 In the most commonly used sense. A. Heinzmann, N. Ronzel, 'Luxembourg Loans Investment Structures: Alternative Investment Funds or Securitisation?' (2017) *Journal of International Banking Law and Regulation*, 247–252.

26 The Latin expression *nummo uno*, literally meaning "one penny," should reflect more broadly the scenario of a company which, again, is thinly capitalised, rather than totally missing a share-capital.

A second type of securitisation, termed "pass-through," is characterised by the presence of a transferee company that manages the portfolio of credits, without being a holder or an owner. In this configuration, the credits, albeit managed by the transferee as a trustee, are bought *pro quota* by the subscribers of the securities. The role of the trustee, in this alternative configuration, the "pass-through," sparks off a conundrum, in legal systems where the trust itself is not a concept duly recognised. Despite this, the fall-back option is still present: the subscribers of the securities, as beneficiaries, will be able to use the categories of the trust of a jurisdiction, where this legal concept is both legally recognised and entrenched,[27] and then be granted a right of compensation. This right can be brought before a Court against the trustee in the event that the trustee has not upheld the claims of the beneficiaries. The SPV can act as a trustee but, needless to say, this is only possible in jurisdictions – the ones governing the specific transaction, the sale of receivables – where the trust is a recognised legal concept.

Ultimately, securitisation, as a financial transaction, is achieved via two potential routes. The first one (pay-through) involves the acquisition by the transferee of the ownership of the portfolio. The transferee commits itself to repay the funding exclusively with the cash flows resulting from the collection of the portfolio of the notes. The second legal route is the one where the structure of payments is not strictly conditioned by the cash flows derived from the "overlying" receivables, since there is not any relationship between the latter and the securities issued. Again, it should be stressed that this second version implies that the transferee manages the credit portfolio without owning it. An articulation of this second mode of execution, that is the pass-through, is realised through the legal instrument of the trust: although the credits are managed by the assignee as a trustee, even if technically it is not, they are bought pro quota by the subscribers of the securities. In a different version of pass-through securitisation, the securities, still owned by the subscribers, are managed by a common fund. Even in the latter circumstance, according to one school of thought, the claims remain the property of the transferor company, but the transferee takes care of the management.[28]

27 The English legal system is the common option.

28 In this case, the element of the sale is missing, therefore the securitisation will result in having synthetic features. About synthetic securitisation, reference can be made from a legal point of view to R. Watson, J. Carter (eds), *Asset Securitisation and Synthetic Structures: Innovations in the European Credit Markets*, Euromoney Books, London, 2006. From a financial point of view, see M. Choudhry, *Structured Credit Products: Credit Derivatives and Synthetic Securitisation*, Wiley-Finance, London, 2010; M. Böhringer, U. Lotz, C. Solbach, J. Wentzler, *Conventional versus Synthetic Securitisation – Trends in the German ABS Market*, Deloitte & Touche Germany, Dusseldorf, 2001; E.J. Podolski, 'Regulating Synthetic Securitisation Following the Global Financial Crisis' (2012) *Australian Economic Review* 45(1), 11–28. This article examines synthetic securitisation in light of the US Subprime Crisis and evaluates whether the regulatory structure in Australia is sufficient to prevent the repetition of the US experience on our shores. I argue that a key problem with securitisation is not the inherent information asymmetry in the programme design, but rather that it allows for uncontrolled growth in risk-taking by over-confident managers. Despite the financial crisis having all the hallmarks of, in Charles Kindleberger's words, "manias, panics

Securitisation in the pay-through "mode"[29] is the most common *modus operandi* in order to finalise securitisations. It should be noted, though, that, despite the declining use of pass-through securitisations, with pay-through being the favourite, alternative contractual structures have been developed in practice, one example being synthetic securitisations. For the sake of completeness, the legal pattern in which the securitised assets coincide with the securitisation bonds is also noteworthy: it is, in essence, the securitisation bond.[30]

Within the various categories of securitisations, STS securitisations, which constitute the focus of this work, do not represent a further *genre* but rather a crosscutting legislation piece, as introduced by the Securitisation Regulation, designed to better protect investors. Under this piece of legislation, the parties involved may decide to arrange their securitisation transaction as STS,[31] by complying with a number of additional requirements. Investors can benefit from investing in STS bonds because holding them would have significant regulatory advantages. In this scenario, STS securitisations, juxtaposed against the traditional categories (pay-through versus pass-through), are consistent with both.

Conversely, in synthetic securitisation, receivables are not transferred to the SPV, since originators are not willing to sever the relationship of trust with

---

and crashes" (C.P. Kindleberger, R.Z. Aliber, Manias, Panics and Crashes. *A History of Fiancial Crises*, London, Macmillan, 1978), the global regulatory response appears to be disproportionately focused on reducing information asymmetry in securitisation programmes, without sufficiently addressing the issue of behavioural biases. It is worth noting that the Australian economy has emerged from the Global Financial Crisis (GFC) stronger than other developed countries. Nonetheless, it seems improbable that Australia is entirely immune from the subprime fallout which has entangled the rest of the world. Securitisation, which contributed significantly towards loosened lending practices in the lead-up to the subprime crisis in the United States, has grown rapidly in Australia over the past decade. In 1997, securitised housing as a portion of all housing loans accounted for roughly 5% of the market. By mid-2007, this figure had risen to 25%. The Australian mortgage securitisation market is the second-largest in the world, second only to the United States in size. The Australian financial sector is therefore very exposed to a potential downturn in the residential housing market. The resilience of the Australian economy to the GFC appears to be attributable more to the mining boom and the fact that the Australian housing market is yet to experience a severe downturn, rather than to exemplary regulation. The housing market is unlikely to stay strong forever, with The Economist finding the Australian property market to be 56% overvalued (The Economist, *Hong Kong Phew-Whee*, March 2011, 34). With this in mind, the article sets out to examine whether the structure and regulation of the securitisation market in Australia is sufficiently robust to avert a severe financial crisis in the future. Although limiting itself to an examination of the Australian legal framework, the evaluation of problems and potential regulatory approaches is applicable to other jurisdictions as well.

29 It expressly provides for and recognises the vehicle as an autonomous legal figure capable of acquiring full capital autonomy and separateness.

30 Y. Altunbasa, L. Gambacorta, D. Marques-Ibanezc, 'Securitisation and the Bank Lending Channel' (2009) *European Economic Review* 53(8), 996–1009; I. Shim, *Development of Asia-Pacific Corporate Bond and Securitisation Markets*, Bank for International Settlements (BIS), BIS Paper No. 63c, 15 Feb 2012; R. Agliardi, 'Green Securitisation' (2021) *Journal of Sustainable Finance & Investment*, online.

31 This type of securitisation will be dealt with in Chapter 4 of the present work.

the debtor. Within this peculiar context, the traditional sale of assets would be regarded, potentially, as the incorrect way to deal with the relationship with the customer.[32] Moreover, in some cases, an undisclosed assignment of claims is not possible because of the prohibitions on the sale of certain types of assets imposed by jurisdictions, where the originator is located and from where receivables originate. Ultimately, in a synthetic securitisation,[33] only the credit risk is transferred to the SPV, via a derivative contract,[34] and the way this virtual transfer is achieved usually consists of credit default swaps (CDSs).

The Securitisation Regulation does not refrain from referring to synthetic securitisations. Specifically, Art. 45, headed "Synthetic securitisations" stipulates, in its first paragraph, that the EBA, by 2 July 2019, is required, in close cooperation with ESMA and EIOPA, to "publish a report on the feasibility of a specific framework for simple, transparent and standardised synthetic securitisation, limited to balance-sheet synthetic securitisation."

Art. 45(2) adds that the same EU Commission, by a later deadline, namely 2 January 2020, based on this EBA report, will "submit a report to the European Parliament and the Council on the creation of a specific framework for simple, transparent and standardised synthetic securitisation, limited to balance-sheet synthetic securitisation, together with a legislative proposal, if appropriate." The EBA report of a framework for STS synthetic securitisation was eventually published on 6 May 2020, with the document officially referred to as Report on STS Framework for Synthetic Securitisation under article 45 of Regulation (EU) 201772402, EBA/OP/2020/07.[35]

Meanwhile, COVID-19 and the turmoil stirred globally have prompted the EU legislature to implement an STS synthetic securitisation, defined as an on-balance-sheet securitisation. Pursuant to Regulation no. 557 of 2021,[36] the synthetic

32 Both cash and synthetic forms of securitisation are assessed from a financial perspective, given the presence of both an arranger and a credit rating agency. Nevertheless, a heightened attention is paid primarily to synthetic securitisation. This approach is motivated by the fact that synthetic securitisation can be achieved in a much cheaper and quicker fashion if compared with cash securitisation. As a result, there is considerably more scope for this form of securitisation to be overused. Securitisation is assessed in light of the incentives it creates for less than perfectly rational managers. There certainly were incentives created for originators of securitisations. There is an underpinning dilemma in all securitisation transactions: the agency problems.

33 J. Benjamin, 'Synthetic, Insurance and Hedge Fund Securitisations' (2005) *Journal of International Business Law and Regulation* 20(7), 354–356.

34 Credits, therefore, are not transferred.

35 This Report has been developed in response to a mandate assigned to the EBA in Article 45 of the Securitisation Regulation (Regulation (EU) 2017/2402), which requires the Authority, in close cooperation with ESMA and EIOPA, to publish a report on the feasibility of a specific framework for simple, transparent and standardised (STS) synthetic securitisation, limited to balance sheet securitisation.

36 In full: "Regulation (EU) 2021/557 of the European Parliament and of the Council of 31 March 2021 amending Regulation (EU) 2017/2402 laying down a general framework for securitisation and creating a specific framework for simple, transparent and standardised securitisation to help the recovery from the COVID-19 crisis" (text with EEA relevance) (OJ L 116/1, 6 April 2021).

securitisation too may fall within the remit of the STS securitisation, so long as it satisfies the requirements under the new Articles 26b and 26c added to the Securitisation Regulation. As clarified later in this work, Art. 26b has now better explained the concept of "simplicity" required for a securitisation, whereas Art. 26c better shapes the concept of standardisation. The new Regulation (hereinafter also referred to as "Securitisation Regulation 2021" or "Regulation no. 557") resulted from the pandemic. Its explicit purpose, on the one hand, is to better contextualise the STS criteria,[37] and on the other hand is to provide synthetic securitisations with a better regulatory framework more consistent with the STS regime.

Some of the Recitals of the Securitisation Regulation 2021 may clarify the complexity of the recent novelty. Synthetic securitisations may involve the transference of the credit risk of a set of loans, typically large corporate loans, or loans to small and medium-sized enterprises, "by means of a credit protection agreement where the originator buys credit protection from the investor" (Recital 11). "Such credit protection is achieved by the use of financial guarantees or credit derivatives while the ownership of the assets remains with the originator and is not transferred to a SSPE, as is the case in traditional securitisations" (Recital 11). "The originator, as protection buyer, commits to pay a credit protection premium, which generates the return for investors. In turn, the investor, as protection seller, commits to a specified credit protection payment when a pre-determined credit event occurs" (Recital 11). Whereas the requirements "for simple, transparent and standardised (STS) on-balance-sheet securitisations should therefore be highly consistent with the STS criteria for traditional true sale securitisations," the overall complexity of the securitisation structures and associated risks "should be appropriately mitigated and no regulatory incentives should be provided to originators which would cause them to prefer synthetic securitisations over traditional securitisations" (Recital 12). In the light of this misalignment, Recital 13 further reads that certain requirements for STS traditional securitisations "are not appropriate for STS on-balance-sheet securitisations due to inherent differences between both types of securitisation, in particular due to the fact that, in synthetic securitisations, the risk transfer is achieved via a credit protection agreement instead of a sale of the underlying assets." Ultimately, the STS criteria should be adapted, where necessary, in order to take those differences into account.

In synthetic structured finance transactions, the risks on receivables materialise in losses, given the fact that, should debtors default, the SPV would repay such losses pursuant to the CDS. The SPV collects the necessary capital to make payments by issuing bonds. However, there is a specific condition according to which, in the case of payment from the SPV to the originator, the same amount is deducted from the bonds.[38] Of these bonds, what is owed to junior notes is the first

37 This will be discussed in the following chapter.

38 That is, the amount is deducted from the bonds, i.e. from the claims that the bondholders have against the SPV.

"bunch" to be deducted, with senior notes being the second and more privileged category.

To the extent that the SPV does not pay, since the obligation to do so has not been sparked off yet, the capital that has been raised by the SPV is invested in low-risk assets such as government bonds issued by financially stable countries or relatively safe goods. The SPV can pay the main capital and interests to bondholders also through the fees that the SPV receives from the originator: when entering into a CDS, the SPV assumes a risk. Other asset items consist of the revenue that the vehicle obtains from credits – low-risk credits purchased with the capital raised through the issuance of bonds.

In the terminology of the Securitisation Regulation 2021, the goal of a credit risk transfer "should be exposures originated or purchased by a Union-regulated institution within its core lending business activity and held on its balance sheet or, in the case of a group structure, on its consolidated balance sheet at the closing date of the transaction" (Recital 14). The requirement for an originator to hold the securitised exposures on the balance sheet should exclude arbitrage securitisations from the scope of the STS label.

Given that with synthetic securitisation credit risk is transferred to the SPV via CDS, synthetic securitisations provide higher capital to the originator: the latter does not have to hold capital against receivables.[39]

The advantages stemming from a synthetic securitisation, in comparison with a traditional one, are summed up in the following way. First and foremost, thanks to synthetic securitisations, it is possible to circumvent the legal restrictions on the transfer of the credits. Quite notoriously, these legal restrictions could give rise to a requalification of the operation.[40] Second, the notice to assigned debtor or consent by the debtor in order to effect a valid transfer of receivable under the laws of some jurisdictions could be by-passed.

A transaction that is executed on a covered bond is very similar to a traditional securitisation, even though it is not possible to turn a blind eye on the potential differences. In covered bond transactions, it is the same bank from which the receivables originate that issues the bonds for the benefit of investors. It is not the SPV as it happens in a genuine securitisation transaction. In the covered bond, the repayment obligations encumbered on the bank, as far as capital and interest are concerned, are merely guaranteed by a vehicle, although the latter is not, formally, a debtor. This vehicle is a bankruptcy remote, special purpose vehicle, in turn defined as a covered bonds company (the "CBC").[41]

CBCs guarantee the payment of the bonds issued by the bank, because it is the bank itself that has transferred a substantial amount of receivables to the CBC.

39 It is evident that a synthetic securitisation is identical to a traditional one.

40 Some legal systems, such as the Italian system, contain prohibitions on the transfer of credits. This means normal disposal transactions, such as financial transactions (factoring and securitisation), are not always feasible.

41 It should be noted that the company may also be held by the arranger with respect to its shareholding in the capital.

Similar to the securitisation transaction, receivables are securely made available thanks to the recourse action that investors have against the guarantor if the vehicle defaulted on its obligations.

Further differences exist with respect to a traditional securitisation transaction. First, covered bond investors have a claim on the bank and its assets[42] and not on the SPV. In fact, it has on its balance sheet only the specific and limited receivables portfolio. Second, covered bond investors have a claim on both the bank and the CBC. The peculiar aspect is that there is not a bond tranching phenomenon: cover bonds, in fact, do not refer to specific classes of receivables as happens, on the contrary, in securitisation. Third, there is not overcollateralisation as there are not hierarchical classes of bonds. In addition, CBC has a dynamic receivables portfolio, in securitisation, whereas SPV receives a more or less static portfolio. Finally, unlike securitisations, the transfer of credits to the CBC does not translate into cash that is provided to the bank in order to pay liabilities that are pending. All these characteristics lead to the claim that the transfer does not involve the off-balance-sheet transfer of the transferred credits.

It is worth pointing out that, through the issuance of bonds by the bank itself and the guarantee of the CBC, investors do not have an action against both the bank and the CBC, namely the dual recourse. All this determines that the related securities have a higher rating than the underlying credits if they are subject to separate valuation. As a result, the investment in covered bonds is considered as having a lower risk profile and, precisely for this reason, those securities receive a more favourable treatment for risk-weighting purposes.

As with securitisations, the collection costs of covered bond transactions may be lower than the collection costs of ordinary loans. As with securitisation transactions, covered bonds qualify as collateral in ECB loans.

2.3 Securitisations and law

Structured finance is one of the areas of UK and corporate law where regulation[43] has not intervened in a disruptive manner by imposing principles and rules within a proper legislation. Opposite to the British approach is the Italian one (to cite one of the civil law systems), where a law on securitisations has been in place for more than four decades, although the purpose of the Italian legislature – setting up a legislative framework for securitisation transactions – has gone far beyond the initial and reasonable intentions, which merely consisted of offering a legislative and contractual safeguard for securitisation transactions.[44]

42 There is also a drawback for creditors who face the competition of the bank creditors, with credit institution being a multi-purpose vehicle, rather than a special-purpose vehicle.

43 D. Annoff, 'Perspectives in Company Law and Financial Regulation: Essays in Honour of Eddy Wymeersch' (2010) *European Business Organization Law Review*, 629–636.

44 At the moment, the Italian securitisation legislation, as a result of (too) many amendments, seems to have become a broad framework, where the SPV caters for public and tax purposes too.

Both the negotiation and the corporate frameworks to be applied to the needs of the arrangers have been elaborated within the standpoint of private law, where the market takes precedence over the legislation.[45]

As far as the regulation is concerned, many critical points must be taken into account when it comes to securitisation. The reference, first and foremost, goes to the requirement to publish the prospectus, the document whereby the issuer makes public the subject matter of the investment, namely securities to consumers. This is a requirement that may be disregarded in specific circumstances. Second, the consumer credit regulation would be an important aspect to be taken into account, given that the SPV holds claims that may relate to debtors who are endowed with consumer status, for example individuals who have contracted mortgages and credit card loans. Third, the rules on the protection of personal data could apply and therefore limit the transfer of credits to the SPV without the possibility of retransfer, particularly in cases where claims relate to consumer positions. In this respect, a mandate can be given to an escrow agent whose job would consist of ensuring compliance with the regulation. In this way, the SPV would be in a position to avoid the application of this regulation. Fourth, the SPV must comply with the financial reporting requirements: the SPV shall make available the information relating to annual financial reports. Pursuant to Art. 7 of the EU Securitisation Regulation, the originator and the SPV are under an obligation

45 It is possible to believe that these models should be considered preferable to the adoption of a granular regulation based on the civil code. This reasoning is propped up by the consideration that these contractual models could also have been adapted to civil law systems. The concept of securitisation, in fact, cannot be tracked back to a specific legal concept of English law or any other Anglo-American legal system. Consequently, operators may simply rely upon concepts available in a given legal system. If the common law appears to be the "usual suspect" for this "borrowing" of contractual concepts, this is simply because investment banks mainly operate between London and New York, therefore in an environment where that law is familiar. It should be added that, in some respects, there are already inconsistencies between English law and the phenomenon of the securitisation and, particularly, with the assignment of receivables. Evidence has it that the contract in the common law principles, apart from the legislative developments that have taken place since 1999, cannot be sold to entities other than those that are the original parties. Additionally, scholars (e.g. T. Burns, 'The Transfer of Future Rights in Securitisations: A Comparative Study of the Law in England and Scotland' (2009) *Journal of International Banking Law and Regulation* 24(1) 35–43) have also shown that there are legal difficulties in transferring future rights, particularly in relation to future flows of securitisations in Britain, including the Anglo-Welsh legal system. Although the English legal system has sorted out these dilemmas more quickly, the solution is still less than ideal. Given the dearth of notice to debtors, the assignee of future rights under an equitable assignment "may incur some risk of a diminution of the value of the assets if, for example, the debtors acquire set-off rights" (*ibidem*). However, the matter is even less satisfactory in Scotland, where the current Scots law of assignment, with its requirement for intimation to debtors as a condition of transferring ownership, "is a product of an old legal transplant from France in the 15th century." The hurdles currently existing in Scots law in the area of securitisation will be overcome once the new proposal of the statutory pledge and the implementation of the pledge on movable assets will be implemented. See T. Burns, *The Transfer of Future Rights in Securitisations*, *ibidem*, 43.

to make available a set of information that, in certain cases, must be submitted to the securitisation repository.[46]

2.4 The purpose of the transactions

At the beginning, securitisations were used nonchalantly, and perhaps even incorrectly, by operators who, faced with extremely complex structures, acted with little transparency. In a number of circumstances, this put the risk assessment of the transaction concerned under serious stress.

Additionally, credit rating agencies did not always play the role assigned to them by the relevant contract, the one existing between them and the arranger, the former being entrusted with the task of assessing the quality of the portfolio to be transferred to the SPV. The role of the credit rating agency was – and it is still – necessary to ensure that securitisation transactions are guided by prudential criteria, suitable to safeguard a "physiological" repayment of securities' holders.[47] It is also important not to forget that a superficial performance, on the part of the credit rating agency, of their contract sparks off serious consequences of a contractual as well as non-contractual nature.[48]

46 Art. 7(2): "where no securitisation repository is registered in accordance with Article 10, the entity designated to fulfil the requirements set out in paragraph 1 of this Article shall make the information available by means of a website that: (a) includes a well-functioning data quality control system; (b) is subject to appropriate governance standards and to maintenance and operation of an adequate organisational structure that ensures the continuity and orderly functioning of the website; (c) is subject to appropriate systems, controls and procedures that identify all relevant sources of operational risk; (d) includes systems that ensure the protection and integrity of the information received and the prompt recording of the information; and (e) makes it possible to keep record of the information for at least five years after the maturity date of the securitisation. The entity responsible for reporting the information, and the securitisation repository where the information is made available shall be indicated in the documentation regarding the securitisation."

47 The literature in this area is very extensive. Among the several scholars, see F. Amtenbrink, J. De Haan, 'Regulating Credit Ratings in the European Union: A Critical First Assessment of Regulation 1060/2009 on Credit Rating Agencies' (2009) *Common Market Law Review* 46, 1915–1949. It is emphasised, among the other things, as follows: "The global financial crisis has triggered a major debate on the effectiveness and efficiency of the current regulatory structures including those governing CRAs. The latter have been severely criticized for having contributed to the current crisis, triggering demands for a regulatory response. In the EU, the Commission clearly wants to be seen acting swiftly and decisively in time of crisis, thereby capturing the new Zeitgeist of legislative intervention in the economic sphere. In doing so, it has notably parted from the recommendations of several high profile expert bodies, all of which advised against the introduction of a comprehensive regulatory framework. The question that arises in this context is whether the new regime for the time being will make a decisive difference compared to the current mix of regulation and self-regulation under the Capital Requirements Directive and the IOSCO code" (F. Amtenbrink, J. De Haan, *ibidem*).

48 As far as the matter of the liability is concerned, see M. Haentjens, P. de Gioia Carabellese, *European Banking and Financial Law*, 2nd ed., *European Banking and Financial Law*, Routledge, London and New York, 2020, *passim*.

The reaction of the legislatures has been to intervene, following the "epiphany" of the financial crisis,[49] via progressive stages, even though this has occurred in a measured and balanced way, in the stereotypical fashion of EU legislation. Centred on these interventions, it is possible to infer: a) secure and simple securitisations have been planned; b) a better approach to the management of securitisations through due diligence[50] and risk retention requirements is envisaged.

From the above, it is not entirely correct to say that the regulation does not have an effect on securitisations. The years leading up to the EU Securitisation Regulation were characterised by copious law-making, and as far as the European Union is concerned, securitisations are regulated in a strict manner within the European market. An entity that securitises and is supervised will have to comply with strict rules of a prudential nature. The Securitisation Regulation, in fact, provides for a risk-sensitive and prudentially sound treatment with regard to activities and investments pursuant to the Capital Requirement Regulation (CRR).[51] The objective is to ensure that risks are appropriately absorbed by the capital requirements of credit institutions.

49 E.F. Gerding, 'Code, Crash, and Open Source: The Outsourcing of Financial Regulation to Risk Models and the Global Financial Crisis' (2009) *Washington University Law Review*, 127.

50 It is possible to observe as follows: "The ability of investors and potential investors to exercise due diligence and thus make an informed assessment of the creditworthiness of a given securitisation instrument depends on their access to information on those instruments. Based on the existing acquis, it is important to create a comprehensive system under which investors and potential investors will have access to all the relevant information over the entire life of the transactions, to reduce originators,' sponsors' and SSPEs' reporting tasks and to facilitate investors' continuous, easy and free access to reliable information on securitisations. To enhance market transparency, a framework for securitisation repositories to collect relevant reports, primarily on underlying exposures in securitisations, should be established. Such securitisation repositories should be authorised and supervised by the European Supervisory Authority (European Securities and Markets Authority) ('ESMA'), established by Regulation (EU) No 1095/2010 of the European Parliament and of the Council. In specifying the details of such reporting tasks, ESMA should ensure that the information required to be reported to such repositories reflects as closely as possible existing templates for disclosures of such information" (Recital No. 12). Moreover, Recital No. 13 spells out: "The main purpose of the general obligation for the originator, sponsor and the SSPE to make available information on securitisations via the securitisation repository is to provide the investors with a single and supervised source of the data necessary for performing their due diligence. Private securitisations are often bespoke. They are important because they allow parties to enter into securitisation transactions without disclosing sensitive commercial information on the transaction (e.g. disclosing that a certain company needs funding to expand production or that an investment firm is entering a new market as part of its strategy) and/or related to the underlying assets (e.g. on the type of trade receivable generated by an industrial firm) to the market and competitors. In those cases, investors are in direct contact with the originator and/or sponsor and receive the information necessary to perform their due diligence directly from them. Therefore, it is appropriate to exempt private securitisations from the requirement to notify the transaction information to a securitisation repository."

51 Recital No. 50 states that "in order to ensure that the risks and risk reductions arising from institutions' securitisation activities and investments are appropriately reflected in the capital requirements of institutions it is necessary to include rules providing for a risk-sensitive and prudentially sound treatment of such activities and investments. To this end, a clear and

The genesis of the new principles is the result of the overall re-assessment of the entire banking sector at a global level. In November 2010, at a time when the consequences of the economic and financial crisis were still being confronted, the G20 leaders met in Seoul. The Financial Stability Board (FSB) was asked to develop suggestions to strengthen oversight and shadow banking regulation.[52]

The FSB, following work developed under this mandate, issued recommendations that affected aspects of the entire shadow banking industry, including securitisations. In this respect, it is appropriate to recall Recommendation No. 7, which is linked, in turn, to securitisation transaction incentives. The FSB drew attention to a specific securitisation issue, namely ensuring that securitisation providers, both originators and sponsors, held part of the underlying assets.

According to the FSB, "skin in the game" was the determining factor in regulatory responses to the financial crisis. This strictly regulatory aspect has been considered increasingly important, ultimately vital, and consistent with the need for securitised products to be transparent and standardised.[53] The specific recommendation, addressed by the International Organization of Securities Commissions (IOSCO), has been incorporated into the regulation of the most advanced jurisdictions[54] but also into the laws of other countries.[55] The obligation to maintain risk, in force in EU law as a result of the EU Securitisation Regulation, is included in several regulatory aspects that, as in the case of due diligence, have the greatest impact on the success of the securitisation transaction.

This system of provisions first defines how the originator will have to calculate the exposure amount for compliance with regulatory capital requirements. The reference goes to both traditional and synthetic securitisations. The modalities by which the originator may exclude the exposure it has securitised from the risk-weighted exposure amount or, if applicable, the expected loss amount shall also be regulated. The transfer of credits, according to a strictly legal interpretation, makes a real and genuine sale.

The maintenance requirement is of crucial importance: it is intended to avoid "loose underwriting" by those involved in the securitisation: arrangers could be

encompassing definition of securitisation is needed that captures any transaction or scheme whereby the credit risk associated with an exposure or pool of exposures is tranched. An exposure that creates a direct payment obligation for a transaction or scheme used to finance or operate physical assets should not be considered an exposure to a securitisation, even if the transaction or scheme has payment obligations of different seniority."

52 www.treasury.gov.

53 FSB, *Shadow Banking: Strengthening Oversight and Regulation*, 27 October 2011, 21.

54 OICU-IOSCO, *The Board of the International Organization of Securities Commissions*, in *Global Developments in Securitisation Regulation Final Report* (FR09/12), 16 November 2012.

55 A. Gelpern, E.F. Gerding, *Rethinking the Law in "Safe Assets,"* in R.P. Buckley, E. Avgouleas, D.W. Arner (eds), *Reconceptualising Global Finance and its Regulation*, Cambridge, Cambridge University Press, 2016, 184. A. Gelpern, E.F. Gerding, 'Private and Public Ordering in Safe Asset Markets' (2015) *Brooklyn Journal of Corporate, Financial & Commercial Law*, 1; A. Gelpern, E.F. Gerding, 'Inside Safe Assets' (2015) *Yale Journal on Regulation*, 363.

those potentially most involved with this behaviour.[56] Scholars already highlighted that the retention requirement should be developed within the regulation: its underpinning philosophy is to avoid the misunderstandings necessitated by some securitisation models, whose objective is the originate-to-distribute.[57] The theme at stake has been the subject matter of a significant reform, which has resulted in an alternative obligation, imposed on both originators and investment banks to maintain, as players, a significant net economic interest in the transaction they are partaking in. The ultimate aim of this stricter requirement is to encourage prudent behaviour on both sides.[58]

According to the Securitisation Regulation, this obligation is substantiated in the legal provisions whereby the main regulated entities are required to assess, in

56 It has been emphasised by the EU legislature that a risk retained by originators ensures the desirable re-alignment and matching of interests between those "players" and the investors themselves. This is confirmed by Recital 10 of the Regulation on Securitisations:

"It is essential that the interests of originators, sponsors, original lenders that are involved in a securitisation and investors be aligned. To achieve this, the originator, sponsor or original lender should retain a significant interest in the underlying exposures of the securitisation. It is therefore important for the originator, sponsor or original lender to retain a material net economic exposure to the underlying risks in question. More generally, securitisation transactions should not be structured in such a way to avoid the application of the retention requirement. That requirement should be applicable in all situations where the economic substance of a securitisation is applicable, whatever legal structures or instruments are used. There is no need for multiple applications of the retention requirement. For any given securitisation, it suffices that only the originator, the sponsor or the original lender is subject to the requirement. Similarly, where securitisation transactions contain other securitisations positions as underlying exposures, the retention requirement should be applied only to the securitisation, which is subject to the investment. The STS notification should indicate to investors that the originator, sponsor or original lender is retaining a material net economic exposure to the underlying risks. Certain exceptions should be made for cases in which securitised exposures are fully, unconditionally and irrevocably guaranteed in particular by public authorities. Where support from public resources is provided in the form of guarantees or by other means, this Regulation is without prejudice to State aid rules."

57 Recital No. 28 of the EU Regulations on Securitisations states as follows: "It is essential to prevent the recurrence of 'originate to distribute' models. In those situations lenders grant credits applying poor and weak underwriting policies, as they know in advance that related risks are eventually sold to third parties. Thus, the exposures to be securitised should be originated in the ordinary course of the originator's or original lender's business pursuant to underwriting standards that should not be less stringent than those the originator or original lender applies at the time of origination to similar exposures which are not securitised. Material changes in underwriting standards should be fully disclosed to potential investors or, in the case of fully supported ABCP programmes, to the sponsor and other parties directly exposed to the ABCP transaction. The originator or original lender should have sufficient experience in originating exposures of a similar nature to those which have been securitised. In the case of securitisations where the underlying exposures are residential loans, the pool of loans should not include any loan that was marketed and underwritten on the premise that the loan applicant, or where applicable intermediaries, were made aware that the information provided might not be verified by the lender. The assessment of the borrower's creditworthiness should also meet, where applicable, the requirements set out in Directive 2008/48/EC or 2014/17/EU of the European Parliament and of the Council or equivalent requirements in third countries."

58 The retention requirement was one of the main conclusions of the G20 Declaration at the Pittsburgh Summit in 2009.

advance and in cases where they decide to invest in securitised securities, whether these obligations to hold an interest in the share capital of the SPV have been fulfilled in a securitisation transaction in which such entities want to invest.[59]

It is noted that the EBA's recommendations on holding requirements[60] contained observations aimed at filling in the potential gap in the implementation of the risk regime, then a transparency requirement. Such a requirement, as originally conceived, could have been circumvented by a broader interpretation of the definition of originator. In detail, it was argued that, for the purposes of Art. 4 of the – then – proposed Securitisation Regulation, an incorporated institution with the sole and final objective of securitisation exposure and without a wider purpose, in other words an *ad hoc* credit institution, could not be considered as an originator.

The transparency requirement for securitisations and underlying exposures is intended to enable investors to understand, assess and compare securitisation transactions. At the same time, this constraint allows investors to act prudently, in accordance with due diligence, in view of the fact that they possess all relevant pieces of information about the securitisation.

A first consequence of the principle of transparency implies the obligation of providing a prospectus, which already exists in the Directive on prospectuses and was subsequently strengthened by the EU with the Prospectus Regulation. Scholars, on the other hand, have largely placed emphasis on the complex phenomenon of shadow banking and the potential risk investors may face, should opacity take over in the offer of securitised products.[61]

Securitised securities are offered on regulated markets where, as a rule, admitted financial instruments are regulated. The concept of a regulated market as a restricted group dealing in financial instruments[62] is referred to in the Securities Market Directive, MiFID II.[63]

Member States should lay down clear and transparent rules concerning the admission of financial instruments to trading. These rules should ensure, in turn, that financial instruments admitted to regulated markets can be traded in a fair, orderly and efficient manner and that they are freely transferable in cases of

59 Within the Securitisation Regulation, the principle of the "neutrality" of the arranger is emphasised by the Recitals, particularly Recital 7: "A sponsor should be able to delegate tasks to a servicer, but should remain responsible for risk management. In particular, a sponsor should not transfer the risk-retention requirement to his servicer. The servicer should be a regulated asset manager such as an undertaking for the collective investment in transferable securities (UCITS) management company, an alternative investment fund manager (AIFM) or an entity referred to in Directive 2014/65/EU of the European Parliament and of the Council (5) (MiFID entity)."

60 *EBA Report on Securitisation Risk Retention, Due Diligence and Disclosure*, 2014, online.

61 S.L. Schwarcz, 'Disclosure's Failure in the Subprime Mortgage Crisis' (2008) *Utah Law Review*, 1109–1122.

62 Art. 51(1) MiFID II.

63 Directive 2014/65/EU of the European Parliament and of The Council of 15 May 2014 on markets in financial instruments and amending Directive 2002/92/EC and Directive 2011/61/EU (recast).

transferability.[64] Since the listing makes the issued securities public, the admission to the securities market is generally accompanied by a prospectus in which both the characteristics of the securities and the issuer legal entity are disclosed to the public.[65]

The Prospectus Directive, which in the past certainly applied to securitised securities issued by the vehicle, has been amended by the Securitisation Regulation. Bearing in mind the general principles on which the Prospectus Directive is built, compliance with the requirements for a prospectus to be published means that the issuer, by publishing it, also discloses to investors pieces of information relating to the securities.[66]

The obligation to publish the prospectus does not stem from one of the alternative circumstances established by Art. 3 of the Prospectus Directive as amended by Directive 2010/73.[67] The exceptions to be applied to securitised securities,

64 Art. 51(1) co.2, MiDIF II.

65 The obligations set out in the prospectus, albeit encapsulated with the MiFID II Directive and previously into MiFID I, were subsequently incorporated into Directive 2003/71/EC of the European Parliament and of the Council, of 4 November 2003 on the prospectus to be published for the public offer or admission to trading of securities and amending Directive 2001/34/EC (Prospectus Directive).

66 In this sense, securitised securities are no exception.

67 Directive 2010/73/EU of the European Parliament and of the Council of 24 November 2010 amending Directive 2003/71/EC on the prospectus to be published for the public offer or admission to trading of securities, and 2004/109/EC, on the harmonisation of transparency requirements concerning information on issuers whose securities are admitted to trading on a regulated market. An analysis on the regulation on prospectus, not limited to the EU regulation, can be read in F. Rossi, 'Prospectus Liability: Implementing Article 6 of the European Community Directive 2003/71/EC in Italy' (2005) *European Business Law Review* 16(6), 1500–1533, where the Italian implications of the Prospectus Regulation is examined; R. Brown, A.V. Ihamuotila, L. Malthasen, 'The Prospectus Directive (Directive 2003/71/EC)' (2013) *International Financial Law Review* 30(28), 97–10; R. Pretorius, J. Ferreira, 'The Implementation of the New Prospectus Directive in the United Kingdom' (2005) *Journal of International Banking Law and Regulation* 20(2), 56–64; P. Faes, H. Vandendael, 'Stock Options on the Verge of Renewed Success?' (2008) *European Lawyer* 59, 58–59; K. Byttebier, J. De Troyer, 'Analysis of the 2017 EU Securitisation Framework – At the Same Time containing an Assessment of the Success or Failure of Establishing a Simple and Safe EU Securitisation Market' (2022) *International Company and Commercial Law Review* 33(2), 79–118; E. Avgouleas, 'EC Securities Regulation, a Single Regime for an Integrated Securities Market: Harmonised We Stand, Harmonised we Fail? Part 2' (2007) *Journal of International Banking Law and Regulation* 22(3), 153–164; L. Minwer Al-Rimawi, 'Securities Disclosure Regime under Shari'a when Contrasted to UK General Law – With Reference to the Principle of Caveat Emptor: Part One' (2020) *Company Lawyer* 41(11), 344–357; P. Schammo, *The Prospectus Approval System* (2006) *European Business Organisations Law Review* 7(2), 501–523; N. Moloney, 'Financial Market Regulation in the Post-Financial Services Action Plan Era' (2006) *International & Comparative Law Quarterly* 55(4), 982–992; J. Herbet, 'Monetary, Banking and Financial Law' (2004) *International Business Law Journal* 5, 695–707; A. Nissen, 'The European Union as a Manager of Global "Business and Human Rights" Regulation: Country-by-Country Reporting Rules' (2019) *UCL Journal of Law and Jurisprudence* 8(2), 141–166; J. Tanega, 'Some Principles of Disclosure for Asset Backed Securities under the EU Prospectus Regulation 2004' (2008) *Journal of International Banking Law and Regulation* 23(6), 294–301;

with the appropriate distinctions, in the light of their particular category, relate to: a) the offer of securitised securities addressed only to qualified investors; b) the offer of securitised securities addressed to less than 150 natural or legal persons per Member State, other than qualified investors;[68] c) the offer of securities addressed to investors who buy securities for less than €100,000.00 per investor, for each offer;[69] d) the offer of securities whose denomination per asset is at least €100,000.00;[70] e) the offer of securitised securities for a total amount of no more than €100,000.00 calculated over a 12-month period.

Art. 7 of the Securitisation Regulation contains more stringent obligations aimed at making the offer more transparent.[71] Moreover, this piece of legislation lays down the pillars on which the prospectus of securitised securities is based. It is precisely for the purposes of this provision that originators, sponsors and SSPEs of a securitisation "shall, in accordance with paragraph 2 of this Article, make at least the following information available to holders of a securitisation position, to the competent authorities referred to in Article 29 and, upon request, to potential investors."[72]

I.H-Y. Chiu, D. Katelouzou, 'Making a Case for Regulating Institutional Shareholders' Corporate Governance Roles' (2018) *Journal of Business Law* 1, 67–99.

68 This limit was raised from 100 to 150 as a result of Directive 2010/73.

69 This limit was initially set at €50,000.00. The new limit takes into account the fact that the previous one no longer reflects "the distinction between retail investors and professional investors in terms of investor capacity, since it appears that even retail investors have recently made investments of more than EUR 50 000 in a single transaction. For that reason it is appropriate to increase the said threshold and amend other provisions in which that threshold is mentioned accordingly. Corresponding adjustments should be made in Directive 2004/109/EC of the European Parliament and of the Council."

70 The previous data referred to €50,000.00.

71 In this respect, see Recital No. 11 of the Securitisation Regulation: "Originators or sponsors should not take advantage of the fact that they could hold more information than investors and potential investors on the assets transferred to the SSPE, and should not transfer to the SSPE, without the knowledge of the investors or potential investors, assets whose credit-risk profile is higher than that of comparable assets held on the balance sheet of the originators. Any breach of that obligation should be subject to sanctions to be imposed by competent authorities, though only when such a breach is intentional. Negligence alone should not be subject to sanctions in that regard. However, that obligation should not prejudice in any way the right of originators or sponsors to select assets to be transferred to the SSPE that ex ante have a higher-than average credit-risk profile compared to the average credit-risk profile of comparable assets that remain on the balance sheet of the originator, as long as the higher credit-risk profile of the assets transferred to the SSPE is clearly communicated to the investors or potential investors. Competent authorities should supervise compliance with this obligation by comparing the assets underlying a securitisation and comparable assets held on the originator's balance sheet. The comparison of performance should be made between assets that are ex ante expected to have similar performances, for example between non-performing residential mortgages transferred to the SSPE and non-performing residential mortgages held on the balance sheet of the originator. There is no presumption that the assets underlying a securitisation should perform similarly to the average assets held on the originator's balance sheet."

72 Fundamentally, there is not an abundance of legal literature as far as the concept of sponsor is concerned. Among the contributions, see P-E. Partsch, 'Sponsoring under the CRR: An Activity

It is possible to distinguish two types of information. The first relates to "information on the underlying exposures on a quarterly basis, or, in the case of ABCP, information on the underlying receivables or credit claims on a monthly basis." The second, by contrast, relates to:

> (i) the final offering document or the prospectus together with the closing transaction documents, excluding legal opinions; (ii) for traditional securitisation, the asset sale agreement, assignment, novation or transfer agreement and any relevant declaration of trust; (iii) the derivatives and guarantee agreements, as well as any relevant documents on collateralisation arrangements where the exposures being securitised remain exposures of the originator; (iv) the servicing, back-up servicing, administration and cash management agreements; (v) the trust deed, security deed, agency agreement, account bank agreement, guaranteed investment contract, incorporated terms or master trust framework or master definitions agreement or such legal documentation with equivalent legal value; (vi) any relevant inter-creditor agreements, derivatives documentation, subordinated loan agreements, start-up loan agreements and liquidity facility agreements.[73]

Now Open to Certain Mancos and AIFMs?' (2014) *Butterworths Journal of International Banking & Financial Law* 29(2), 121–122; M.C. Nwogugu, 'Economic Policy and the Constitutionality of Asset Securitisation' (2009) *International Company and Commercial Law Review* 20(7), 245–254; H. von Reden, 'Regulation of Securitised Products Post the Financial Crisis' (2013) *UCL Journal of Law and Jurisprudence* 2(1), 112–140; B. Ingman, 'Shadow Banking – The Next Wave of Financial Regulation' (2018) *Journal of International Banking Law and Regulation* 33(3), 84–93; V. Bavoso, 'Financial Innovation and Structured Finance: The Case of Securitisation' (n. 6), 3–12; E. Matebalavu, 'The Beginning of the Revival for Structured Debt?' (2010) *Law & Financial Markets Review* 4(2), 99–101; M.P. Atzwanger, 'Securitising Commercial Loans by Pooling: Part 2' (1993) *Journal of International Banking Law* 8(12), 499–507; J.D. Feinberg, Paul T. Scheuerman, 'Revision of US Risk-Based Capital Rules' (2000) *Journal of International Banking Law* 15(4/5), 121–123; J.D. Feinberg, P.T. Scheuerman, *Revision of US Risk-Based Capital Rules* (2000) *Journal of International Banking Law* 15(4/5), 121–123; P. Zijp, J.P. Franx, 'Finding a Special Purpose' (2008) *European Lawyer* 83, 33–35; G. Penn, 'Promoting Liquidity in the Secondary Loan Market: Is Sub-Participation Still Fit for Purpose?' (2022) *Journal of International Banking Law and Regulation* 37(3), 85–102; K. Vyas, K. Cummings, 'Securitising Distressed Debt' (2012) *Tax Journal* 1120, 17–20.

73 About the underlying exposures, Recital No. 26 of the Securitisation Regulation stresses the concept: "Underlying exposures should not include exposures in default or exposures to obligors or guarantors that, to the best of the originator's or original lender's knowledge, are in specified situations of credit-impairedness (for example, obligors that have been declared insolvent). The 'best knowledge' standard should be considered to be fulfilled on the basis of information obtained from debtors on origination of the exposures, information obtained from the originator in the course of its servicing of the exposures or in the course of its risk-management procedure or information notified to the originator by a third party. A prudent approach should apply to exposures which have been non-performing and have subsequently been restructured. However, the inclusion of the latter in the pool of underlying exposure should not be excluded where such exposures have not presented new arrears since the date of the restructuring, which should have taken place at least one year prior to the date of transfer or assignment of the underlying exposures to the SSPE. In such cases, adequate disclosure should ensure full transparency." With regards to legal opinion,

Art. 7 also requires supporting information to be provided to the investor if the prospectus has been drawn up in accordance with Directive 2003/71. In this case, it is stipulated that:

> where a prospectus has not been drawn up in compliance with Directive 2003/71/EC of the European Parliament and of the Council, a transaction summary or overview of the main features of the securitisation, including, where applicable: (i) details regarding the structure of the deal, including the structure diagrams containing an overview of the transaction, the cash flows and the ownership structure; (ii) details regarding the exposure characteristics, cash flows, loss waterfall, credit enhancement and liquidity support features; (iii) details regarding the voting rights of the holders of a securitisation position and their relationship to other secured creditors; (iv) a list of all triggers and events referred to in the documents provided in accordance with point (b) that could have a material impact on the performance of the securitisation position.[74]

In the case of STS securitisations, notification and reporting shall be on a quarterly basis; alternatively, in the case of ABCPs, monthly reporting shall include: a) all credit quality and underlying exposure performance data; b) cash flow data generated by the underlying exposures and securitisation liabilities;[75] c) information on the maintenance of risk.

2.5 The dynamics of securitisations

The economic objective of the originator is to obtain a credit surplus. This goal will be achieved, seemingly, after the securitisation transaction has exhausted its effects and the investors have received the repayment of both the principal and the interest. A surplus could emerge in the event of overcollateralisation too, therefore, a transfer of receivables significantly higher than the securitised financial instruments. From the standpoint of contractual law, it can be quite certainly stated that the SPV is under an obligation to transfer the surplus resulting from the completion of the securitisation transaction to the originator.

Likewise, from a legal point of view several issues arise from securitisation, such as a regulatory conundrum and ownership issues, including public policy rules. These mandatory aspects cannot be derogated by the parties.

---

the Securitisation Regulation, at its Recital No. 23, seems to provide a very helpful definition: "A legal opinion provided by a qualified legal counsel could confirm the true sale or assignment or transfer with the same legal effect of the underlying exposures and the enforceability of that true sale, assignment or transfer with the same legal effect under the applicable law."

74 Art. 7(1), lett. c.

75 Exceptions to this are ABCPs and information on breaches of events involving a change in the order of priority of payments or replacement of counterparties.

First and foremost, the transfer of receivables from the originator to the SPV must qualify as true sale.[76] This is essential to ensure that the sale is genuine and that the originator shall return the price received. A consequent aspect is that, according to certain legal systems, a transfer for fiduciary purposes that takes place only for the purpose of security is prohibited.[77] From this perspective, true sale is also instrumental in ensuring that the amount paid by the SPV to the originator does not qualify as a loan, secured by the claims.

Should this re-characterisation[78] take place, the results for the parties involved would be catastrophic.[79] Specifically, the off-balance-sheet treatment of receivables will be affected and the originator will be left with responsibility for the receivable credit risk. In addition, all the requirements for the provision of credit-related securities will be applied and, as a result of re-characterisation, they will no longer have to be met.[80] Investors who do not subscribe the securitised financial instruments as they rely on the creditworthiness of the company will see their money in jeopardy.

This combination of unexpected events leads to a number of difficulties, such as the reversal of publication or registration requirements linked with the ostensive sale. Also depending on the different property rights regimes, any surplus on collateral will have to be returned to the creditors, following activation and enforcement of the collateral, whereas, conversely, the surplus in a securitisation transaction is reserved for bondholders. Finally, the enforcement of the security is subject to restrictive rules that are absent in the hypothesis of full transfer in the case of a securitisation.

76 The Securitisation Regulation, in this matter, is adamant: "This Regulation only allows for 'true-sale' securitisations to be designated as STS. In a true-sale securitisation, the ownership of the underlying exposures is transferred or effectively assigned to an issuer entity which is a SSPE. The transfer or assignment of the underlying exposures to the SSPE should not be subject to clawback provisions in the event of the seller's insolvency, without prejudice to provisions of national insolvency laws under which the sale of underlying exposures concluded within a certain period before the declaration of the seller's insolvency can, under strict conditions, be invalidated" (Recital No. 22).

77 Art. 3:84(3) del *Dutch Civil Code*. M. Haentjens, P. de Gioia Carabellese, *European Banking and Financial Law*, 2nd ed. (n. 48), 255.

78 That is, if the trust transfer is not the result of a true sale but has taken place solely for the purpose of guarantee.

79 P.R. Wood, *Law and Practice of International Finance*, Sweet & Maxwell, London, 2008, 468–470; P.R. Wood, *Law and Practice of International Finance Series*, 3rd ed., Sweet & Maxwell, London, 2019.

80 In the Italian legal system, an attempt was made by the Financial Administration (Sassari Provincial Tax Commission, 10 June 2004, no. 67). The dispute concerned the fact that the guarantee given by the originator in relation to the junior notes affected the genuine nature of the transaction as a sale. The decision was not favourable to the Financial Administration, because it was established that there was nothing abnormal in the actual contractual package of the securitisation compared to the usual dynamics of a standard securitisation transaction. A. Scano, 'Credit Enhancement e Riqualificazione della Cessione di Crediti nell'Ambito delle Operazioni di Asset Securitisation' (2006) *Banca, borsa e titoli di credito*, 87 ff.

In order to prevent re-characterisation, the transaction in question should not possess the main characteristics of a credit-related security interest. This goal could be achieved via different strategies. First, the fact that the originator has residual liability for the assets that are transferred to the SPV must be ruled out. The originator, in other words, cannot guarantee the repayment of the principal and the interest of the receivables and, therefore, is not encumbered by any obligation to repurchase the securities in the event of losses on the receivables. Second, it is essential for the SPV to obtain exclusive control over the assets and for the vehicle to be allowed to take any action that a normal owner is authorised to take.[81] Third, from an accounting point of view, the assets must be solidly included within the perimeter of the SPV and therefore isolated from the originator in the event of its insolvency. Finally, depending on the applicable law, a court might consider other circumstances to assess whether a securitisation transaction can be qualified as a secured loan.[82] Fourth, the originator could still be liable for the underlying claims even if indirectly. This would be the case with a subordinated loan to the vehicle, the SPV, if the originator's creditor bears credit losses before the bondholders are forced to do so.[83] The above-described situation would integrate a delicate circumstance which could be appreciated differently depending on the legal regime applicable in a specific legal order. In other words, one element will be regarded as decisive on the basis of the sensitivity of a legal order.

Legal aspects may also apply to the transfer of the security rights that guarantee claims to the security trustee. As a rule of ownership, security rights are ancillary; in other words they follow the claims they guarantee. In this way, the security rights that guarantee the credits are generally transferred with the same credits from the originator to the SPV. Quite commonly, the security rights that guarantee receivables are land mortgages or bank mortgages. Such mortgages are connected with properties, each guaranteeing the loan that finances the property.

81 The SPV should obtain full disposal power of assets to sell or secure assets. This principle does not appear to be affected by the fact that the originator may continue to collect the revenues of the assets as a servicer. In fact, it is common, within securitisation transactions, that a servicing contract is entered into between the originator and the SPV, whereby the collection of the receivables, including the request of payment from the assigned debtors, is entrusted to the originator. However, if the originator continued servicing and collecting the claims after the transfer to the SPV, this could be consistent with re-characterisation, if there was not any contract of service or if the sale and purchase agreement prohibited any servicing.

82 Under the law of securities, the surety is entitled to benefit from the security, as long as the proceeds of the sale of either the pledged item or the secured assets do not exceed the initially guaranteed debt. Accordingly, the surety will return any surplus on the sale to the debtor. It must be added that in a classic securitisation transaction, the SPV returns the surplus to the originator with the aim of making a profit, while other profits are for the benefit of investors. All these aspects will depend on the specific arrangements existing for each transaction. Therefore, much will depend on whether to consider its material profit with its re-characterisation. Sometimes the originator has a right to repurchase any surplus on receivables. Whether this is material or not will depend on the particular conditions of the transaction concretely put in place. In any case, the repurchase of credits cannot be without consideration.

83 This operation is defined as equity price.

However, like bank's mortgages, they may also guarantee other claims, not necessarily loans on properties (therefore, real estate), that a bank can claim against the debtor, for example those connected with overdraft or current accounts. When a loan on a property is secured and is transferred to an SPV, it becomes attackable to the extent that the mortgage, which guarantees the bank, refers to the SPV. In these circumstances, the mortgage branches out into two parts. The first is *pro rata* and concerns the percentage of the loan that is transferred to the SPV, while the originator retains the rest for the part that guarantees the other relationships.

When credit security interests are transferred to the SPV, they need to be transferred to the security trustee. As regards the aspect of the applicable law, there could be different solutions. Under Dutch law, for example, the most commonly used method is parallel debt construction. This means that the SPV obliges itself to pay the same amount to the security trustee and bondholders so that the debts are parallel. The SPV, therefore, constitutes a pledge on receivables in favour of the security trustee to guarantee the payment of the debt concurrently created. In the application of the ancillary principle, the security interests that guarantee the mortgages become available with the pledge in favour of the security trustee. Therefore, the latter will have the power, in the event of default of the SPV, to activate the security interest and recover the losses in place of the investors.

2.6 Securitisations and assignment of receivables

The reference to the notion of shadow banking makes it possible to understand, more in-depth, how simple, transparent and standardised structured finance transactions should be interpreted from the point of view of the general law theory.[84]

It is possible to affirm that shadow banking[85] draws a perimeter for the financial activities that intermediaries are allowed to exercise because this business is not strictly prohibited.[86] The definition refers to the discrepancy existing between the action of the banking industry and its players, on the one hand, and the absence of immediate understanding by the legislature, on the other hand.[87]

With these premises, it is recalled that securitisations are usually attached to the concept of shadow banking. These operations were not regulated until 2010 and are currently subject to the capital market realm, in the EU the debt capital market. The main features of this new approach are the requirements of due diligence and retention.

At present, it is possible to argue that securitisations benefit from full regulatory harmonisation in major world markets. In this context, securitisations

84 I.H-Y. Chiu, J. Wilson, *Banking Law and Regulation*, Oxford University Press, Oxford, 2019.

85 P. de Gioia Carabellese, C. Chessa, 'The So-Called Pan-European Depositors' Protection Scheme: A Further Euro Own-Goal? A Critical Analysis of Directive 2014/49' (2016) *Maastricht Journal of European and Comparative Law*, 241.

86 The enacting terms can be defined as "loose."

87 E.F. Gerding, *Law, Bubbles, and Financial Regulation* (n. 18), 139–195.

are now subject to extensive regulation.[88] The ultimate goal of the regulation is to formalise the process whereby a market of securitised simple, transparent and standardised securities is created and shaped. From this, it can also be said that the STS requirements will be designed to create two categories of securitisations: one in the short term (ABCP) and one in the long term. The two categories will be strengthened "on the basis of existing requirements in the Liquidity Coverage ratio and Solvency II delegated acts, on the EBA advice and on the BCBS-IOSCO standard." It should be added that these structured finance transactions, once attention is paid to the new genre of STS securitisations, could hardly qualify as shadow banking transactions. In a global and harmonised context, in which regulated entities have necessarily to comply with burdens and procedures in order to buy securitised products and in which SPVs are regulated, the term shadow banking could sound anachronistic.

Starting from these premises, at least two reflections are addressed in this work.

The first bears on the fact that overregulation of the banking and financial system does not necessarily prevent crises.[89] It is possible that a strict discipline can, even, unleash the so-called bubble.[90] The second observation is that unbalanced and "emotional" financial regulation can produce a squeeze on growth and investment. It should be noted in this regard that they fulfil their function, provided that they are complied with in the long term.[91]

A further, albeit intertwined, reflection originates from this. While regulatory harmonisation has pervaded structured finance, on the one hand, legal harmonisation of the financial industry is an objective on the other. It should be stressed that, as regards contracts and transactions that are cross-border by definition, the legal risks that the investor may incur are not totally avoided. In a strictly legal perspective, the accountability of "securitisers"[92] is left to the discretion of the various courts and legal systems, that is of the nations or juridical systems in which the various contractual phases of the operation are put in place.

Following this reasoning, a "new" legislative framework in the territory of the European Union could function to better identify the area of responsibility of "securitisers" towards private investors. From this would derive, also, an

88 It is possible that this will be less and less sectoral and more and more uniform, as the Rules of Procedure have shown.

89 L. Enriques, 'Regulators' Response to the Current Crisis and the Upcoming Regulation of Financial Markets: One Reluctant Regulator's View' (2009) *University of Pennsylvania Journal of International Law*, 1147–1155; R. Roberta, 'Regulating in the Dark and a Postscript Assessment of the Iron Law of Financial Regulation' (2014) *Hofstra Law Review* 43(1), Article 2.

90 E.F. Gerding, *Law, Bubbles, and Financial Regulation* (n. 18), 62–135.

91 F.A. Hayek, *Law, Legislation, and Liberty. Volume II: The Mirage of Social Justice*, University of Chicago Press, Chicago, 1977, 29.

92 Reference is made to the securitisation players.

elevation of the level of protection of the investor to whom securitised securities are expected to be returned safely.[93]

This prompts a more robust[94] legislation in the territory of the European Union: it should be interpreted as more incisive than that MiFID II. Due to the gap in the current regulation, a bank that offers or distributes structured products is not considered immediately liable for the damages that are suffered by ordinary investors, although for institutional ones the outcome can be debated.

This provision is a shortcoming of the current framework, which could be overcome by means of an explicit regulation that makes the distributor of financial products objectively liable for the damages caused to investors. The objective of the proposed legislative action would be to strengthen the standards of diligence and professionalism of operators. The potential legal action that they would face, as well as the risk of reputational damage, could be a very persuasive deterrent.[95]

The legal liability of the main securitisation players, and its uniform criteria across the main markets and jurisdictions, may become the new frontier of structured finance analysis, together with the real support that investors lack when buying these financial instruments. In other words, the *caveat emptor*[96] principle should be reaffirmed when an individual approaches the capital market.

The concept of financial stability can be considered a mere utopia since financial bubbles and crises are connected with human and financial market history. After the crisis of 2008, securitisation, thanks to the STS regulation, could enjoy a new season.

2.7 Financial disintermediation and structured finance

It is well-known that the traditional function of the bank, with its ancillary activities, is based on the activities of savings collection and the exercise of credit. If this is true, it is equally correct to point out that in recent years banks have been the target of a phenomenon of disintermediation and, precisely, credit disintermediation.

This term does not precisely refer to the possibility for borrowers to carry out a bank's typical functions but rather to the possibility of resorting to credit players

93 A. Gelpern, E.F. Gerding, *Rethinking the Law in "Safe Assets,"* (n. 55), *passim*.

94 In this robust sense it is understood as an alternative to the concept of regulation. R.P. Buckley, E. Avgouleas, D.W. Arner (eds), *Reconceptualising Global Finance and its Regulation*, Cambridge University Press, Cambridge, 2016; N. Moloney, E. Ferran, J. Payne (eds), *The Oxford Handbook of Financial Regulation*, Oxford University Press, Oxford, 2015; D. Busch, G. Ferrarini (eds), *European Banking Union*, Oxford University Press, Oxford, 2015.

95 In this regard, it should be noted that a decision of the Court of Justice of the European Union did not recognise this responsibility. Case-604/11 *Genil 48 SL and another v Bankinter SA* (2013) CMLR 43.

96 M. Haentjens, P. de Gioia Carabellese, *European Banking and Financial Law*, 2nd ed. (n. 48), 56–75.

that operate informally. In some legal systems, they are not subject to any regulation at all.[97] On a less dynamic side, the phenomenon of disintermediation also occurs when current account holders invest their savings in the form of deposits other than with banks, such as bonds issued by large companies.[98]

Securitisation and disintermediation are connected because the former represents an extreme form of the latter. The vehicle, in fact, whilst collecting the savings across the capital markets, does not guarantee anything with its own capital, which is *de facto* non-existent. In turn, the investor makes an alternative investment in bank deposits or bank bonds or both.

In a structured finance transaction, the restitution stems from the assets transferred to the vehicle by the originator and on a set of contractual documentation that caters to an essential function: to ensure that the assets sold are linked to the fulfilment of the obligations undertaken vis-à-vis securities underwriters. The tool through which this activity is carried out also contributes to disintermediation. Assets based on a bank's balance sheets[99] are allowed to be transferred to separate companies.

The traditional paradigm of a bank, hinged on the concept of deposit-funded corporation as well as non-bank financial intermediary, in both cases funded via equity capital, results in being replaced by an asset-backed vehicle. In the extreme form of disintermediation, this takes bank credit outside both the banking perimeter itself and intermediation. The vehicle does not have any assets, since it is not part of the traditional "supervisory network." Despite this, the strict contractual liability, based on the concept of true sale,[100] means that the market investor is more sensitive to these investments than the more traditional forms of investment, although the latter are carried out within the most traditional "banking circuit."

97 The reference is to micro lending. K. Alexander, *Principles of Banking Regulation* (n. 10), 24.

98 This has been achieved partly through the liberalisation of exchange controls and cross-border capital movements. This allows one to invest in large amounts of credit exposures in other jurisdictions and/or markets to achieve both diversification of risk and potentially higher returns.

99 These assets are, at the same time, recorded in the bank's financial statements.

100 This liability is coupled with the "trust" placed on the credit rating agency and the reliance on its reasonable care in carrying out its functions. It should be noted that in the EU legal system, this trust is enforceable from a legal point of view. In essence, the European legislation has introduced a public regime for authorising credit rating agencies with specific supervisory powers granted to ESMA. This supervision is combined with a contractual liability regime that is activated in the event that the evaluation of the assets transferred and the related securitised securities are not considered adequate. As far as the CRAs literature is concerned, see among others J. De Haan, F. Amtenbrink, *Credit Rating Agencies*, in S. Eijffinger, D. Masciandaro (eds), *Handbook of Central Banking, Financial Regulation and Supervision*, Edward Elgar, Cheltenham and Northampton (MA), 2011.

2.8 Traditional, new and prospective themes: data protection securitisations

Certain legal systems, especially those with a civil law tradition,[101] require a notice of assignment of claims, or, in other cases, the consent of the debtor ceded[102] so that the transaction can also be effective vis-à-vis third parties.

Given that in a traditional securitisation a copious number of claims are involved and many debtor counterparties are affected, the notice cannot be considered a viable solution. Indeed, the mechanism described above could undermine the effectiveness of the operation and, if it were to be carried out in practice, it would become extremely expensive. The solution could be the use of a pledge or the creation of a synthetic securitisation.

If reference is made to the different systems of transfer of ownership that allow undisclosed assignment to become effective against third parties via public forms of publicity, debtors remain entitled to fulfil their obligations via a payment to be made to the original owner, therefore the originator. This would be possible until the notification of the sale to the SPV takes place.

In common law systems, debtors' payments to the originator, prior to the notification of the assignment, may be made to a trust. The related amount of money flowing into the trust cannot be "attacked" by other creditors of the originator in case of insolvency.[103]

Specifically, because of the difference between common law and civil law systems, it becomes crucial to define which law is applicable to the transfer of receivables from the originator to the SPV. This is a controversial issue as the Rome I Regulation does not provide a definitive answer.[104]

101 T.C. Hartley, 'Choice of Law regarding Voluntary Assignment of Contractual Obligations under the Rome I Regulation' (2011) *International & Comparative Law Quarterly*, 29–56.

102 The term "ceded" is used as a synonym for assigned. "Cedent" and "ceded" are used in the EU jargon, although it is well known that in some common law jurisdictions, such as Scotland, the concept of "cession" means that both terms, albeit nearly obsolete, are still used among jurists.

103 It should be noted that, as far as civil law systems are concerned, should a similar trust not be allowed, the relevant legal issue could be problematic. In the event of the originator's insolvency, the payment of the debtors becomes part of the originator's bankruptcy assets and, consequently, available for distribution to the originator's creditors.

104 A.J. Belohlavek, *Rome Convention – Rome I Regulation*, Juris Publishing, Huntington (NY), 2011; O. Lando, P.A. Nielsen, 'The Rome I Proposal' (2007) *Journal of Private International Law* 3(1), 29–51; M. Wilderspin, 'The Rome I Regulation: Communitarisation and Modernisation of the Rome Convention' (2008) *ERA Forum* 9, 259–274; E. Chvika, 'Rome I: Uncertainty on the Horizon of Cross-Border Finance Transactions' (2009) *Butterworths Journal of International Banking & Financial Law* 24(3), 152–154; R. Fentiman, 'Assignment and Rome I: Towards a Principled Solution' (2010) *Law & Financial Markets Review* 4(4), 405–412; J. Ramage, 'All Roads Lead to Rome' (2009) *Solicitors Journal* 153(8), 11–12; F.J. Garcimartin Alferez, 'The Rome I Regulation: Exceptions to the Rule on Consumer Contracts and Financial Instruments' (2009) *Journal of Private International Law* 5(1), 85–103; P. Kiesselbach, 'Financial Transactions in the Crossfire of Rome II' (2011) *Butterworths Journal of International Banking & Financial Law* 26(1), 25–27; A. Haynes, 'The Law Relating to International Banking' (2020) *Journal of International Banking Law and Regulation* 35(5), 220–222; R. Merkin, 'The Rome I Regulation

Art. 14[105] clarifies the law applicable to the assigned claims and determines their assignability, the relationship between the assignee and debtor, the conditions under which the assignment can be enforced against the debtor and whether the debtor's obligations have been fulfilled. According to Art. 14(2), the law of the State in which the claims were created could also define the regulation to be followed for their transfer. Another hypothesis concerns the application of the law of the legal system in which the transferor habitually resides. Finally, the same law could stipulate that the law to be applied for the transfer of ownership of claims is that of the legal system in which the assignment agreement was concluded.[106]

This third possible solution has positive aspects. The parties to the securitisation agreements do not have to verify, from a strictly legal point of view, the law to be applied to each assignment. They should only comply with the statutory ownership requirements of the comprehensive divestiture agreement alone. Another positive aspect is linked with the circumstance that the players of a securitisation will not have to construe which law they need to apply on claims or receivables subject to assignment. It is the global credit transfer agreement[107] that will determine the law to be applied.

A further issue related to the assignment of the claims is whether a set-off between the debtors and the originator can take place, therefore the debts on the one hand, and receivables on the other, albeit belonging to these parties even after the transfer to the SPV. This is related to the determination of the law to be applied to the assignment of claims. Most jurisdictions provide that debtors can effectively offset their claims against the originator, even at a time after the transfer, but within a period when the notice has been assigned.

---

and Reinsurance' (2019) *Journal of Private International Law* 5(1), 69–84; A. Arora, 'Unfair Contract Terms in International Banking Contracts' (2001) *Journal of Business Law*, Sep, 553–565; S. James, 'Rome I – The Uncertainty Remains' (2007) *Butterworths Journal of International Banking & Financial Law* 22(5), 256–257; J. Kane, 'Regulation (EC) No 593/2008 (Rome I Regulation) – Choice of Law – Conflicts of Law – Assignment of Security for Debts – Law Applicable to Third-Party Effects of Assignment' (2019) *Commercial Law Practitioner* 26(10), 195; J. Fleming, 'Legal Catenaccio' (2009) *European Lawyer* 86 32–34, 36; G. Thieffry, J. Walsh, 'Securitisation: The New Opportunities Offered by Economic and Monetary Union' (1997) *Journal of International Banking Law* 12(12), 463–472.

105 "Voluntary assignment and contractual subrogation: 1. The relationship between assignor and assignee under a voluntary assignment or contractual subrogation of a claim against another person (the debtor) shall be governed by the law that applies to the contract between the assignor and assignee under this Regulation. 2. The law governing the assigned or subrogated claim shall determine its assignability, the relationship between the assignee and the debtor, the conditions under which the assignment or subrogation can be invoked against the debtor and whether the debtor's obligations have been discharged. 3. The concept of assignment in this Article includes outright transfers of claims, transfers of claims by way of security and pledges or other security rights over claims." P. Torremans (ed), *Cheshire, North & Fawcett: Private International Law*, 15° ed., Oxford University Press, Oxford, 2017, 686–775.

106 M. Haentjens, P. de Gioia Carabellese, *European Banking and Financial Law*, 2° ed. (n. 48), 255.

107 It is the "Master" encompassing the general clauses governing the sale and purchase for securitisation purposes.

Within a securitisation transaction, an important number of parties could have access to pieces of information about the assets, which are the subject matter of the principal transaction (the sale of receivables). In this way, for example, a rating agency, an SPV and trustees are only potential parties that could have access to information belonging to the originator.

This aspect may be assessed within the GDPR legislative framework:[108] the aim of the GDPR Regulation is to have a global legal measure in the European Union area about Personal Data Protection.[109] Recital No. 1 therein stipulates that the protection of natural persons in relation to the processing of personal data "is a fundamental right." Furthermore, Art. 8(1) of the Charter of Fundamental Rights of the European Union (the "Charter") and Art. 16(1) of the Treaty on the Functioning of the European Union (TFEU) provide that "everyone has the right to the protection of personal data concerning him or her."

The GDPR "applies to the processing of personal data wholly or partly processed by automated means and to the processing other than by automated means of personal data which form part of a filing system or are intended to form part of a filing system." It should also be mentioned that Art. 2(2) of the GDPR Regulation highlights that the relevant piece of legislation

> does not apply to the processing of personal data: (a) in the course of an activity which falls outside the scope of Union law; (b) by the Member States when carrying out activities which fall within the scope of Chapter 2 of Title V of the TEU; (c) by a natural person in the course of a purely personal or household activity; (d) by competent authorities for the purposes of the prevention, investigation, detection or prosecution of criminal offences or the execution of criminal penalties, including the safeguarding against and the prevention of threats to public security.[110]

108 Regulation (EU) 2016/679 of the European Parliament and of the Council of 27 April 2016 on the protection of natural persons with regard to the processing of personal data and on the free movement of such data, and repealing Directive 95/46/EC (General Data Protection Regulation).

109 In this way see Recital No. (2): "The principles of, and rules on the protection of natural persons with regard to the processing of their personal data should, whatever their nationality or residence, respect their fundamental rights and freedoms, in particular their right to the protection of personal data. This Regulation is intended to contribute to the accomplishment of an area of freedom, security and justice and of an economic union, to economic and social progress, to the strengthening and the convergence of the economies within the internal market, and to the well-being of natural persons."

110 S. O'Brien, 'European Data Protection Board Publishes Draft Guidelines on the Contractual Necessity Basis for Processing Personal Data in the Context of Online Services' (2019) *Computer and Telecommunications Law Review* 25(5), 130–134; L. Scaife, 'General Data Protection Regulation: The Principles and Grounds for Processing' (2017) *Compliance & Risk* 6(5), 6–9; S. Stokes, 'Data Protection, Information Security Risk Management and Operational Resilience' (2020) *Compliance Officer Bulletin* 177(Jun), 1–36; H. Johnson, 'Boundaries of Data Protection Law' (2007) *Communications Law* 12(3), 99–101; R. Marchini, 'Processing, Unfair Processing and Compensation' (2006) *Computers & Law* 17(1), 28–31; M.D. Lorenzo, 'Processing of Personal Data ("processing") – Personal Data Filing System ("Filing System") – Structured Set'

Personal data, in the terms of Art. 4(1) of the GDPR,

> means any information relating to an identified or identifiable natural person ("data subject"); an identifiable natural person is one who can be identified, directly or indirectly, in particular by reference to an identifier such as a name, an identification number, location data, an online identifier or to one or more factors specific to the physical, physiological, genetic, mental, economic, cultural or social identity of that natural person.

In this concept it is feasible to include username, password, pseudonyms, date of birth, age, employment, civil status, ID number, etc. Processing, in the terms of Art. 4(2), means "any operation or set of operations which is performed on personal data or on sets of personal data, whether or not by automated means, such as collection, recording, organisation, structuring, storage, adaptation or alteration, retrieval, consultation, use, disclosure by transmission, dissemination or otherwise making available, alignment or combination, restriction, erasure or destruction." In the structure and aim of GDPR, processing, of which either

---

(2011) *European Law Forum* 3(4), 154; E. Lievens, S. van der Hof, 'The Importance of Privacy by Design and Data Protection Impact Assessments in Strengthening Protection of Children's Personal Data under the GDPR' (2018) *Communications Law* 23(1), 33–43; C. Sellars, 'UK Information Commissioner's Opinion on the Use of Live Facial Recognition Technology by Law Enforcement' (2020) *Computer and Telecommunications Law Review* 26(2), 27–30; J. Reichel, 'The GDPR and Processing of Personal Data for Research Purposes: What about Case Law?' (2021) *European Public Law* 27(1), 167–190; Commonwealth Law Bulletin (editorial), 'Draft Model Law on the Protection of Personal Information' (2003) *Commonwealth Law Bulletin* 29(1), 387–411; D.P. Cooper, 'Data Privacy and Corporate Transactions: Dos and Don'ts' (2005) *Company Lawyer* 26(4), 104–110; F. Good, S. Sayers, O. Wint, 'GDPR Series: How to Legitimise Your Profiling Activities' (2018) *Privacy & Data Protection* 18(3), 7–10; S. Bhaimia, 'The General Data Protection Regulation: The Next Generation of EU Data Protection' (2018) *Legal Information Management* 18(1), 21–28; C. Docherty, F. McLean, D. van Der Merwe, 'GDPR Series: The New Data Subject Rights' (2017) *Privacy & Data Protection* 17(8), 9–11; A. Schreiber, 'Mere Access to Personal Data: Is It Processing?' (2020) *International Data Privacy Law* 10(3), 269–277; M. Webber, 'The GDPR's Impact on the Cloud Service Provider as a Processor' (2016) *Privacy & Data Protection* 16(4), 11–14; A. Bevitt, 'Sensitive Personal Data – Current and Future' (2015) *Privacy & Data Protection* 15(5), 6–7; L. Wyeth, 'GDPR Series: Record of Processing Activities' (2017) *Privacy & Data Protection* 18(1), 15–16; R. Jones, 'Data Protection Provisions for Outsourcing Contracts' (2012) *Privacy & Data Protection* 12(6), 3–6; R. Thomas, 'Risk, Accountability, and Binding Corporate Codes: A "Smarter" Approach to Data Protection' (2013) *Privacy & Data Protection* 13(7), 3–6; R. Marchini, 'Data Processing' (2007) *Computers & Law* 18(2), 31–33; S. Doe, 'Practical Privacy: Report from the GDPR World' (2018) *Legal Information Management* 18(2), 76–79.

the controller[111] or the processor is in charge,[112] shall "stick" to the principles contained in Art. 5 therein, namely "lawfulness, fairness and transparency."

In turning the focus on securitisations, the privacy aspect and its underpinning legal "universe," at least in the EU, entails that the correct information to interested parties shall be verified. Every securitisation transaction implies the processing of personal data pertaining to the debtor and, more generally, their successors thereto. Such elements consist of basic information or personal data, earnings, capital (or assets). They are usually included in paper and electronic documents which are passed by the transferor to the transferee.

From this perspective, the privacy policy has two dimensions. First, the debtor will be made aware of the privacy policy pursuant to Art. 13 and Art. 14 of GDPR. At a later time, the controller/processor should explain the processing of personal data, bearing in mind the organisation and the relation between the parties of the transaction.

However, there appears to be a crucial problem: it is extremely complex to provide a privacy policy to a considerable number of people. In other words, the performance required of the servicer appears to be excessive when put in relation to the protected right.

The way out, in this scenario, thanks to a business practice that materialised later, is to obtain a statement from the debtor in which they give an authorisation to the processing of personal data by the surety. The duty of the bank, in compliance with the principle of due diligence, shall lie in the assessment as to whether this authorisation has been given.

2.9 Regulation and supervision

The global financial crisis, with its widespread "wrecks," became, quite unceremoniously, the milestone for the launch of a new set of regulation in the financial and banking sector: after the 2008 financial crisis, indeed, the European legislature has attempted to create a safe harbour, in the financial and banking sector, in the European Union and elsewhere.

The academic debate has been focused for a long time on the possible development of prudential regulation, with the aim to prevent banking crises. Thus, a more stringent framework has been urged, in order to reduce the intensity of banking crises. In order to "resuscitate the securitisation market,"[113] the EU

111 Art. 4(7) is "the natural or legal person, public authority, agency or other body which, alone or jointly with others, determines the purposes and means of the processing of personal data; where the purposes and means of such processing are determined by Union or Member State law, the controller or the specific criteria for its nomination may be provided for by Union or Member State law."

112 It is the "natural or legal person, public authority, agency or other body which processes personal data on behalf of the controller," pursuant to Art. 4(8).

113 V. Bavoso, 'Market-Based Finance, Debt and Systemic Risk: A Critique of the EU Capital Markets Union' (2018) *Accounting, Economics, and Law: A Convivium* 11(3), 6.

legislature, at that time still including the UK, took a legal approach to this market, previously informed by total *laissez-faire*. The aim is to promote securitisations transactions, albeit with more rigorous regulation, informed by market discipline. This will avoid the negative consequences of shadow banking.

Bearing this in mind, Art. 29 of the EU Securitisation Regulation contains a list of competent Authorities to supervise the fulfilment of the obligations laid down in Art. 5. The duty of these Authorities is to "review the arrangements, processes and mechanisms that originators, sponsors, SSPEs and original lenders have implemented in order to comply with this Regulation" (Art. 30(2) of the Securitisation Regulation).[114] It can be affirmed, therefore, that the norms, previously regarded as moral persuasion, have been made binding legal provisions, thanks to a supervisory regime, to be implemented at the EU level.[115]

The review powers include:

> (a) the processes and mechanisms to correctly measure and retain the material net economic interest on an ongoing basis, the gathering and timely disclosure of all information to be made available in accordance with Article 7 and the credit-granting criteria in accordance with Article 9; (b) for STS securitisations which are not securitisations within an ABCP programme, the processes and mechanisms to ensure compliance with Article 20(7) to (12), Article 21(7), and Article 22; and (c) for STS securitisations which are securitisations within an ABCP programme, the processes and mechanisms to ensure, with regard to ABCP transactions, compliance with Article 24 and, with regard to ABCP programmes, compliance with Article 26(7) and (8).[116]

Another additional task entrusted to the competent authority is to assess the participation in the securitisation market and its impact:

> on the stability of the financial institution that operates as original lender, originator, sponsor or investor as part of its prudential supervision in the field of securitisation, taking into account, without prejudice to stricter sectoral regulation: (a) the size of capital buffers; (b) the size of the liquidity buffers;

114 The competent authorities are "(a) for insurance and reinsurance undertakings, the competent authority designated in accordance with point (10) of Article 13 of Directive 2009/138/EC; (b) for alternative investment fund managers, the competent authority responsible designated in accordance with Article 44 of Directive 2011/61/EU; (c) for UCITS and UCITS management companies, the competent authority designated in accordance with Article 97 of Directive 2009/65/EC; (d) for institutions for occupational retirement provision, the competent authority designated in accordance with point (g) of Article 6 of Directive 2003/41/EC of the European Parliament and of the Council (1); (e) for credit institutions or investments firms, the competent authority designated in accordance with Article 4 of Directive 2013/36/EU, including the ECB with regard to specific tasks conferred on it by Regulation (EU) No 1024/2013" (Art. 29(1)).

115 A more in-depth analysis of this both regulatory and supervisory regime is within Chapter 4, below.

116 Art. 30 (2).

and (c) the liquidity risk for investors due to a maturity mismatch between their funding and investments.[117]

The Securitisation Regulation stipulates that the competent authorities are "responsible for the supervision of sponsors in accordance with Article 4 of Directive 2013/36/EU, including the ECB with regard to specific tasks conferred on it by Regulation (EU) No 1024/2013."[118] Should the authority find a risk, that is a material one, posed on either the financial stability or the financial system, "it shall take action to mitigate those risks, report its findings to the designated authority competent for macroprudential instruments under Regulation (EU) No 575/2013 and the ESRB."[119] Additionally, the Authorities[120] have to supervise compliance by the sponsor with some legal duties: a) risk retention (Art. 6); b) transparency requirements (Art. 7); c) ban of resecuritisation (Art. 8); d) the application of criteria for credit-granting (Art. 9).

117 Art. 30(4).
118 Art. 29(2).
119 Art. 30(4), second part.
120 Art. 29(2).

3 The new EU "certified" securitisations

3.1 The European dimension of securitisations

In this work, the term "crisis" all but axiomatically refers to the 2007–2008 period and what is commonly called "2008 financial crisis." It is well-known that the EU legislators, in reacting to this crisis, have strengthened the regulation of capital markets. Although this regime has been heralded by the motto "more regulation is better," the ensuing – yet burning – questions encompass the dilemma: "Better for who? Better for what?" As of today, the only reasonable response is: better for a) capital market stability; b) the European market's peaceful operation; and c) the financial markets more generally.

Bearing this in mind, the EU Securitisation Regulation has engendered, essentially, three changes. At the first level, financial markets have to comply with stringent measures; at the second level, a more pervasive supervision is carried out by the Authority; and, finally, harmonisation and, to a certain extent, a full unification of national rules has been achieved.[1] The latter two elements are closely related to each other.

In the light of the scenario depicted above, it is possible to infer that the central principle of the overall regulation lies in the quintessential importance of the "health" of credit institutions. In this respect, scholars highlight that "sound and safe operation of the banking system is of strategic importance not only in fostering economic development but also in ensuring social and economic stability."[2]

In interpreting the EU Securitisation Regulation in a literal way, particularly as regards the STS concept, this piece of legislation aims to make the securitisation market a more secure one.[3] It is obvious that STS securitisations aim at

1 M. Haentijens, P. de Gioia Carabellese, *European Banking and Financial Law*, 2nd ed., Routledge, London and New York, 2020.

2 R. Craston, A. Avgouleas, K. van Zwieten, C. Hart, T. van Sante, *Principle of Banking Law*, 3rd ed., Oxford University Press, Oxford, 2018, 6.

3 Based on the words of the EU Commission, the approach is to put in place a more risk-sensitive regulatory framework (Proposal for a REGULATION OF THE EUROPEAN PARLIAMENT AND OF THE COUNCIL laying down common rules on securitisation and creating a European framework for simple and transparent securitisation and amending Directives 2009/65/EC, 2009/138/

DOI: 10.4324/9780429293436-3

minimising risks, with such "dangers" being immanent to all financial systems. As a result, asset-backed securities, linked with STS securitisations, in the original "picture" of the Securitisation Regulation, should bear a lower level of both risk and, in exceptionally negative circumstances, losses, at least for financial institutions, which have to hold these assets.[4] Ultimately, this is the "terrain" on which the pillars of the STS Regulation firmly lie. However, as highlighted in this chapter and elsewhere in this work, one pillar has been demolished during the COVID-19 crisis: synthetic securitisations, which in the original plan of the Securitisation Regulation were expected to drive a coach and horses through the "STS" concept, have now seen their "redemption," albeit subject to some caveats. Therefore, synthetic securitisation, euphemistically defined as "on-balance-sheet" structured finance transactions, may now fall within the remit of the STS legal framework.[5]

To elaborate on this, the underpinning philosophy of the Securitisation Regulation has not been altered by some recent developments, prompted by the COVID-19 crisis, the *casus belli* of the passing of a new piece of legislation from Brussels.[6] Although it is true that Regulation 2021/557 encapsulates a slightly more flexible regime, as regards the criteria of simplicity, transparency and standardisation,[7] the need for market discipline and investors' protection, the spark of that legislation, has not changed, although securitisations, more generally, are viewed as the ideal means, for credit institutions, of dealing with the

EC, 2011/61/EU and Regulations (EC) No 1060/2009 and (EU) No 648/2012 and Proposal for a REGULATION OF THE EUROPEAN PARLIAMENT AND OF THE COUNCIL amending Regulation (EU) No 575/2013 on prudential requirements for credit institutions and investment firms {COM(2015) 472 final} {COM(2015) 473 final} {SWD(2015) 186 final}).

4 V. Bavoso, 'High Quality Securitisation and EU Capital Markets Union – Is it Possible?' (2016) *Accounting, Economics, and Law: A Convivium* 7(3), 1–29.

5 This is spelt out by Recital 14 of Regulation n. 557 of 2021: "The object of a credit risk transfer should be exposures originated or purchased by a Union regulated institution within its core lending business activity and held on its balance sheet or, in the case of a group structure, on its consolidated balance sheet at the closing date of the transaction. The requirement for an originator to hold the securitised exposures on the balance sheet should exclude arbitrage securitisations from the scope of the STS label."

6 This is made explicit in the first two Recitals of Regulation no. 557 of 2021: The COVID-19 crisis is severely affecting people, companies, health systems and the economies of Member States. In its Communication of 27 May 2020 entitled 'Europe's Moment: Repair and Prepare for the Next Generation,' the Commission stressed that liquidity and access to finance will continue to be a challenge in the months to come. It is therefore crucial to support the recovery from the severe economic shock caused by the COVID-19 pandemic by introducing targeted amendments to existing pieces of financial legislation" (Recital 1). "The severe economic shock caused by the COVID-19 pandemic and the exceptional containment measures required are having a far-reaching impact on the economy. Businesses are facing disruption to supply chains, temporary closures and reduced demand, while households are confronted with unemployment and a fall in income. Public authorities at Union and Member State level have taken far-reaching action to support households and solvent undertakings in withstanding the severe but temporary slowdown in economic activity and the resulting liquidity shortages" (Recital 2).

7 The principles and norms of Regulation no. 557 of 2021 are also dissected in Chapter 2 and Chapter 4.

increasing number of non-performing exposures which are fundamentally the outcome of the COVID-19 crisis.[8]

Art. 2 of the Securitisation Regulation, the already mentioned EU Regulation 2017/2402, takes pains to draw a perimeter around the securitisation phenomenon from a legal perspective. The article in question, by using the term "definitions," stipulates that securitisations shall be intended and interpreted as transactions or schemes

> whereby the credit risk associated with an exposure or a pool of exposures is tranched, having all of the following characteristics: (a) payments in the transaction or scheme are dependent upon the performance of the exposure or of the pool of exposures; (b) the subordination of tranches determines the distribution of losses during the ongoing life of the transaction or scheme; (c) the transaction or scheme does not create exposures which possess all of the characteristics listed in Article 147(8) of Regulation (EU) No 575/2013.[9]

It stems from this legal provision that mono-tranche securitisation transactions, namely those involving the issue of a single class of ABS securities, are excluded from the scope of the Securitisation Regulation.[10]

Therefore, the "new" EU Regulation is applicable only where the segmentation of the risk associated with the securitised exposure occurs through the issuance of at least two tranches: the senior[11] and the junior,[12] even if, in practice, the tranches usually unfold in not less than groups of three.

Remarkably, a further legal provision, Art. 2(9–10) of the Securitisation Regulation, clarifies the demarcation line between the concepts of traditional[13] and synthetic securitisation.[14] Yet, it is worth emphasising that, from a purely theoretical point of view, the whole body of law encompassed with the ultimate piece

8 In this respect, Recital 5 is self-explanatory: "The COVID-19 crisis risks increasing the number of non-performing exposures (NPEs), and increases the need for institutions to manage and deal with their NPEs. One way for institutions to do so is to trade their NPEs on the market through securitisation. Additionally, in the current context, it is vital that risks are moved away from the systemically important parts of the financial system and that lenders strengthen their capital positions. Synthetic securitisation is one way of achieving this, as well as, for example, raising new own funds."

9 D. Ramos-Munoz, *The Law of Transnational Securitisation*, Oxford University Press, Oxford, 2010.

10 The reference is to Asset-Backed Securities, i.e. the issue of securities by the vehicle that are based not on the guarantee of the capital of the company but on the assets bought by the originator.

11 This bears a lower risk because the payment is based on the currency value prior to the date of the transaction, and has a lower interest rate.

12 The payment of these results in being subordinated to that of the senior notes. Should an intermediate class be present, the payment would be subordinated to that of all the other tranches. As a result, the interest that is promised to investors in the junior class is higher than in the other classes.

13 "Traditional securitisation means a securitisation involving the transfer of the economic interest in the exposures being securitised through the transfer of ownership of those exposures from the originator to an SSPE or through sub-participation by an SSPE, where the securities issued do not represent payment obligations of the originator."

14 "Synthetic means a securitisation where the transfer of risk is achieved by the use of credit derivatives or guarantees, and the exposures being securitised remain exposures of the originator."

of legislation being analysed is limited in its scope: the rules therein contained apply exclusively to credit institutions, insurance undertakings, pension funds and mutual fund managers, as long as they act as institutional investors, originators, promoters, lenders and special purpose vehicles in securitisation transactions. Upon a closer view, this is not a revolutionary statement, as securitisations would not stand without the presence of at least one of those players.

It is a trite view, among scholars, that discipline has a subjective scope: when the securitisation involves institutional entities, such as, for example, banks and financial institutions, the legislation of the Union ensures that the private sector business is integrated with the regulatory framework. The legal provisions encompassed within Directives/Regulations are more stringent in nature, since, in the name of the market stability mantra, they are designed to protect both the investor and the stability of supervised entities. It should be added that the scope of this new legislative framework is straightforward and self-explanatory: the involvement of business banks, which are by definition supervised subjects, acting as advisors too, enjoins the view that even the sale of portfolios of commercial receivables will fall within the realm of the new legislation, as well as the pertinent supervision. Ultimately, the logical consequence is that almost all securitisation transactions will be governed by the rules set out in EU Regulation 2017/2402.

With regard to the time of the application, and therefore its applicability, the Securitisation Regulation has become effective for securitisation transactions whose securities were issued after 1 January 2019. Consequently, even if the relevant contractual documentation was signed before that date, in all cases in which the relevant securities were issued later the new legislative framework applies. This is a peculiarity that would support the view that the main rationale of the EU regulation is to protect the investor by introducing new transparency requirements for the securities that the investor has purchased or may possibly buy. The regulatory regime for STS securitisations may also be beneficial for securitisations with securities issued before 1 January 2019. Securities issued on a previous date may qualify as STS securitisations, provided that they meet certain criteria at the time of notification of the status. In the latter case, ontologically the securities would not be eligible, although they become so after complying with this *ex post* process.

A further aspect that must be addressed relates to both a subjective and a negative condition. Specifically, the Securitisation Regulation stipulates that it is not possible to sell securities to retail customers: these are non-professional investors falling within the meaning of MiFID II. However, there is an exception to this norm, which is subject to two conditions: "a) a verification of suitability has been carried out pursuant to Art. 25.2 MiFID, with a specific written report;" "b) the prudential limit of impact of the investment on the client's portfolio has been respected";[15] c) "the transaction or scheme does not create exposures that possess all the characteristics listed above in Art. 147(8) of Regulation (EU) No.

15 If the investor's portfolio turns out to be €500,000.00, the incidence of the investment in securitisation securities may not exceed 10% of that portfolio with a minimum cut that cannot be less than €10,000.00.

575/2013." Should these conditions be met in a cumulative way, the securities can be offered to these investors too.

In perusing these conditions, it must be pointed out that the last requirement (lett. c) excludes from the definition of securitisation all those transactions that engender exposures resulting, in turn, from "specialised funding," as they have been defined and identified by Art. 147(8) Regulation (EU) No. 575/2013 (Capital Requirement Regulation or CRR).[16] Regarding the exact definition of the concept of "specialised financing," it is also possible to recall the guidelines proposed by the Bank for International Settlements in the Basel III document, which was finalised during the post-crisis reforms. Using these guidelines, it is possible to determine which transactions are excluded from the scope of the Securitisation Regulation – fundamentally complex financial transactions such as project finance.[17]

The wording of the EU Regulation seems to go beyond the aforementioned limit, as it seems to be directed towards a conceptualisation of all the typical subjects of securitisation.

In essence, within the perimeter drawn by the European Union legislature, the SPV is defined as a "securitisation special purpose entity" or "SSPE," i.e. "a corporation, trust or other entity, other than an originator or sponsor, established for the purpose of carrying out one or more securitisations, the activities of which are limited to those appropriate to accomplishing that objective, the structure of which is intended to isolate the obligations of the SSPE from those of the originator."[18] In this definition, the functional aspects of the vehicle, as well as the activities it pursues, are instrumental in the "achievement of this objective," therefore, in the realisation of one or more securitisation operations. Therefore, this definition is not totally aligned to the quintessence of the vehicle frequently suggested and even recommended by scholars: having a single corporate purpose that usually coincides with a single securitisation transaction and, often, not even having an actual corporate structure.[19]

16 The reference is to exposures that: a) are made to an entity created *ad hoc* to finance or administer physical assets or economically similar exposures; b) have contractual conditions that give the lender substantial control over the assets and income generated by them; c) the primary source of repayment of the obligation is the credit generated by the assets financed rather than the autonomous capacity of a larger commercial enterprise.

17 More specifically, the Regulation lists five categories of "specialised financing:" project finance, high volatility commercial real estate, object finance, commodities finance, income-producing real estate (IPRE).

18 Art. 2(2) of the Securitisation Regulation.

19 Owing to these elements, it would differ from the classical corporate model, where there is a plurality of objects, therefore of creditors, as well as a real structure; R. Cranston, E. Avgouleas, K. Van Zwiten, C. Hare, T. van Sante, *Principles of Banking Law*, 3rd ed., Oxford, Oxford University Press, 2018, 491. The most efficient structure of a securitisation would be one where there are as many vehicles as the number of securitisations organised by an arrangement and/or involving the same originator. Thanks to the SPV in charge of a specific securitisation, investors would be protected to the full extent. By contrast, in an SPV in charge of purchasing different pools from

Further elements of linguistic originality can be found in the definitions of an originator and promoter.

As regards the former, it is classified as a "cedent," to be interpreted as "an entity which: (a) itself or through related entities, directly or indirectly, was involved in the original agreement which created the obligations or potential obligations of the debtor or potential debtor giving rise to the exposures being securitised; or (b) purchases a third party's exposures on its own account and then securitises them."[20]

In this regard, through this line of reasoning, the concept of cedent turns out to be pertinent, given that a different terminology, perhaps semantically alluding to the concept of seller, would not have implied the peculiarity of the originator in a securitisation transaction. Ultimately, this is a subject that simply transfers, *ergo* cedes, the risk, although it is not necessarily the owner of the claims.

In relation to the latter, it is defined as a "sponsor," to be understood as a

> credit institution, whether located in the Union or not [...],[21] or an investment firm [...][22] other than an originator, that: (a) establishes and manages an asset-backed commercial paper programme or other securitisation that purchases exposures from third-party entities, or (b) establishes an asset-backed commercial paper programme or other securitisation that purchases exposures from third-party entities and delegates the day-to-day active portfolio management involved in that securitisation to an entity authorised to perform such activity in accordance with Directive 2009/65/EC, Directive 2011/61/EU or Directive 2014/65/EU (Art. 2(5)).

The paradox lies in the overlap between the rigid nature of the Regulation and the perimeter of the bank business.

3.2 The antecedents of the Securitisation Regulation: the financial crisis 2007–2008

The macro-category of structured finance transactions includes the main forms of securitisation and cover bonds.[23] These two variations have as a common feature

different originators, the controversy among different classes of creditors would be highly likely. In common law jurisdictions, the different companies, with different legal personalities, entail that the creditors of each company are separate.

20 Art. 2(3) of the Securitisation Regulation.

21 Credit institution as defined in point (1) of Article 4(1) of Regulation (EU) No. 575/2013.

22 Investment firm as defined in point (1) of Article 4(1) of Directive 2014/65/EU.

23 M. Huertas, K. Lyaskova, 'Bundling Bonds as Safe Assets: An Update on the Eurozone's Sovereign Bond-Backed Securities Proposal' (2018) *Journal of International Banking Law and Regulation* 33(6), 200–207; J. Tribe, S. Hunt, 'Insolvency Bonds: History, Policy and Substance' (2012) *Insolvency Intelligence* 25(3), 37–45; W.W. Bratton, 'Bond Covenants and Creditor Protection: Economics and Law, Theory and Practice, Substance and Process' (2006) *European Business Organization Law Review* 7(1), 39–87; K. Graham, 'The Parent Company Guarantee v Bonds

the fact that economic assets and risks are included in a corporate body, namely a financial vehicle *de facto* exempt from the risk of insolvency, linked, in turn, to a bond issue. The proceeds from issuing such bonds are used to finance or pay for the transfer of assets.

The type of transactions described above, from the standpoint of the transferor, therefore the originator, allows one to replace illiquid assets with financial resources, therefore cash. For investors, however, by using this transaction it is possible to access assets that could not have been otherwise available for investment. Moreover, with this type of transaction, assets can be invested in bonds that carry a lower risk than the underlying assets.[24]

Accordingly, securitisations are not the only instrument through which structured finance transactions can be shaped and moulded, and these instruments as a whole are aimed at creating a capital market union.[25]

Covered bonds represent a form of securitisation too, as they lead to the creation of collateral debts. If a regulatory perspective is adopted, securitisation is a tool that has been expressly adopted by Basel II to be interpreted as a means of credit mitigation.[26] It should be clarified that if covered bonds can meet regulatory requirements despite the absence of SPV, theoretically direct bond issuance by

Debate' (2006) *Construction Newsletter*, Oct, 171–172; Company Lawyer (case comment), 'Payment of Bond on Default' (1989) *Company Lawyer* 10(8), 170; N. Mugarura, 'Different Types of Guarantee Schemes and Their Usage in Safeguarding against Default Risks in International Commercial Practice' (2016) *International Journal of Law and Management* 58(5), 507–522; Journal of International Banking Law (case comment), 'Performance Bonds: Nature of Bank's Obligation to Pay' (1986) *Journal of International Banking Law* 1(4), n. 158–n. 159; A. Herbert, 'Why Have a Trustee for a Eurobond Issue?' (1987) *Journal of International Banking Law* 2(1), 48–49; Construction Law Journal (case comment), 'Bond – Condition that Contractors Shall Fully Comply with All Terms, Covenants and Conditions of the Contract' (1994) *Construction Law Journal* 10(2), 157–165; G.J-Y. Thieffry, 'Fungible Bond Issues: Legal Issues and Market Practice on the Eurobond Market' (1994) *International Business Law Journal* 3, 291–296; W. Seung Chong, 'The Abusive Calling of Performance Bonds' (1990) *Journal of Business Law*, Sep, 414–427; B. Liu, 'Why Are Bond Trustees Sued More Often in New Zealand? An Analysis of the Duty to Monitor under New Zealand Law' (2016) *Journal of International Banking Law and Regulation* 31(2), 75–79; H.A. Hirte, 'Convertible Bonds and Option Bonds: A Comparative Study' (2000) *European Business Organization Law Review* 1(3), 507–537; G.A. Penn, 'On-Demand Bonds – Primary or Secondary Obligations?' (1986) *Journal of International Banking Law* 1(4), 224–230; C. Debattista, 'Performance Bonds and Letters of Credit: A Cracked Mirror Image' (1997) *Journal of Business Law*, 289–305; J.J. Rankin, 'Road Bond Regulations' (1986) *Scottish Planning Law & Practice* 17(Feb), 7–8; P.R. Wood, 'International Convertible Bond Issues' (1986) *Journal of International Banking Law* 1(2), 69–76.

24 See Chapter 1.

25 P. Dorin, M. Vojtko, 'Simple, Transparent and Standardised Synthetic Securitisation – The Next Step Ahead?' (2017) *Journal of International Banking Law and Regulation*, 299–306.

26 Basel II and Basel III, also following the implementation of the EU Securitisation Regulation, encourage banks to operate actively in securitisations for liquidity purposes.

banks may not be part of this list, since the requirement of true sale in Basel II and III would not be met.[27]

In a classical securitisation transaction, bonds are issued with different risk profiles, i.e. in different tranches. According to the opinion of most economists, securitisation transactions and the repackaging of loans on real estate bonds, which in turn have different tranches, caused, albeit partially, the financial crisis of 2008. Subprime mortgage receivables are loans that derive from mortgage-backed real estate loans with a relatively high probability of default. Through the use of securitisation operations, these claims were reorganised as "residential mortgage-backed securities" (RMBS) bonds, which were assessed, in a positive way, as valuable bonds to be marketed to the global market, and with a very high rating, generously given by credit rating agencies. Thanks to this mechanism, investors used to base their decisions on the rating given to such bonds, without taking into consideration the risks of the underlying assets, which, by contrast, were high-risk loans.

As soon as real estate prices plummeted and the risk of subprime loans defaulting materialised, the RMBS lost much of their value and determined, as a result, the collapse of different financial institutions as they had massively invested in such products.[28] Following the collapse of Lehman Brothers, the securitisation market even stopped for ten years after the outbreak of the financial crisis, when the European legislator issued the Securitisation Regulation.

The latter, as already mentioned, is a piece of legislation that lays down a broad framework[29] with regard to securitisation transactions by establishing due

27 Again, Regulation No. 557 of 2021 has changed the original framework of the Securitisation Regulation, by making the true sale requirement for STS securitisations less rigid.

28 The Lehman Brothers case encapsulates this paradigm.

29 With regard to the regulatory reaction that has taken place in the European Union, "the limits and negative externalities of regulation should also be borne in mind. Prescriptive laws, as are common in European regulation, are generally past-looking. This is adequate to prevent the reiteration repetition of the same crisis. Nevertheless, regulation rarely helps to anticipate the next crisis. It is a paradox that regulators are now regulating the securitisation market, which was the innovative side-effect of capital regulation in Basel I. This raises the question whether the currently enacted regulatory regime will lead to a future crisis. Another side effect is that it is unlikely to achieve deterrence of certain transactions. Instead, it might force business activities into unregulated markets. As the CRD, and thus most of the measures discussed, only apply to credit institutions, it is very likely that transactions will move to nonregulated entities and markets, such as shadow banks and hedge funds. Then, regulators will not even be in a position to monitor and intervene. An alternative to imposing prescriptive rule for the regulator could be supporting structural and market-led reforms. Rules need to be enforced via supervisors. This aspect warrants the question of regulatory capacity in times of tight public budgets. This problem becomes especially apparent for the CRA Regulation. Here, a market-led solution might be more appropriate if it were able to restore the CRA's reputational constraint, which has proven to work well in the bond market. The market should also be more engaged in standardisation setting of loan-level data. It would avoid useless information being disclosed, provide for flexibility, enhance the potential for effective benchmarking, and more likely make standards internationally convergent. Nonetheless, regulators or public institutions could give start-up aid in cases where initial set-up costs are too great." H. von Reden,

diligence, risk-retention and, finally, transparency requirements for the parties involved with such structured finance transactions. In principle, the sale of securitised products to retail clients, re-securitisation and hence the repackaging of bonds issued in a securitisation such as other bonds are prohibited. This firm prohibition is coupled with the nomenclature of securitisations as simple, transparent and standardised structured market transactions.

3.3 STS securitisations

Arguably, the quintessence of the EU Securitisation Regulation deals with a set of rules whose final objective is the establishment of a European register of "quality" securitisations, called "STS" securitisations.[30] Admittedly, there is a further goal in this body of law, namely fixing a microsystem of sanctions, with even a Supervisory Authority. To further elaborate, as far as the pursuit of the first objective is concerned, namely the set-up of both the register and the move towards the stringent requirements that a securitisation shall comply with,[31] the "players" of the transaction, therefore the "securitisers," are tasked with the duty of genuine, timely and prompt communications. Failure to comply with them involves the activation of a sanction system that has both administrative and potentially criminal connotations.[32]

The core aspect of the Securitisation Regulation is contained in Chapter IV of the Securitisation Regulation and is concerned with the concept of simple, transparent and standardised securitisation. As far as the latter features are concerned, Art. 18 stipulates that the originator, sponsor and vehicle may use the name "simple, transparent and standardised securitisation" only if it meets the requirements of Section 1 or Section 2 of the chapter of the Securitisation Regulation in which the legal provision under discussion has been added. Furthermore, it is necessary to notify the transaction to ESMA[33] and, finally, it is essential for this transaction to be included in a specific list.[34]

'Regulation of Securitised Products Post the Financial Crisis' (2013) *UCL Journal of Law and Jurisprudence*, 112–140.

30 The literature on the STS securitisation is not as vast as one would expect. In addition to the authors cited elsewhere in this work, reference can be made to J. Cullen, 'Securitisation, Ring-Fencing, and Housing Bubbles: Financial Stability Implications of UK and EU Bank Reforms Get Access Arrow' (2018) *Journal of Financial Regulation* 4(1), 73–118; P. Katner 'Simple, Transparent and Standardised Securitisation (STS Securitisation) as a Specific Type of Securitisation under the Regulation 2017/2402' (2020) *Studia Iuridica Lublinensia* 5, 103–116.

31 Namely the requirements of simplicity, transparency and standardisation investigated in this chapter.

32 A potential problem entailed to the European legal framework in this area deals with the potential risk of an unlevelled playing field, instead of a desirable level playing field, given that the discretion enjoyed by each Member State is very wide.

33 This duty is expected by Art. 27(1) of EU Securitisation Regulation.

34 The reference is to the list of simple, transparent and standardised transactions referred to in Art. 27(5) of the Regulation at stake. The sponsor and the originator are jointly responsible for the

The STS brand recognised for securitisation transactions is the outcome of a sustainable securitisation market[35] where the multifarious benefits coming from securitisation transactions can be achieved. On the other hand, this brand shortens the information asymmetries and the excessive risk that can result from them.[36] Entailed to this is a further advantage: the consistency between the *nomen iuris* of the products at stake, the legal form and/or category, and from a more substantial perspective, the "calibration" of the risk on the part of the investor. In other words, it can be inferred that "sustainable securitisation is high-quality securitisation, based on transnational trading structures, with transparent underlying assets, predictability of risk and investor performance."[37]

Bearing this in mind, it must be recalled that, in the context of the European Union regulation, the financial crisis that occurred in 2007–2008 was the result, among other reasons, of the lack of rules governing structured finance transactions. Therefore, new European Union securitisation rules to promote so-called sustainable securitisations may be the prediction of a new world to come. Nevertheless, sustainability, in this context, should be interpreted as a recommendation and not a duty to the financial community.

3.4 The simplicity criterion

Securitisation that is not an asset-backed commercial paper will be simple, transparent and standardised provided that, pursuant to Art. 19 of the Securitisation Regulation, it complies with the requirements of Articles 20, 21 and 22, each containing a criterion or parameter.

First, the requirement of simplicity for securitisations aspiring to the STS trademark is contained in Art. 20 of the Securitisation Regulation which requires that "the title to the underlying exposures shall be acquired by the SSPE by means of a true sale or assignment or transfer with the same legal effect in a manner that is enforceable against the seller or any other third party. The transfer of the title to the SSPE shall not be subject to severe clawback provisions in the event of the seller's insolvency."[38]

This first legal provision encompassed within Art. 20 sets out the concept of true sale, which, until the adoption of the Securitisation Regulation, had never been made explicit, simply because it was always considered implicit and recurrent in every securitisation transaction. A true sale, more specifically, consists of

notification: in the event that the securitisation consists of a commercial paper programme, only the sponsor will be responsible for the notification.

35 Entailed to this is the need to build a quality market for securitisation transactions; those which contributed to this programme are the European Central Bank and the Bank of England.

36 V. Bavoso, *Market-Based Finance, Debt and Systemic Risk: A Critique of the EU Capital Markets Union* (June 5, 2018), University of Oslo Faculty of Law Research Paper No. 2018–19.

37 Out translation, albeit not literal, from Italian. P. de Gioia Carabellese, *Cartolarizzazioni semplici, trasparenti e standardizzate. Dallo shadow banking al techno banking*, Cacucci, Bari, 2020, 67.

38 Art. 20 (1).

the certification often provided by the lawyers who assist the transferor: the purpose is to attest the genuineness of the sale as well as the absence of circumstances likely to force the transferor to buy back the securities sold.[39]

The true sale to be referred to, in this specific case, is concerned with the separateness of the vehicle; in its turn, this ensures that, in case of insolvency of the vehicle, the assessment of the Court departs from the traditional criteria of insolvency law. Thus, the examination of the Court should be limited in its scope, since the judiciary would be devoid, in this area, of any power to classify the assets transferred to the vehicle as fraudulent transfer.[40] In other words, the true sale refers to the concept of "derecognition,"[41] because it allows the transferor to eschew the reversal of the sale, but in very limited circumstances.

In the light of this, the different legal provisions, which do exist in various legal systems, whose purpose is the clawback of securitisation transactions (therefore, their invalidity), should be limited in their actual application. Recital 22 states that this Regulation

> only allows for 'true-sale' securitisations to be designated as STS. In a true-sale securitisation, the ownership of the underlying exposures is transferred or effectively assigned to an issuer entity, which is a SSPE. The transfer or assignment of the underlying exposures to the SSPE should not be subject to clawback provisions in the event of the seller's insolvency, without prejudice to provisions of national insolvency laws under which the sale of underlying exposures concluded within a certain period before the declaration of the seller's insolvency can, under strict conditions, be invalidated.[42]

Pursuant to this legal provision, creditors of the originator, as well as any other entity, should not be allowed to invalidate the purchase by the vehicle on the basis that the facts took place and were performed before the declaration of insolvency

39 Should this not be realised, the amount payable by the vehicle to the originator could be reclassified as an asset-backed loan. By way of example, the US Court and the Federal Deposit Insurance Corporation (FDIC) will normally examine the transfer, the documentation of the transfer, the accounting, the timing and the price in order to determine if a sale can really be defined as genuine. H.S. Scott, *International Finance: Transaction, Policy and Regulation*, 17th ed., Foundation Press, New York, 2010, 634. It should be added that in those jurisdictions a fiduciary transfer which is not the result of a sale but is made for the sole guarantee purpose is prohibited. A similar provision is also found in Art. 3:84 of the Dutch Civil Code. M. Haentjens, P. de Gioia Carabellese, *European Banking and Financial Law*, 2nd ed. (n. 1), 233. As regards the Italian legal system, the most common view of scholars is that the assignment of claims for the purpose of security is not admissible, see in Italian P. Perlingeri, *Cessione dei crediti*, ESI, Napoli, 2010, 39–40.

40 H.S. Scott, *International Finance: Transaction, Policy and Regulation* (n. 29), 634.

41 S. Gleeson, *International Regulation of Banking*, 2nd ed., Oxford University Press, Oxford, 2012, 286.

42 As far as the concept of bankruptcy remoteness of the vehicle is concerned, see K. Ayotte, S. Gaon, 'Asset-Backed Securities: Costs and Benefits of "Bankruptcy Remoteness"' (2011) *Review of Financial Studies*, 1299 ff.

of the originator. The rationale behind this lies in the fact that the STS securitisation provisions are strict because they interfere with the securitisation market and the legal certainty expected by the markets themselves and those taking part in them.[43] Thus, the rigidity apparently needs to be better understood and adapted to the "real world": in this, concrete experience prevails on abstract ideals. In this sense, it seems that the real functioning of regulated markets and the interest of investors in the certainty of the investment cannot tolerate that complex transactions such as securitisation transactions may be invalidated at a later date.

The scope of what can be defined as the "EU clawback action" is limited by Art. 20(2),[44] a legal provision which is based on two fundamental assumptions. First, there are those that allow the seller's liquidator to invalidate the sales of underlying exposures solely on the basis of the idea that such sales of underlying exposures took place within a certain period preceding the declaration of bankruptcy. The reference, quite obviously, is to the legal provisions that allow for the invalidation of transactional documents on the basis of unrebuttable presumptions. One of them is that the transfer took place before the insolvency of the transferor. The second hypothesis suggests the possibility, for the transferee, to avoid the invalidation of the assignment of the receivables, on condition that the same is able to prove that it was not aware of the state of insolvency of the relevant counterparty.

As regards the exact perimeter of the national clawback legal provisions, it is necessary to refer to Art. 20(3), according to which

> for the purpose of paragraph 1, clawback provisions in national insolvency laws that allow the liquidator or a court to invalidate the sale of underlying exposures in the case of fraudulent transfers, unfair prejudice to creditors or transfers intended to improperly favour particular creditors over others shall not constitute severe clawback provisions.

43 It should be pointed out that, albeit indirectly, the recent European Union legislation has stepped up to the plate in this area. Insolvency laws, historically, take an orthodox and rigid approach to transactions, via an automatic invalidation, at a later stage, once the insolvency of the affected party unfolds. This invalidation stems from the presumption that such a transaction was performed in the suspect period, therefore during a certain period preceding the declaration of insolvency. By contrast, the latest legislative measures coming from Brussels, within the Securitisation Regulation, do not have an "abrogative" impact on the insolvency laws existing in various Member States. As a result, the internal corresponding rules shall be simply disregarded by the Court (or an administrative Authority, such as the Resolution Authority), should this be required to adjudicate on an STS securitisation. It follows that, in the event of the insolvency of a credit institution, the Authority (either judicial or administrative) will simply have to apply the "Brussels rules," by overlooking the national rules existing in the legal system of the originator.

44 "For the purpose of paragraph 1, any of the following shall constitute severe clawback provisions: (a) provisions which allow the liquidator of the seller to invalidate the sale of the underlying exposures solely on the basis that it was concluded within a certain period before the declaration of the seller's insolvency; (b) provisions where the SSPE can only prevent the invalidation referred to in point (a) if it can prove that it was not aware of the insolvency of the seller at the time of sale."

Based on this, the strict provisions should be those relating to the protection of public policy interests and which, as a result, become mandatory as in the case of fraud or fraud of the assignment. On the contrary, provisions intended to protect interests, legal assets that deserve less absolute protection than the potential slowdown in business practice, should be regarded as derogating. In other words, in the area of STS securitisations – complex financial transactions where by definition there is a predominance of market interests over the protection of the originator's creditors – the strict provisions are disregarded. In contrast, the flexible provisions continue to remain in force because they are considered tolerable in the context of a complex financial transaction.[45]

At present it is known that the effects of a re-characterisation[46] can be difficult for the parties involved to bear and the financial transaction itself can certainly not be considered a commercial success.[47] The re-characterisation, in particular, turns out to be an interpretative instrument left to the discretion of the judicial power belonging to the jurisdiction of the originator or the vehicle according to the applicable law.

The consequences that could result from a re-characterisation can be avoided, from a contractual point of view, provided that the parties can count on a legal opinion.[48]

If it qualifies as a closing legal opinion, it contains an examination of the transaction and the relating contractual documentation. It is carried out by a qualified lawyer in the jurisdiction or jurisdictions in which the transaction took place or where it is expected to be carried out, and it is ultimately focused on specific circumstances and documents.[49]

Until now, the legal opinion was relied upon exclusively by the persons or entities to which it was addressed, therefore principally by the bank in charge of the economic transaction. Thanks to this document, they received assurances that the securitised securities and the entity issuing them, the vehicle, were immune from

45 The norms, if flexible, are designed to protect the originator's creditors in limited cases, namely when the transaction can be defined as truly fraudulent, because, for example, it is intended to deprive the originator's creditors of their property guarantees.

46 P.R. Wood, *International Loans, Bonds, Guarantees, Legal Opinions: The Law and Practice of International Financial Series*, Sweet & Maxwell, London, 2007, 468 ff.

47 H.S. Scott, *International Finance: Transaction, Policy and Regulation* (no. 29), 630.

48 It tends to be based on very precise assumptions and caveats, many of which are of an extremely technical nature. In other words, it is a legal assessment, the preparation and presentation of which may be qualified as a condition precedent for the granting of financing or the issuance of securities. The opinion will be issued by a lawyer appointed by the bank or the consortium of banks acting as arrangers or promoters: the submission of the legal opinion guarantees that the underlying issues are excluded from the transaction, with redevelopment to be understood as a transaction other than the sale.

49 R. McCormick, *Legal Risk in the Financial Markets*, 2nd ed., Oxford University Press, Oxford, 2010, 419; P.R. Wood, *International Loans, Bonds, Guarantees, Legal Opinions: The Law and Practice of International Financial Series*, III, Sweet & Maxwell, London, 2007, 413; P.R. Wood, *International Loans, Bonds, Guarantees, Legal Opinions*, 3rd ed., Sweet & Maxwell, London, 2019.

a declaration of insolvency of the seller. Nevertheless, investors, in actual terms the real beneficiaries of the Securitisation Regulation, could not rely on the same statement, as lawyers used to include a disclaimer in the legal opinion. It pointed out that the legal opinion was intended only for the people it was addressed to, and no-one else could place trust on it.[50]

In common law jurisdictions it is very unlikely that an investor is entitled to sue a lawyer on the basis of an erroneous legal opinion.[51] By contrast, within the European Union, any error of a professional nature in a securitisation procedure may take the shape of a quasi strict liability for the lawyers who issue a legal opinion to investors. At the present time, it is possible to say that such a hypothesis can be considered remote, if not utopian.

More generally, re-characterisation shall be granted to the creditors if it can be assumed that the originator continues to maintain effective control over the exposure of the transferred credit risk. This is a circumstance that could be potentially met, should the originator be in a position to repurchase the previously transferred exposures from the transferee, so that the latter may receive the related benefits. An alternative to this legal consequence is where the originator is obliged to hold the risk of the transferred exposures.[52]

As regards the first provision, this could be the case where the transferor and the business bank have agreed, on the basis of a side letter, on a commitment to repurchase the receivables as if they exceed a certain physiological threshold. As regards the second case, it is clear that the appointment of the originator as a service provider of management duties connected with the securitised assets cannot be considered as a presumption of control over the transferred transactions. It is

50 In addition, the opinion could not be disclosed to third parties without the issuance of prior written consent. The beneficiary's limited liability is confirmed, in England and Wales, in the case *Allied Finance & Investments Ltd v. Haddow & Co*, 1983, NZLR 22 CA.

51 P.R. Wood, *International Loans, Bonds, Guarantees, Legal Opinions: The Law and Practice of International Financial Series*, III, Sweet & Maxwell, London, 2007, 424. The case is *Hedley Byrne & Co. Ltd v. Heller & Partners Ltd*, 1964, AC 465. As far as the numerous commentaries on this precedent are concerned, see *inter alia*: D. Campbell, 'The Absence of Negligence in Hedley Byrne v Heller' (2016) *Law Quarterly Review* 132(Apr), 266–277; R. Buxton, 'How the Common Law Gets Made: Hedley Byrne and Other Cautionary Tales' (2009) *Law Quarterly Review* 125(Jan), 60–78; J. Komorowski, 'Donoghue v Stevenson: Myths and Reality' (2013) *Juridical Review* 3, 451–467; K.R. Handley, 'Some Unsettled Aspects of the Hedley Byrne Doctrine and Commonwealth Perspectives' (2002) *Common Law World Review* 31(2), 177–188; T. Foxton, 'Second Degree Byrne' (2019) *Cambridge Law Journal* 78(1), 18–21; J.A.W. Grower, O.F. Sherman, 'Equivalent to Contract? Confronting the Nature of the Duty Arising under Hedley Byrne v Heller' (2019) *Law Quarterly Review* 135(Apr), 177–182; J. Castle, G. Mortimer, 'Professional Negligence: Tortious Liability' (1995) *International Insurance Law Review* 3(4), G58–61; R. Mullender, 'Negligent Misstatement, Threats and the Scope of the Hedley Byrne Principle' (1999) *Modern Law Review* 62(3), 425–434; K.M. Stanton, 'Hedley Byrne and Heller: The Relationship Factor' (2007) *Professional Negligence* 23(2), 94–107; E. Gordon, 'Out with the Old, in with the Older? Hedley Byrne Reliance Takes Centre Stage' (2018) *Cambridge Law Journal* 77(2), 251–255; D. Brodie, 'Hedley Byrne and Public Authorities' (1997) *Reparation Bulletin* 18(Nov), 2–3.

52 S. Gleeson, *International Regulation of Banking* (n. 31).

therefore self-evident that the originator should not have any remaining liability for the assets that have been transferred to the vehicle.

On such a ground, it is possible to reach at least three conclusions. First, the vehicle cannot be considered as under an obligation to repurchase claims in the event of losses, nor can it guarantee capital and interest on loans to investors in the securities issued by the vehicle.

Second, the vehicle must be able to exercise, in an exclusive way, control over the assets in the evolutionary aspects: it is any type of action that a normal holder would be allowed to carry out. In other words, it means that the vehicle should be given full dominical power by including the exercise in selling, foreclosing or managing the assets owned by it.

Third and finally, the transferred assets must be isolated from the originator, in the event of its insolvency: securitisation is a transaction that ensures that the vehicle is protected from possible insolvency of the originator, even where, formally, the securitisation is "endowed" with the remote bankruptcy brand.[53] To achieve this objective, third parties will request agreements of a contractual nature, as well as credit and liquidity enhancement.[54]

The general rules of property law existing in different countries stipulate that collateral rights are an accessory feature and, therefore, follow the claims that are secured. Based on this, therefore, the securities of the receivables[55] are transferred, with the same credits, from the originator to the vehicle.[56]

The most recent debate seems to focus on the question of the possible transfer of a loan granted for a first home purchase to the vehicle in the event that it is securitised. The answer will be that, depending on the applicable law, the mortgage is divided *pro rata*: the share of the mortgage that concerns the loan will be transferred to the vehicle, while the originator will handle the remaining.[57] Conversely, in common law systems, the vehicle will be considered the beneficiary of the entire mortgage.[58]

In continuing with the examination of Art. 20(5) of the Securitisation Regulation, it is worth noting that, in cases in which the transfer of underlying

53 S. Franken, 'Creditor – and Debtor-Oriented, Bankruptcy Regimes Revised' (2004) *European Business Organization Law Review*, 645–676.

54 H.S. Scott, *International Finance: Transaction, Policy and Regulation* (n. 29), 634.

55 The term securities refers to guarantees.

56 As regards securitisation, guarantee rights are bank mortgages, which in turn are charged to real estate. See W. Johnston, *Security over Receivables: An International Handbook*, Oxford University Press, Oxford, 2008.

57 M. Haentjens, P. de Gioia Carabellese, *European Banking and Financial Law*, 2nd ed. (n. 1), 234.

58 It should be added that security interests, such as, for example, pledges and mortgages, may be transferred under the common law. Since in the securitisation the claims are transferred to the vehicle, the guarantee claims must be transferred to the collateral beneficiary. P. de Gioia Carabellese, *Securitisation and Structured Finance: From Shadow Banking to Legal Harmonization*, in I.H-Y. Chiu, I. MacNeil (eds), *Research Handbook on Shadow Banking: Legal and Regulatory Aspects*, Edward Elgar, Cheltenham, 2018, 136.

exposures is performed by means of an assignment and perfected at a later stage than the closing of the transaction,

> the triggers to effect such perfection shall include at least the following events: (a) severe deterioration in the seller credit quality standing; (b) insolvency of the seller; and (c) unremedied breaches of contractual obligations by the seller, including the seller's default.

It is known, in fact, that in securitisation transactions it is theoretically possible to distinguish between two different moments: one, the closing, coincides with the signing of the different contracts; the other, the settlement, is the moment devoted to the settlement of the different transactions underlying the different contracts entered into.

On such premises, the European Union framework points to the fact that, in the event that the underlying transactions are transferred by means of a divestment, i.e. by means of a real, non-synthetic securitisation transaction, and the related settlement occurs at a later time, the latter should depend on a number of events, such as the serious deterioration of the seller's merit classes, the insolvency of the seller, the breach of contractual obligations by the seller. In other words, the provision in question results in a recommendation, albeit indirect, to operators to give priority – in order to be able to benefit from the STS trademark – to securitisation transactions, where there is a chronological coincidence between the closing and the settlement.[59]

It is prescribed, by Art. 20(6) of the Securitisation Regulation, that the seller

> shall provide representations and warranties that, to the best of its knowledge, the underlying exposures included in the securitisation are not encumbered or otherwise in a condition that can be foreseen to adversely affect the enforceability of the true sale or assignment or transfer with the same legal effect.

The content of this provision seems to be rooted in the experience gained during the economic crisis of 2007–2008 to avoid the superficial nature of structured finance transactions carried out by credit institutions during that period.[60]

The obligation introduced by Art. 20(6) of the Securitisation Regulation has several purposes: first, it confers the "quality" trademark on the operation in question, and second, it appears to be intended to draw the attention of the supervised entity in relation to the importance of the verification to be carried out. The control activity that should be carried out by the originator in this matter appears to be

59 This should facilitate the same transparency as the transaction, given that uncertainty between the two periods would decrease. Where this correspondence is not possible, the favour of the legislator can also be obtained when the conditions described are satisfied.

60 In that context, securitisation transactions were lacking in declarations by the originator to ensure the lack of constraints on the purchased portfolio.

tricky: if omitted or superficially released, the same may result in the imposition of sanctions on the transferor which are of such a magnitude as to act as a deterrent for other operators. In addition, it is possible to foresee the emergence of a form of concurrent liability of the business bank that organises the transaction. Although it is true that the supervised entity directly reports to the supervisory authority, in the internal contractual relations between the transferring intermediary (the principal) and the business bank (the agent), the latter is subject to the legal initiatives of the transferor, albeit via the equivalent form of damages.

Underlying exposures that are transferred or disposed of by the seller to the SSPE shall meet the established eligibility criteria, which shall be clear and documented and not allow for discretionary asset management of the portfolio of such exposures.[61]

The following paragraph of Art. 20 stipulates that the securitisation

> shall be backed by a pool of underlying exposures that are homogeneous in terms of asset type, taking into account the specific characteristics relating to the cash flows of the asset type including their contractual, credit risk and prepayment characteristics. A pool of underlying exposures shall comprise only one asset type. The underlying exposures shall contain obligations that are contractually binding and enforceable, with full recourse to debtors and, where applicable, guarantors.

This was intended to make securitisation transactions less complex: historically, the heterogeneity of securitisation transactions was a problem, particularly for the regulation to be applied to them, given the dearth of a suitable legal framework to prevent the occurrence of risks. The above is further supported by the fact that in the second part of the paragraph it is said that the underlying portfolio of exposures should be related to only one type of divested assets.[62] It is also added that the underlying exposures should involve binding contractual obligations with a full right of recourse against debtors and, where appropriate, against collaterals. Underlying exposures should also present predetermined periodic payment flows, the instalments of which may differ in terms of amount, for the payment of leases, the principal or interest or any other right to obtain an income from the assets supporting the payments: the underlying exposures may also generate revenues from the sale of financed or leased assets.

61 The reference is to Art. 20(7): "The underlying exposures transferred from, or assigned by, the seller to the SSPE shall meet predetermined, clear and documented eligibility criteria which do not allow for active portfolio management of those exposures on a discretionary basis. For the purpose of this paragraph, substitution of exposures that are in breach of representations and warranties shall not be considered active portfolio management. Exposures transferred to the SSPE after the closing of the transaction shall meet the eligibility criteria applied to the initial underlying exposures."

62 The homogeneity of the divested assets should also allow for a better analysis of the portfolio by the securitisation operator, including credit rating agencies.

Paragraph 8[63] also specifies that exposures that are disposed of in the context of a transaction intended to fall within the concept of simplicity shall not include "transferable securities, as defined in point (44) of Article 4(1) of Directive 2014/65/EU, other than corporate bonds that are not listed on a trading venue."[64]

In order to receive a quality certification, "the underlying exposures shall not include any securitisation position," pursuant to Art. 20(9) of the Securitisation Regulation. An exposure to the securitisation that is to be divested under the same securitisation transaction would give rise to an accounting situation that is misleading for credit rating agencies and investors alike.

A very original legal provision is the one encompassed within Art. 20(10) according to which the underlying exposures

> shall be originated in the ordinary course of the originator's or original lender's business pursuant to underwriting standards that are no less stringent than those that the originator or original lender applied at the time of origination to similar exposures that are not securitised. The underwriting standards pursuant to which the underlying exposures are originated and any material changes from prior underwriting standards shall be fully disclosed to potential investors without undue delay. In the case of securitisations where the underlying exposures are residential loans, the pool of loans shall not include any loan that was marketed and underwritten on the premise that the loan applicant or, where applicable, intermediaries were made aware that the information provided might not be verified by the lender. The assessment of the borrower's creditworthiness shall meet the requirements set out in Article 8 of Directive 2008/48/EC or paragraphs 1 to 4, point (a) of paragraph 5, and paragraph 6 of Article 18 of Directive 2014/17/EU or, where applicable, equivalent requirements in third countries. The originator or original lender shall have expertise in originating exposures of a similar nature to those securitised.

63 It has been significantly implemented by the European Banking Authority (EBA) which is required to develop, in cooperation with the European Insurance and Occupational Pension Authority (EIOPA), draft regulatory technical standards. See Art. 20(14) "The EBA, in close cooperation with ESMA and EIOPA, shall develop draft regulatory technical standards further specifying which underlying exposures referred to in paragraph 8 are deemed to be homogeneous. The EBA shall submit those draft regulatory technical standards to the Commission by 18 July 2018. The Commission is empowered to supplement this Regulation by adopting the regulatory technical standards referred to in this paragraph in accordance with Articles 10 to 14 of Regulation (EU) No 1093/2010."

64 It must be pointed out that securities, because of their high variability and the risk that is implied by them, are not very compatible with that element of simplicity towards which the provision in question is directed. The only exception concerns "corporate bonds not listed on a trading venue" which, although they may be defined as real estate, cannot be defined as simple securitisation in order to benefit from the relevant regulations.

The rationale of the provision is to maintain a balance between the portfolio that is held by the bank and the one that is securitised, in quantitative terms, to ensure that virtuous securitisation does not create an opportunity for the disposal of low-value portfolios at the expense of the market.[65]

Once portfolio selection has been made, the underlying exposures shall be transferred without delay to the SSPE,[66] as they cannot include defaulted exposures at the time of their selection, pursuant to Art. 178(1) of Regulation 575/2013, nor exposures to a debtor or a guarantor of non-performing credit standing which, on the basis of the knowledge of the original originator or lender, do not find themselves in any of the following conditions. First, the debtor or guarantor who

> has been declared insolvent or had a court grant his creditors a final non-appealable right of enforcement or material damages as a result of a missed payment within three years prior to the date of origination or has undergone a debt restructuring process with regard to his non-performing exposures within three years prior to the date of transfer or assignment of the underlying exposures to the SSPE.[67]

Second, it is recalled that the debtor does not enjoy an adequate credit scoring.[68] Specifically, reference shall be made to the fact that the assigned debtor should not be included in a specific public register relating to people affected by negative credit references. Finally, an automatic exclusion from the portfolio of assigned claims of a debtor who "has a credit assessment or a credit score indicating that the risk of contractually agreed payments not being made is significantly higher than for comparable exposures held by the originator which are not securitised."

More generally, the prescriptions of Art. 11 must be interpreted as intended to preserve the quality of the transferred portfolio and, indirectly, its simplicity: the presence of non-performing loans, to be related to the quality of the transferred

65 As a result, this new constraint should be functional to make the future market direct to risk containment.

66 In this respect, see also the following paragraph: "The underlying exposures shall be transferred to the SSPE after selection without undue delay and shall not include, at the time of selection, exposures in default within the meaning of Article 178(1) of Regulation (EU) No 575/2013 or exposures to a credit-impaired debtor or guarantor, who, to the best of the originator's or original lender's knowledge." Article 178(1) of Regulation (EU) No 575/2013.

67 The following situations are exceptions: "(i) a restructured underlying exposure has not presented new arrears since the date of the restructuring, which must have taken place at least one year prior to the date of transfer or assignment of the underlying exposures to the SSPE; and (ii) the information provided by the originator, sponsor and SSPE in accordance with points (a) and (e)(i) of the first subparagraph of Article 7(1) explicitly sets out the proportion of restructured underlying exposures, the time and details of the restructuring as well as their performance since the date of the restructuring." As far as the British legal system is concerned, reference is made to the Insolvency Act 1986.

68 "At the time of origination, where applicable, on a public credit registry of persons with adverse credit history or, where there is no such public credit registry, another credit registry that is available to the originator or original lender."

debtors, could affect the requirement of simplicity.[69] Credit scoring, in fact, on the one hand can provide an objective assessment of the debtor but on the other it does not appear to be presently supported by suitable regulations to make the use of the same objective and effective. In other words, there is a risk that the debtor may be adversely affected by this provision, which would have the credit terminated, indirectly, at the occurrence of events that prevent the same assignment of the credit.

Paragraph 12 seems to resolve an issue which, prior to the financial crisis, gave rise to a number of problems. The reference goes to the elusive tendency of some operators to sell the portfolio of credits as soon as they have arisen: in this, the originator, especially a credit institution, does not appear to be the originator of the credit but the distributor. This aspect is superseded given that, according to the regulation, "The debtors shall, at the time of transfer of the exposures, have made at least one payment, except in the case of revolving securitisations backed by exposures payable in a single instalment or having a maturity of less than one year, including without limitation monthly payments on revolving credits."[70] It is considered that this measure, aimed at tightening the securitisation system, cannot be considered to be stringent. Providing for at least one instalment of the transferred credit to be paid as a condition of assignment may also be reconciled with a bank or financial credit transfer arising from a contract in which the first instalment, with a six-month maturity, occurred one month after delivery. In this respect, the legislator could have foreseen a more appropriate period between the date of conclusion of the contract and the date from which the transfer to vehicles could be carried out as part of the securitisation transactions.

The EU regulation which is the subject of this analysis deals with a practice that can be defined as pathological and not physiological, since the main objective concerns the introduction of corrections to securitisation transactions in order to overcome the relative criticalities. There is a reference to the repayment which, in the structure of these transactions, may depend to a large extent on the guarantees rather than the quality of the assets with all the risks that could arise. The promoter appears to be uninterested in the selection of the portfolio of claims according to the possibility of their recovery at maturity, which relies exclusively on guarantees. In this case, the securitisation transaction could not be defined as genuine because the cause would be the guarantee and not the sale.

69 It should be noted that the parameters mentioned above may be too rigid and even counterproductive. Requesting that a debt is not entered in the public register of negative references or that it does not have a negative credit scoring rating could accentuate a form of credit crunch. This phenomenon leads banks to demand excessively strict requirements from their potential debtors, even and perhaps especially in anticipation of a subsequent securitisation of the credit portfolio. This excessive formalism could also give rise to negative phenomena such as the recourse by the debtor to forms of credit that can be defined as alien to the official channel of legal intermediation.

70 The only exception concerns revolving and secured securitisation by exposures payable in a single instalment or with a maturity of less than one year, also including the monthly payments under revolving credits.

In order to recover the core aspects of the securitisation transaction, the legislator introduced the criterion of preponderance stating that "the repayment of the holders of the securitisation positions shall not have been structured to depend predominantly on the sale of assets securing the underlying exposures. This shall not prevent such assets from being subsequently rolled-over or refinanced" (Art. 20(13)). The measure stems from the need to avoid a division between the guarantor and the debtor as part of the lending activity.

Paragraph 14 contains a "plan B" legal provision that leaves to the Commission the task to supplement this Regulation by adopting regulatory technical standards in a manner consistent with Articles 10 to 14 of Regulation (EU) No. 1093/2010.

3.5 The standardisation requirement

The standardisation requirement is laid down in Art. 21 of the EU Regulation. Three parameters can be found that qualify a securitisation as standardised. The first parameter is the obligation to maintain risk.

Art. 21(1) of the Securitisation Regulation stipulates that originators, promoters and original lenders, in an alternative way, have the obligation to retain the risk in accordance with Art. 6.[71] This legal provision lays down a principle whereby the originator, sponsor or original lender of a securitisation "shall retain on an ongoing basis a material net economic interest in the securitisation of not less than 5 %." This norm is instrumental to a fundamental objective: to ensure that at least one of the strategic players of the securitisation transaction maintains an interest in such transaction. In doing so, a *de facto* security (the compliance with this legal provision) is offered to the investor, in the light of the fact that there is a minimisation of the risk of the securitisation itself. Otherwise, the transferor or promoter would be penalised. Nevertheless, it can be noted that the link between the obligation to retain risk and the standardisation criterion is not clear, since the first requirement seems to be a ramification of an autonomous principle, the function of which would be to implement a better risk weight.

The second parameter to define a securitisation as standardised is mentioned in Art. 21(2) of the Securitisation Regulation. It is therein requested, in detail, that the interest rate and currency risks arising from the securitisation "shall be appropriately mitigated and any measures taken to that effect shall be disclosed." Therefore, apart from the purpose of hedging interest-rate or currency risk, "the SSPE shall not enter into derivative contracts and shall ensure that the pool of underlying exposures does not include derivatives."[72] However, if speculative

71 "The originator, sponsor or original lender shall satisfy the risk-retention requirement in accordance with Article 6."

72 *Ibidem*.

contracts are included, those derivatives "shall be underwritten and documented according to common standards in international finance."[73]

From the joint reading of the latest two paragraphs it can be inferred that the standardisation requirement should be also interpreted as a "transparency requirement." This statement is supported by the rationale behind the two different legal provisions, namely to inform the investor about the risks involved with the securitisation investment. In other words, there is a gut feeling that the need for standardisation is functional to pursue a strategic goal, rather than a tactical one.

The third parameter defining a securitisation as standardised is closely linked to enforcement actions.[74] The purpose of this norm is connected with the implementation of general rules the purpose of which is to ensure that, in the event of enforcement actions against the vehicle, the cash available to it is not less than the amount required for the transaction of the vehicle.[75] It is obvious that the capital gains originating from the underlying exposures are passed on to investors as serial repayment of securitisation positions, according to the seniority of each of them. In doing so, the matching existing between the liquidity held by the vehicle and the seniority of the credits (and the enforcement procedures imposed on them) should keep any financial imbalance at bay.

According to the prescriptions encapsulated in Art. 21(5) of the Securitisation Regulation, transactions which feature non-sequential priority of payments "shall include triggers relating to the performance of the underlying exposures resulting in the priority of payments reverting to sequential payments in order of seniority. Such performance-related triggers shall include at least the deterioration in the credit quality of the underlying exposures below a predetermined threshold." The non-sequential payment priority, as set out in that legal provision, could potentially lead to an imbalance in the liquidity of the vehicle. In light of this, it is required that the payment be made on the basis of underlying performance to ensure, quickly, the return to the original equilibrium of the liquidity of the vehicle itself.

73 *Ibidem*. This legal provision should be interpreted in conjunction with the following paragraph, where it is specified that any referenced interest payments under the securitisation assets and liabilities "shall be based on generally used market interest rates, or generally used sectoral rates reflective of the cost of funds, and shall not reference complex formulae or derivatives."

74 In this respect, Art. 21(4) helps clarify: "where an enforcement or an acceleration notice has been delivered: (a) no amount of cash shall be trapped in the SSPE beyond what is necessary to ensure the operational functioning of the SSPE or the orderly repayment of investors in accordance with the contractual terms of the securitisation, unless exceptional circumstances require that an amount be trapped to be used, in the best interests of investors, for expenses in order to avoid the deterioration in the credit quality of the underlying exposures; (b) principal receipts from the underlying exposures shall be passed to investors via sequential amortisation of the securitisation positions, as determined by the seniority of the securitisation position; (c) repayment of the securitisation positions shall not be reversed with regard to their seniority; and (d) no provisions shall require automatic liquidation of the underlying exposures at market value."

75 It is necessary to include this requirement in the light, in particular, of the general principle of separation of assets.

Given the above, it is possible to conclude that standardisation is remarkably effective on the negotiating power of the parties with regard to certain clauses normally included in the securitisation documentation. It is well-known that investors in securitised instruments need to wait for their maturity, simply because they cannot rely on potential accelerations, given the lack of *ad hoc* clauses to such an end.

This aspect, when legislation was still missing in this area, used to represent a risk for investors: in fact, they needed to fundamentally bet on the underlying assets. At the moment, the problem seems to have been overcome: if the securitisation is a "quality one" (i.e. it is STS), it must be accompanied by early repayment clauses or, alternatively, in the case of roll-over securitisation, by trigger events, coinciding with the end of each revolving period. Both these methods may provide the investors with the entitlement to activate an early repayment if this is required.[76]

The standardisation requirement may have the positive effect of making the content of the documentation accompanying the transaction more precise.[77] In this respect, Art. 21(8) of the Securitisation Regulation requires that the servicer "shall have expertise in servicing exposures of a similar nature to those securitised and shall have well documented and adequate policies, procedures and risk-management controls relating to the servicing of exposures."

On the subject of standardisation, it is also laid down that the transaction documentation

> shall set out in clear and consistent terms definitions, remedies and actions relating to delinquency and default of debtors, debt restructuring, debt forgiveness, forbearance, payment holidays, losses, charge offs, recoveries and other asset performance remedies. The transaction documentation shall clearly specify the priorities of payment, events which trigger changes in such priorities of payment as well as the obligation to report such events. Any change in the priorities of payments which will materially adversely

76 Art. 21(6) clarifies the matter. More in detail: "the transaction documentation shall include appropriate early amortisation provisions or triggers for termination of the revolving period where the securitisation is a revolving securitisation, including at least the following: (a) a deterioration in the credit quality of the underlying exposures to or below a predetermined threshold; (b) the occurrence of an insolvency-related event with regard to the originator or the servicer; (c) the value of the underlying exposures held by the SSPE falls below a predetermined threshold (early amortisation event); and (d) a failure to generate sufficient new underlying exposures that meet the predetermined credit quality (trigger for termination of the revolving period)."

77 In this respect, Art. 21(7) points out: "the transaction documentation shall clearly specify: (a) the contractual obligations, duties and responsibilities of the servicer and the trustee, if any, and other ancillary service providers; (b) the processes and responsibilities necessary to ensure that a default by or an insolvency of the servicer does not result in a termination of servicing, such as a contractual provision which enables the replacement of the servicer in such cases; and (c) provisions that ensure the replacement of derivative counterparties, liquidity providers and the account bank in the case of their default, insolvency, and other specified events, where applicable."

affect the repayment of the securitisation position shall be reported to investors without undue delay.[78]

These used to be actual signs that could have been observed in the practice of securitisation transactions before regulation was passed in this matter in 2017. From a strictly practical point of view, though, legal advisors should now be more careful in complying with these requirements too. The risk, in case of non-compliance, is that the Supervisory Authority may raise objections when it is requested to issue a certification.

Standardisation also requires compliance with corporate governance rules. In this respect, Art. 21(10) of the Securitisation Regulation requires that the transaction documentation "shall include clear provisions that facilitate the timely resolution of conflicts between different classes of investors, voting rights shall be clearly defined and allocated to bondholders and the responsibilities of the trustee and other entities with fiduciary duties to investors shall be clearly identified." This may mean that third-party arbitrators are appointed when a dispute is not easily resolved. The arbitrator could be the same business bank that sets up the securitisation transaction. While it is recognised that a different entity, which should be a "third party" to both parties, is better placed to settle a dispute, it is also recognised that it would be too burdensome a mechanism for the securitisation transaction. In this case, the entire costs would be borne by the intermediary.

Finally, it is worth noting that it is stipulated – still in the area of standardisation – that in the contractual documentation voting rights "shall be clearly defined and allocated to bondholders and the responsibilities of the trustee and other entities with fiduciary duties to investors shall be clearly identified." Indeed, classes of investors in securitised securities are not always expected to have a voting right. Consequently, it can be assumed that the standard has indirect preceptive content. In other words, standardisation requires each category of investor (senior, mezzanine, junior) to appoint a representative at a specific meeting.

3.6 The criterion of transparency

The requirement of transparency is the third requirement of "quality securitisation" in the 2017 EU Regulation and is set forth under Art. 22. As mentioned above, it is difficult to draw a line between standardisation and transparency as independent criteria. In the previous paragraph, in dealing with the standardisation requirement, it has already been pointed out that many of its characteristics may fall within the transparency requirement. The choice made by the EU legislator is not an easy one. If one analysed real business practice, it would become obvious that the conceptualisation of the different parameters does not totally comply with logic.

78 Art. 21(9) of the Securitisation Regulation.

As regards the requirement of transparency, first of all, Art. 22(1) stipulates that both sponsors and originators "shall make available data on static and dynamic historical default and loss performance, such as delinquency and default data, for substantially similar exposures to those being securitised, and the sources of those data and the basis for claiming similarity, to potential investors before pricing. Those data shall cover a period of at least five years."

There is, therefore, an obligation on the part of the originator, and jointly of the promoter, to make available the data mentioned in the provision to potential investors. As regards the offer and, more specifically, the fixing of the price of assignment of the claims, they cannot take place in the absence of detailed information covering a period of at least five years.

The aim of this legal provision is to avoid bad practices which became obvious in the financial crisis of 2007–2008. The reference is made to a modus operandi that led to the transfer of low-quality and, quite soon defaulted, residential loans which, in turn, had a negative impact on the repayment possibilities of the corresponding securitised financial instruments. In this respect, it is vital to clarify that the rule under consideration does not prohibit a transfer of claims of this kind, but it dissuades from doing so, due to the report obligations arising from non-compliance practices.[79] Thus, it is also crucial to clarify that the underlying securitised instruments pegged with a – later – unpaid credit may have economic advantages for investors.

First, the investor may have the opportunity to benefit from a higher interest rate, given that the transaction is riskier. In this regard, the aspect stressed by the European Union legislature concerns the respect of the principle of *caveat emptor*. The buyer, in fact, must be informed of the risk, and the correct *modus operandi* for the "securitisers" is the disclosure: should this be missing, it would not be possible to benefit from the STS qualification of the securitisation.

Secondly, transparency is connected with an additional obligation, i.e. the one enshrined in Art. 22(2): "a sample of the underlying exposures shall be subject to external verification prior to issuance of the securities resulting from the securitisation by an appropriate and independent party, including verification that the data disclosed in respect of the underlying exposures is accurate." It is not clear which party is required to fulfil this obligation, namely whether the reference is to the originator or the promoter. In view of the technical nature of the obligation, it is not too speculative to say that it should be imposed on the sponsor, in view of the mandate that the sponsor has received from the principal, the originator, who conceived the securitisation transaction.

79 It is possible to observe that Art. 22(5) is strictly linked to paragraph 1 of the same article. This legal provision is intended for information to be made available to potential investors upon request from potential investors prior to pricing. Art. 22(5) states that the information required by point (a) of the first subparagraph of Article 7(1) "shall be made available to potential investors before pricing upon request. The information required by points (b) to (d) of the first subparagraph of Article 7(1) shall be made available before pricing at least in draft or initial form. The final documentation shall be made available to investors at the latest 15 days after closing of the transaction."

Notwithstanding the above, paragraph 5 holds that both originator and sponsor are liable for non-compliance with this obligation. More specifically, it could be argued that the independent entity which the European legislator refers to is – precisely because it is independent – outside the scope of securitisation players. Consequently, it shall be different from both the originator and the sponsor. Since the latter is in charge of the transaction, as fundamentally the arranger of the operation, it may incur an indirect conflict of interest, thus the arranger could potentially come up with a too superficial appraisal of the sample. This interest is linked to the need to achieve an objective that is considered profitable for the securitisation transaction itself. The subjects that could carry out this activity in a more fruitful way are the auditing companies or, alternatively, qualified professionals such as chartered accountants. The credit rating agency itself could play this role, despite the same being in an obvious conflict of interest position. In fact, at a further stage, the credit rating agency must carry out the evaluation of the securitised instruments.

Clearer on the subjects held from a contractual perspective is Art. 22(3), which states that:

> the originator or the sponsor shall, before the pricing of the securitisation, make available to potential investors a liability cash flow model which precisely represents the contractual relationship between the underlying exposures and the payments flowing between the originator, sponsor, investors, other third parties and the SSPE, and shall, after pricing, make that model available to investors on an ongoing basis and to potential investors upon request.

Although this is a continuous and not occasional obligation, this activity must be carried out before the price is fixed: the parties are required to fulfil it even after the price has been fixed.

Paragraph 4 requires that

> in the case of a securitisation where the underlying exposures are residential loans or auto loans or leases, the originator and sponsor shall publish the available information related to the environmental performance of the assets financed by such residential loans or auto loans or leases, as part of the information disclosed pursuant to point (a) of the first subparagraph of Article 7(1).

The investor in securitised securities should be able to assess whether the underlying credit meets ethical requirements, for example those related to the environment. Although it is an ideal prescription, it is difficult to implement from a practical point of view.

If a common law perspective is adopted, this legal provision recalls the ways in which the British legislation of the Companies Act 2006 tried to implement the principle of corporate social responsibility within the duties of the directors of capitals. Sect. 172 provides for enlightened shareholder's value, and obliges directors to take into account, when they make management choices, the ultimate objectives extraneous to the primary goals which include, for example, respect for the environment.[80]

80 L. Linklater, 'Promoting Success: The Companies Act 2006' (2007) *Company Lawyer* 28(5), 129–130; W.S. Robinson, 'A Change in the Legal Wind – How a New Direction for Corporate Governance Could Affect Takeover Regulation' (2012) *International Company and Commercial Law Review* 23(9), 292–307; D.K.C. Wu, 'Managerial Behaviour, Company Law, and the Problem of Enlightened Shareholder Value' (2010) *Company Lawyer* 31(2), 53–61; A. Keay, 'Office-Holders and the Duty of Directors to Promote the Success of the Company' (2010) *Insolvency Intelligence* 23(9), 129–134; D. Ahern, 'Nominee Directors' Duty to Promote the Success of the Company: Commercial Pragmatism and Legal Orthodoxy' (2011) *Law Quarterly Review* 127(Jan), 118–146; A. Keay, 'Section 172(1) of the Companies Act 2006: An Interpretation and Assessment' (2007) *Company Lawyer* 28(4), 106–110; C. Lam, S. Goo, 'Confucianism and the Duty to Promote the Success of the Company' (2014) *International Company and Commercial Law Review* 25(12), 418–422; A. Al-Hawamdeh, I.H-Y. Chiu, M. Goergen, C. Mallin, E. Mitleton-Kelly, 'The Interpretation of the Director's Duty under Section 172 Companies Act 2006: Insights from Complexity Theory' (2013) *Journal of Business Law* 4, 417–433; J. Lowry, 'The Duty of Loyalty of Company Directors: Bridging the Accountability Gap through Efficient Disclosure' (2009) *Cambridge Law Journal* 68(3), 607–622; E. Ndzi, 'UK Company Law and Precarious Employment Contracts' (2017) *International Journal of Law and Management* 59(4), 571–583; R. Alexander, 'Duty to Promote the "Success of the Company": Time for Greater Emphasis on All Factors' (2017) *Company Lawyer* 38(9), 269–270; J.P. Sykes, 'The Continuing Paradox: A Critique of Minority Shareholder and Derivative Claims under the Companies Act 2006' (2010) *Civil Justice Quarterly* 29(2), 205–234; J. Kong, S. Ho, 'Director's Duty to Promote the Success of the Company: Should Hong Kong Implement a Similar Provision?' (2010) *Journal of Corporate Law Studies* 10(1), 17–33; E. Lynch, 'Section 172: A Ground-Breaking Reform of Director's Duties, or the Emperor's New Clothes?' (2012) *Company Lawyer* 33(7), 196–203; D. Pollard, 'The Short-Form "Best Interests Duty" – Mad, Bad and Dangerous to Know: Part 2: The Problems and a Suggested Better Formulation' (2018) *Trust Law International* 32(3), 176–220; D. Attenborough, 'The Company Law Reform Bill: An Analysis of Directors' Duties and the Objective of the Company' (2006) *Company Lawyer* 27(6), 162–169; E. Ndzi, 'Directors' Duties and Employee Interest: The Case of Zero Hour Contracts' (2016) *Company Lawyer* 37(5), 135–138; S.F. Copp, 'S.172 of the Companies Act 2006 Fails People and Planet?' (2010) *Company Lawyer* 31(12), 406–408; A. Keay, J. Loughrey, 'Something Old, Something New, Something Borrowed: An Analysis of the New Derivative Action under the Companies Act 2006' (2008) *Law Quarterly Review* 124(Jul), 469–500; S. Griffin, 'The Regulation of Directors under the Companies Act 2006' (2008) *Company Law Newsletter* 224, 1–4; J. McCalman, A. Young, 'Another Round of Corporate Governance Reforms in the UK: Implications for Directors in the Financial Sector' (2018) *Journal of International Banking Law and Regulation* 33(8), 286–292; T. Ashraf, 'Directors' Duties with a Particular Focus on the Companies Act 2006' (2012) *International Journal of Law and Management* 54(2), 125–140; I.H-Y. Chiu, 'Regulatory Duties for Directors in the Financial Services Sector and Directors' Duties in Company Law: Bifurcation and Interfaces' (2016) *Journal of Business Law* 6, 465–490; A. Keay, 'Applications to Continue Derivative Proceedings on behalf of Companies and the Hypothetical Director Test' (2015) *Civil Justice Quarterly* 34(4), 346–365; H. Warwick, 'For Whom Should Bank Directors Promote the Success of the Bank?' (2014) *Butterworths Journal of International Banking & Financial Law* 29(4), 222–224; L. Miles, M. Lower, 'Giving Effect to the Statutory Duty of Loyalty' (2006) *Company Law Newsletter* 5, 1–4; R. Craig, '"The Enormous Turnip": A Discussion on the Companies Act 2006 which like Topsy in the Child's Fairy Tale is still Growing' (2008) *Company Lawyer* 29(12), 360–364; R. Davidson, 'The Companies Act 2006:

The actual problem that arises, with regard to both the EU and UK legislations, is concerned with the possibility of concretely implementing the precept. The stakeholder, who is outside the company – and in this case the community – has an expectation and/or relies on the company in terms of respect for the environment. Nevertheless, they do not have an action in Court, nor therefore an entitlement to file a lawsuit against the company or even against the promoters in the case of EU securitisations.

In light of this, therefore, information about the environmental sustainability of financial activities could be assessed by the investor as sensitive to the values that are protected by the body of law under analysis.

3.7 The "Third Parties Verifiers" and STS criteria

There is no doubt that Art. 28 of the EU Securitisation Regulation engenders a regulatory microsystem whose general principles are within the broader legislation, i.e. the EU Securitisation Regulation and its main pillars. The common

Directors' Duties and Promoting the Company's Success' (2007) *Butterworths Journal of International Banking & Financial Law* 22(11), 631–632; J. Mukwiri, 'Directors' Duties in Takeover Bids and English Company Law' (2008) *International Company and Commercial Law Review* 19(9), 281–289; R. Goddard, 'Directors' Duties' (2008) *Edinburgh Law Review* 12(3), 468–472; M. Almadani, 'Derivative Actions: Does the Companies Act 2006 Offer a Way Forward?' (2009) *Company Lawyer* 30(5), 131–140; J. Green, L. Johnston, B. Williams, 'Corporate Governance in Financial Institutions' (2017) *Compliance Officer Bulletin* 146(May), 1–30; S. Paulo, 'The United Kingdom's Companies Act of 2006 and the Capital Asset Pricing Model: Attaining the Corporate Objective' (2010) *International Journal of Law and Management* 52(4), 253–264; C. Jones, 'Directors' Duties – A Supporting Statement' (2005) *International Company and Commercial Law Review* 16(9), 364–368; J. Green, L. Johnston, B. Williams, 'Corporate Governance in Financial Institutions' (2020) *Compliance Officer Bulletin* 180(Oct), 1–42; B. Perry, L. Gregory, 'The European Panorama: Directors' Economic and Social Responsibilities' (2009) *International Company and Commercial Law Review* 20(2), 25–36; A. Keay, 'Directors' Duties' (2014) *International Company and Commercial Law Review* 2014, 25(12), 436–437; A. Berg, 'The Company Law Review: Legislating Directors' Duties' (2007) *Journal of Business Law*, Sep, 472–491; J. Zhao, 'Promoting More Socially Responsible Corporations through UK Company Law after the 2008 Financial Crisis: The Turning of the Crisis Compass' (2011) *International Company and Commercial Law Review* 22(9), 275–284; R. Teele Langford, 'General Law and Statutory Directors' Duties: "Unmixed Oil and Water" or "Integrated Parts of the Whole Law"?' (2015) *Law Quarterly Review* 131(Oct), 635–651; J. Quinn, 'The Duty of Good Faith in Light of the Business Judgment Rule' (2016) *International Company and Commercial Law Review* 27(4), 120–128; A. Keay, 'The Duty of Directors to Exercise Independent Judgment' (2008) *Company Lawyer* 29(10), 290–296; P. Davies, 'Directors' Creditor-Regarding Duties in Respect of Trading Decisions Taken in the Vicinity of Insolvency' (2006) *European Business Organization Law Review* 7(1), 301–337; D. Pollard, 'The Short-Form "Best Interests Duty" – Mad, Bad and Dangerous to Know: Part 1 – Background, Cowan v Scargill and MNRPF' (2018) *Trust Law International* 32(2), 106–156; J.M. Wood, 'Directors' Duties Post Insolvency' (2021) *International Company and Commercial Law Review* 32(7), 371–386; R. Mundy, 'Directors' Duties during Administration and Liquidation' (2021) *Insolvency Intelligence* 34(3), 58–61; R. Goddard, 'Promoting the Success of the Company' (2010) *Company Secretary's Review* 34(17), 136.

threads of these two layers are the structured transactions and the way they are organised, from a transactional point of view too.

Admittedly, the complexity of these legal provisions could potentially be a factor that may discourage players from using securitisations. However, the response to this theoretical objection is that, on the one hand, the architecture, albeit intricate, is nonetheless instrumental in safeguarding the credibility of the STS brand. On the other hand, not only does this result in an extremely complex mechanism, but it also requires compliance with possible increased costs. An image of Art. 28 of the EU Securitisation Regulation could be one of a Russian doll: the outer is the regulation, whereas within a deeper frame it is possible to find the rules applicable to independent authorities; finally, in the innermost layer there are private and independent third parties.

In a nutshell, an STS securitisation shall be subject to a threefold verification process: first and foremost, it shall comply with the EU Securitisation Regulation, although at a further stage it shall be subject to a double-check by both a public independent authority and a private independent party. Not without a certain degree of irony, it is possible to say that the EU legislator tried to answer, perhaps in a brilliant way, an ancient dilemma: "who controls the controller."

Art. 27(2) of the EU Securitisation Regulations states that, if the originator, sponsor or SSPE want to have the STS label, they have to use the service of a third party authorised by virtue of Article 28.[81]

If the originator or original lender cannot qualify as a credit institution or investment firm,[82] as established by the Union, the notification shall be accompanied by the following. First, "a confirmation by the originator or original lender that its credit granting is done on the basis of sound and well-defined criteria and clearly established processes for approving, amending, renewing and financing credits and that the originator or original lender has effective tools in place to apply such processes in accordance with Article 9 of this Regulation." Second, "a declaration by the originator or original lender as to whether credit granting referred to in point (a) is subject to supervision."[83]

Art. 28 of the EU Securitisation Regulation stipulates that a third party[84] could be authorised by the Authority to certify that an STS securitisation complies with the criteria established by this regulation.[85] The role of the competent authority

81 "However, the use of such a service shall not, under any circumstances, affect the liability of the originator, sponsor or SSPE in respect of their legal obligations under this Regulation. The use of such service shall not affect the obligations imposed on institutional investors as set out in Article 5. Where the originator, sponsor or SSPE use the service of a third party authorised pursuant to Article 28 to assess whether a securitisation complies with Articles 19 to 22 or Articles 23 to 26, the STS notification shall include a statement that compliance with the STS criteria was confirmed by that authorised third party. The notification shall include the name of the authorised third party, its place of establishment and the name of the competent authority that authorised it."

82 The reference is to points (1) and (2) of Article 4(1) of Regulation (EU) No 575/2013.

83 Art. 27(3), lett. a) and lett. b).

84 See Art. 27(2).

85 More specifically, compliance with criteria of Articles 19 to 22 and Articles 23 to 26 is necessary.

is to release the authorisation only if the criteria are respected.[86] An independent third party may become such if it aligns with the technical standards defined by ESMA.[87]

The second part of Art. 28(1) stipulates that this authorisation may be withdrawn by the competent authority if the third party is not in accordance with the previous provisions. The duty of the third party is to notify to the authority every change to the information that is required.[88] The authority will be empowered to charge the cost to the third party in order to cover the necessary expenditure linked to the assessment of applications.[89]

86 Pursuant to Art. 28(1), these conditions are: "a) the third party only charges non-discriminatory and cost-based fees to the originators, sponsors or SSPEs involved in the securitisations which the third party assesses without differentiating fees depending on, or correlated to, the results of its assessment; (b) the third party is neither a regulated entity as defined in point (4) of Article 2 of Directive 2002/87/EC nor a credit rating agency as defined in point (b) of Article 3(1) of Regulation (EC) No 1060/2009, and the performance of the third party's other activities does not compromise the independence or integrity of its assessment; (c) the third party shall not provide any form of advisory, audit or equivalent service to the originator, sponsor or SSPE involved in the securitisations which the third party assesses; (d) the members of the management body of the third party have professional qualifications, knowledge and experience that are adequate for the task of the third party and they are of good repute and integrity; (e) the management body of the third party includes at least one third, but no fewer than two, independent directors; (f) the third party takes all necessary steps to ensure that the verification of STS compliance is not affected by any existing or potential conflicts of interest or business relationship involving the third party, its shareholders or members, managers, employees or any other natural person whose services are placed at the disposal or under the control of the third party. To that end, the third party shall establish, maintain, enforce and document an effective internal control system governing the implementation of policies and procedures to identify and prevent potential conflicts of interest. Potential or existing conflicts of interest which have been identified shall be eliminated or mitigated and disclosed without delay. The third party shall establish, maintain, enforce and document adequate procedures and processes to ensure the independence of the assessment of STS compliance. The third party shall periodically monitor and review those policies and procedures in order to evaluate their effectiveness and assess whether it is necessary to update them; and (g) the third party can demonstrate that it has proper operational safeguards and internal processes that enable it to assess STS compliance."

87 See the first part of 28(4), which states: "ESMA shall develop draft regulatory technical standards specifying the information to be provided to the competent authorities in the application for the authorisation of a third party in accordance with paragraph 1."

88 Article 28(2): "A third party authorised in accordance with paragraph 1 shall notify its competent authority without delay of any material changes to the information provided under that paragraph, or any other changes that could reasonably be considered to affect the assessment of its competent authority."

89 Article 28(3): "The competent authority may charge cost-based fees to the third party referred to in paragraph 1, in order to cover necessary expenditure relating to the assessment of applications for authorisation and to the subsequent monitoring of compliance with the conditions set out in paragraph 1."

3.8 Structured finance and commercial papers

The requirements of transparency, simplicity and standardisation can be applied not only to securitisations, in the way they are perceived in a traditional and orthodox way, but also to commercial papers (ABCP). These are securities with a shorter maturity than a traditional transaction. In this case, the required criteria of STS shall be based, as far as the objective parameters are concerned, on those enshrined in Art. 24 of the EU regulation and, as regards the subjective ones, those encapsulated in Art. 25, since they are, in fact, transferor's assets.

With regard to the first legal provision, namely Art. 24, the latter does not contain any different criteria from those laid down for general STS securitisations. Consequently, the principle that the contract for the assignment of claims between seller and the vehicle must be a true sale will also apply to the ABCP securitisation case. No obligation shall be inferable, for the originator, to repurchase the receivables.

Furthermore, the transfer of titles is not subject to the clawback rules[90] in the case of insolvency of the seller. In this respect, it is stipulated that, if the seller is an entity different from the assignor, the effective sale or transfer must comply with the same requirements as the direct assignment of receivables. Essentially, the "second degree" assignment will have to comply with the requirement of true sale required for the "first degree" sale.[91] The reason for this norm is to prevent

90 The reference is to those rules which cannot be derogated from. It should be noted that, even in the case of ABCP securitisations, the norms protecting public policy interests are not mandatory. Among these is Art. 24(3), in force of which, "for the purpose of paragraph 1, clawback provisions in national insolvency laws that allow the liquidator or a court to invalidate the sale of underlying exposures in the case of fraudulent transfers, unfair prejudice to creditors or transfers intended to improperly favour particular creditors over others shall not constitute severe clawback provisions." These may be regarded as "untouchable," i.e. rules that cannot be derogated. They are not rigid, nor flexible. They would belong to the realm of the public policy rules. The literature on this area is unfettered: without pretence of completeness, see D. Milman, 'Clawback and Limited Liability Partnerships' (2021) *Insolvency Lawyer* 5(Nov), 178–179; D. Livshiz, 'At the Ocean's Edge? The Extraterritorial Reach of the Avoidance and Recovery Provisions of the US Bankruptcy Code' (2017) *Butterworths Journal of International Banking & Financial Law* 32(3), 146–148; Clifford Chance, 'Insolvency Regulation: Local Law Defences' (2017) *PLC Magazine* 28(7), 67; S. Bonfatti, 'Rescue Culture in Italy: the Introduction of Key Incentives to Companies in Crisis to Restructure Their Business and Future Perspectives' (2018) *International Company and Commercial Law Review* 29(3), 195–208; S. Sax, A.M. Swierczok, 'European Court of Justice Decision on the Scope of Article 13 European Insolvency Regulation: Lutz v Bauerle (C-557/13)' (2016) *Insolvency Intelligence* 29(2), 25–26; I.F. Fletcher, '"Better Late than Never": The UNCITRAL Model Law Enters into Force in Great Britain' (2006) *Insolvency Intelligence* 19(6), 86–93; I.F. Fletcher, 'The European Insolvency Regulation Recast: The Main Features of the New Law' (2015) *Insolvency Intelligence* 28(7), 97–103; S. Fennell, 'Cash-Flow and Balance Sheet Insolvency for Claims by Office-Holders' (2014) *Insolvency Intelligence* 27(8), 121–123; D. Milman, 'Bankruptcy in the Courts: Continuity in an Era of Change?' (2017) *Insolvency Intelligence* 30(6), 91–93.

91 The reference is to Art 24(4), namely: "where the seller is not the original lender, the true sale or assignment or transfer with the same legal effect of the underlying exposures to the seller, whether

second-degree selling from becoming an opportunity to avoid the application of mandatory rules. These rules are applicable to the first instance transfer and could, therefore, be circumvented in the subsequent sale.

Paragraph 5 applies to the situation in which the transfer of the underlying exposures occurs in two different times, namely whether it is in coincidence with the closing of the transaction or thereafter.[92]

This particular technique is seen as unfavourable by the European legislator; in fact, it has stated that the subsequent improvement will take place on condition of the following three events occurring: the serious deterioration of the credit quality of the seller, the insolvency of the seller, and finally the breach of contractual obligations by the seller. This confirms the tendency of the regulation to favour forms of securitisation in which the conclusion of contracts and the completion of the transaction, then closing and settlement, coincide in chronological terms.

Further characteristic elements of the ABCP securitisation are: a) the seller's statement that the underlying exposures are not binding;[93] and b) "the underlying exposures transferred from, or assigned by, the seller to the SSPE shall meet predetermined, clear and documented eligibility criteria which do not allow for active portfolio management of those exposures on a discretionary basis."[94] Art. 24(8) requires that the underlying exposures not be included in any securitisation position.

The regulation also requires that once the portfolio selection has been made, the underlying exposures are transferred without delay to the vehicle and shall not include, at the time of selection, default exposures[95] and no exposures to a debtor or a non-performing credit rating authority. With respect to the latter, the original originator or lender is required to be aware that he:

(a) has been declared insolvent or had a court grant his creditors a final non-appealable right of enforcement or material damages as a result of a missed payment within three years prior to the date of origination or has undergone a debt restructuring process with regard to his non-performing exposures within three years prior to the date of transfer or assignment of the underlying exposures to the SSPE, except if: (i) a restructured

that true sale or assignment or transfer with the same legal effect is direct or through one or more intermediate steps, shall meet the requirements set out in paragraphs 1 to 3."

92 The relevant legal provision stipulates as follows: "where the transfer of the underlying exposures is performed by means of an assignment and perfected at a later stage than at the closing of the transaction, the triggers to effect such perfection shall include at least the following events: (a) severe deterioration in the seller credit quality standing; (b) insolvency of the seller; and (c) unremedied breaches of contractual obligations by the seller, including the seller's default."

93 See Art. 24(6): "the seller shall provide representations and warranties that, to the best of its knowledge, the underlying exposures included in the securitisation are not encumbered or otherwise in a condition that can be foreseen to adversely affect the enforceability of the true sale or assignment or transfer with the same legal effect."

94 Art. 24(7).

95 The reference is to Art. 178(1) of Regulation (EU) No. 575/2013.

underlying exposure has not presented new arrears since the date of the restructuring, which must have taken place at least one year prior to the date of transfer or assignment of the underlying exposures to the SSPE; and (ii) the information provided by the originator, sponsor and SSPE in accordance with points (a) and (e)(i) of the first subparagraph of Article 7(1) explicitly sets out the proportion of restructured underlying exposures, the time and details of the restructuring as well as their performance since the date of the restructuring;

(b) was, at the time of origination, where applicable, on a public credit registry of persons with adverse credit history or, where there is no such public credit registry, another credit registry that is available to the originator or original lender; or

(c) has a credit assessment or a credit score indicating that the risk of contractually agreed payments not being made is significantly higher than for comparable exposures held by the originator which are not securitised.[96]

Additional requirements in respect of ABCP securitisations seem to recall those already prescribed in respect of ordinary securitisations.[97] These include: a) the mandatory condition that, at the time of transfer, the debtor in the portfolio has paid at least one instalment (Art. 24(10)); b) the repayment of securitised positions is not primarily dependent on the sale of collateral (Art. 24(10)); c) interest rate risk and exchange rate risk are adequately mitigated also through the conclusion of derivative contracts, signed for hedging purposes between a vehicle and an investment bank.[98] It is worth adding that, apart from these exceptions, the Union legislator is not supportive of overly speculative securitisations. Therefore, the vehicle cannot enter into derivative contracts and more in general, cannot securitise positions on derivatives.

Norms that relate more in depth to ABCP securitisations are those encompassed within Art. 24(15).

Starting from paragraph 15, it is prescribed that ABCP transactions are guaranteed by a homogeneous portfolio, including one asset only. This is a requirement for transparency. Consistent with the short-term nature of the commercial papers, it is expected that "the pool of underlying exposures shall have a remaining

96 Art. 24(9).

97 L. Walters, 'ABCP Set to Grow Again' (2002) *International Securitisation Report* 64, 50–51; International Securitisation Report (editorial), 'The ABC of ABCP' (2004) *International Securitisation Report* 89(Jun), 49–58; International Securitisation Report (editorial), 'ABCP Loan-Backed Vehicles' (2002) *International Securitisation Report* 70(Sep), 11; M. Kaur, T. Fritz, 'US ABCP Market Greets New Regulations with Cautious Optimism' (2005) *International Securitisation Report* 101(Jun) Supp, 3–4; A. Quirk, 'Restructuring Imminent in Europe's ABCP Market as Structural and Regulatory Issues Loom Large' (2005) *International Securitisation Report* 101(Jun) Supp, 7–8.

98 This is the only hypothesis where the vehicle is entitled to conclude derivative contracts that, otherwise, would be excluded in the same *sedes materiae*, therefore the area of law, which is the subject matter of current analysis.

weighted average life of not more than one year, and none of the underlying exposures shall have a residual maturity of more than three years." Assuming that the portfolio relates to loans of a specific type, those for instrumental vehicles, the securitisation transactions will have "life of not more than three and a half years, and none of the underlying exposures shall have a residual maturity of more than six years."

The 2007–2008 financial crisis was marked by a quintessential problem: the technical complexity of securitisation operations, which made the contractual packages extremely opaque. As a result, it is now required that the interest rate, both for the assets and liabilities of a securitisation transaction, must be intelligible. More specifically, it is necessary that a specific market is indicated, insofar as to avoid the use "of complex formulas or derivatives." Art. 24(17) stipulates that, in the wake of the seller's default or an acceleration event:

> (a) no amount of cash shall be trapped in the SSPE beyond what is necessary to ensure the operational functioning of the SSPE or the orderly repayment of investors in accordance with the contractual terms of the securitisation unless exceptional circumstances require that an amount be trapped to be used, in the best interests of investors, for expenses in order to avoid the deterioration in the credit quality of the underlying exposures; (b) principal receipts from the underlying exposures shall be passed to investors holding a securitisation position via sequential payment of the securitisation positions, as determined by the seniority of the securitisation position; and (c) no provisions shall require automatic liquidation of the underlying exposures at market value.

As far as the subjective criterion to conduct an ABCP transaction is concerned, it refers to the "character" of the arranger. It must be a supervised credit institution within the meaning of Directive 2013/36/EU.[99] This requirement is derived from Art. 25(1) of the Securitisation Regulation. This provision is certainly stringent, but justified by the fact that the registration of an entity as a credit institution should be a measure of credibility and a guarantee of compliance with the rules of the entire transaction. In fact, the ABCP operation is different from the securitisation operation in that it requires a guarantee which, in turn, should reduce the risks to investors.

The EU regulation regulates two forms of guaranteed European securitisation: the fully guaranteed ABCP scheme and the fully guaranteed ABCP operation.

99 "Directive 2013/36/EU of the European Parliament and of the Council of 26 June 2013 on access to the activity of credit institutions and the prudential supervision of credit institutions and investment firms, amending Directive 2002/87/EC and repealing Directives 2006/48/EC and 2006/49/EC (text with EEA relevance)" (7.6.2013 Official Journal of the European Union L 176/338 of 7 June 2013). On this piece of legislation, see M. Haentjens, P. de Gioia Carabellese, *European Banking and Financial Law*, 2nd ed. (n. 1), 105 ff.; A. Hudson, *Hudson The Law of Finance*, 2nd ed., Sweet & Maxwell, London, 2013, 851 ff.; J. Odgers QC, *Paget's Law of Banking*, 15th ed., LexisNexis, London, 2018, 4 ff.

In the first case:

> its sponsor directly and fully supports by providing to the SSPE(s) one or more liquidity facilities covering at least all of the following: (a) all liquidity and credit risks of the ABCP programme; (b) any material dilution risks of the exposures being securitised; (c) any other ABCP transaction-level and ABCP programme-level costs if necessary to guarantee to the investor the full payment of any amount under the ABCP.[100]

The second, in contrast:

> ABCP transaction supported by a liquidity facility, at transaction level or at ABCP programme level, that covers at least all of the following: (a) all liquidity and credit risks of the ABCP transaction; (b) any material dilution risks of the exposures being securitised in the ABCP transaction; (c) any other ABCP transaction-level and ABCP programme-level costs if necessary to guarantee to the investor the full payment of any amount under the ABCP.[101]

Again, the transaction must contain the above-mentioned elements jointly.

The definition of this operation is similar to that of the programme with a guarantee from the promoter, although there is a difference. In the first case, the guarantee is issued by the promoter and therefore presents the characteristics of a personal guarantee. In the second case, the guarantee appears to be linked to the same liquidity facility that could be made available to the party.

The role of the promoter, that is to be a supervised and European entity, is also explained according to the specific mandate that, in a given ABCP securitisation operation, the same promoter is given. The arranger,[102] in fact, is not only the entity that provides assistance to the organisation of the operation but also the entity that must provide liquidity in the light of the short-term nature of the operation. In this logic, liquidity becomes the essential element for the subsistence and credibility of the operation.

The European Union legislative concern, according to the definition provided by the arranger, is to ensure that they, in the case of ABCP securitisation, are more involved than a normal securitisation transaction. In this sense the arranger assumes not only a contractual role as agent, therefore responsible for the

100 Art. 2(21).
101 Art. 2(22).
102 It is defined by Art. 25(2) as "a liquidity facility provider and shall support all securitisation positions on an ABCP programme level by covering all liquidity and credit risks and any material dilution risks of the securitised exposures as well as any other transaction- and programme-level costs if necessary to guarantee to the investor the full payment of any amount under the ABCP with such support. The sponsor shall disclose a description of the support provided at transaction level to the investors including a description of the liquidity facilities provided."

structuring of the operation, but also assumes the function of being co-responsible for the economic success of the operation, as far as this is possible.

The role of guarantor of the transaction appears to be an excessive legal qualification for the ABCP securitisation promoter. It is believed that he has a weak role, a *patronant* who, with his authority, albeit without taking on contractual commitments of any kind, provides the transaction with an *aura* of credibility.

In conclusion, it should be emphasised that not all securitisations covered by the trading system of the Securitisation Regulation are eligible for STS status. This eligibility is linked to the actual transfer. It follows that synthetic securitisations are excluded:

> in securitisations which are not true-sale, the underlying exposures are not transferred to an issuer entity which is an SSPE, but rather the credit risk related to the underlying exposures is transferred by means of a derivative contract or guarantees. This introduces an additional counterparty credit risk and potential complexity related in particular to the content of the derivative contract. For those reasons, the STS criteria should not allow synthetic securitisation.[103]

3.9 The European context: between private and administrative law

The European Securitisation Regulation heralds a new set of norms which could be defined as a microsystem of rules of an administrative nature.[104]

The registration in the roll of STS securitisations shall be preceded by a notification to ESMA jointly made by the originator and the promoter in accordance with the provisions of Art. 27(1) of the Rules of Procedure.[105] In the case of an ABCP programme, only the promoter is responsible for the notification of such a

103 Recital 24 of the Securitisation Regulation.

104 It is an expression used in a "cosmetic" way. The STS trademark, which is recognised for securitisations with a high quality, caters to both a substantial and a formal goal. The main practical objective is the need for financial instruments duly presenting the characteristics of simplicity, transparency and standardisation. As far as the formal one is concerned, it substantiates in the preparation of a mandatory register for STS securitised securities. Only in this case will the relevant operators, namely investors, be able to benefit from it for balance sheet and supervisory capital purposes. It should be recalled that the registration in question does not confer the STS status on a securitisation that does not meet the substantial requirements. Therefore, the registration with the roll of the European authority and the related publicity that follows therefrom does not have a substantive law nature, nor does it "cure" *ex post* any flaw that may affect the relevant requirements. The substantial requirement, in other words, shall be subject to continuous and careful assessment by investors.

105 "Originators and sponsors shall jointly notify ESMA by means of the template referred to in paragraph 7 of this Article where a securitisation meets the requirements of Articles 19 to 22 or Articles 23 to 26 ('STS notification'). In the case of an ABCP programme, only the sponsor shall be responsible for the notification of that programme and, within that programme, of the ABCP transactions complying with Article 24."

programme and of the ABCP transactions pursuant to Art. 24. It follows from this that the registration has a mere informative nature.

With the notification of the STS securitisation, the originator and the sponsor shall communicate how each of the STS criteria has been met, namely: simplicity, transparency, standardisation. The *ratio essendi* of the notification of the start of the STS securitisation status and its termination is referred to in Recital 31 of the Securitisation Regulation. It states that:

> where originators, sponsors and SSPEs would like their securitisations to use the STS designation, investors, competent authorities and ESMA should be notified that the securitisation meets the STS requirements. The notification should include an explanation on how each of the STS criteria has been complied with. ESMA should then publish it on a list of notified STS securitisations made available on its website for information purposes. The inclusion of a securitisation issuance in ESMA's list of notified STS securitisations does not imply that ESMA or other competent authorities have certified that the securitisation meets the STS requirements. Compliance with the STS requirements remains solely the responsibility of the originators, sponsors and SSPEs. This should ensure that originators, sponsors and SSPEs take responsibility for their claim that the securitisation is STS and that there is transparency on the market.

At a later stage, ESMA, as a result of the notification, should ensure that the securitisation is included in a list of STS securitisations, subsequently published for information purposes on its website. In this sense, it seems, therefore, that ESMA fulfils the function of notary of registration of the securitisation.

In interpreting this provision, the feeling is that there is an intention to limit, if not to exclude, a liability of ESMA in the event that a securitisation presented as STS is not recognised as such at a later date. In any event, in accordance with general principles of law, ESMA should be held liable for professional damages if it is established that ESMA has intentionally entered the apparent STS securitisation. As a result, compliance with STS requirements remains the sole responsibility of originators, promoters and SSPs. In doing so, it should be ensured that originators, promoters and SSPs assume responsibility for the STS securitisation status and market transparency declaration.

When it comes to the publication procedure, ESMA shall publish the STS notification on its official website. In order to achieve the ultimate objective of ensuring the best agreement with the National Authority, it is provided that the originator and the sponsor inform the respective competent authorities of the notification in question. Although the notification is jointly made, it is mandatory that the originator and promoter[106] designate the entity that acts as the "first point of contact" for both investors and competent authorities.

106 This element will be released on the website of the Authority.

The certification of coherence, which proves to be a very technical operation, can also be performed by a third party.[107] In order to ensure that the task entrusted to third parties does not result in the liability of the primary obligated parties, the responsibility of the originator, the sponsor or the SSPE remains with the originator. This is a liability that must be related to the legal obligations incumbent on such entities under the Securitisation Regulation. In addition, investors will continue to be subject to the obligations contained in Art. 5 of the Securitisation Regulation.

In further looking at the matter from the perspective of the authorising third party, it is worth mentioning that Art. 27(2) sets forth the principle that the STS notification "shall include a statement that compliance with the STS criteria was confirmed by that authorised third party." This precept is compounded by the legal provision pursuant to which the notification "shall include the name of the authorised third party, its place of establishment and the name of the competent authority that authorised it."[108]

If the originator or the original lender is not an EU credit institution, there are even more stringent requirements. The reference, in this respect, is Art. 27(3), pursuant to which:

> if the originator or original lender is not a credit institution or investment firm [...],[109] the notification [...] shall be accompanied by the following: (a) confirmation by the originator or original lender that its credit granting is done on the basis of sound and well defined criteria and clearly established processes for approving, amending, renewing and financing credits and that the originator or original lender has effective systems in place to apply such processes in accordance with Article 9 of this Regulation; and (b) a declaration by the originator or original lender as to whether credit granting referred to in point (a) is subject to supervision.

107 This idea is also referenced in Art. 27(2) by virtue of which the originator, sponsor or SSPE "may use the service of a third party authorised under Art. 28 to check whether a securitisation complies with Articles 19 to 22 or Articles 23 to 26."

108 The *ratio essendi* of this legal provision is similar to the one in Recital 34 pursuant to which "the involvement of third parties in helping to check compliance of a securitisation with the STS requirements could be useful for investors, originators, sponsors and SSPEs and contribute to increasing confidence in the market for STS securitisations. Originators, sponsors and SSPEs could also use the services of a third party authorised in accordance with this Regulation to assess whether their securitisation complies with the STS criteria. Those third parties should be subject to authorisation by competent authorities. The notification to ESMA and the subsequent publication on ESMA's website should mention whether STS compliance was confirmed by an authorised third party. However, it is essential that investors make their own assessment, take responsibility for their investment decisions and do not mechanistically rely on such third parties. The involvement of a third party should not in any way shift away from originators, sponsors and institutional investors the ultimate legal responsibility for notifying and treating a securitisation transaction as STS."

109 As defined in points (1) and (2) of Art. 4(1) of Regulation (EU) No. 575/2013, therefore an entity established in the Union.

The notification of the STS securitisation compliance requirements which, from a strictly formal point of view, provide the transaction with the mark of quality, is not concerned exclusively with the "genetic" phase (the conferral of such a status and the ensuing acquisition of the "quality brand"), but also with the demise of the status.[110] The notification of termination, therefore, is provided for and explained by Recital 32, according to which, where a securitisation no longer meets the STS requirements, "the originator and sponsor should immediately notify ESMA and the relevant competent authority."

Also during the process, therefore from the approval of the STS status until its end, the competent authority should impose administrative sanctions with regard to a securitisation notified as being STS, "that competent authority should immediately notify ESMA for their inclusion on the STS notifications list allowing investors to be informed about such sanctions and about the reliability of STS notifications."[111] Ultimately originators and sponsors are required to be the watchdogs, for administrative purposes, of the STS securitisation, and these legal provisions take precedence over contractual provisions to the contrary embedded in the securitisation documentation.

While the latter is concerned with the regime of the notifications, the publicity regime of the STS securitisation is hinged upon Art. 27(5) of the EU Securitisation Regulation,[112] based on websites and catering for adequate information to be provided to the public.

The administrative system that characterises the securitisation discipline is also implemented by what could be defined as a "micro-system of operating rules" which has the function to harmonise the framework of secondary discipline. The first reference goes to Art. 27(7), whereby:

> in order to ensure uniform conditions for the implementation of this Regulation, ESMA, in close cooperation with the EBA and EIOPA, shall develop draft implementing technical standards to establish the templates to be used for the provision of the information referred to in paragraph 6. ESMA shall submit those draft implementing technical standards to the Commission by 18 July 2018. Power is conferred on the Commission to

110 This is the interpretation of Art. 27(4): "The originator and sponsor shall immediately notify ESMA and inform their competent authority when a securitisation no longer meets the requirements of either Articles 19 to 22 or Articles 23 to 26."

111 *Ibidem.*

112 "ESMA shall maintain on its official website a list of all securitisations which the originators and sponsors have notified to it as meeting the requirements of Articles 19 to 22 or Articles 23 to 26. ESMA shall add each securitisation so notified to that list immediately and shall update the list where the securitisations are no longer considered to be STS following a decision of competent authorities or a notification by the originator or sponsor. Where the competent authority has imposed administrative sanctions in accordance with Article 32, it shall notify ESMA thereof immediately. ESMA shall immediately indicate on the list that a competent authority has imposed administrative sanctions in relation to the securitisation concerned."

> adopt the implementing technical standards referred to in this paragraph in accordance with Article 15 of Regulation (EU) No 1095/2010.

At the second stage it is necessary to recall Recital 35, pursuant to which:

> Member States should designate competent authorities and provide them with the necessary supervisory, investigative and sanctioning powers. Administrative sanctions should, in principle, be published. Since investors, originators, sponsors, original lenders and SSPEs can be established in different Member States and supervised by different sectoral competent authorities, close cooperation between relevant competent authorities, including the European Central Bank (ECB) with regard to specific tasks conferred on it by Council Regulation (EU) No 1024/2013 (1), and with the ESAs should be ensured by the mutual exchange of information and assistance in supervisory activities. Competent authorities should apply sanctions only in the case of intentional or negligent infringements. The application of remedial measures should not depend on evidence of intention or negligence. In determining the appropriate type and level of sanction or remedial measure, when taking into account the financial strength of the responsible natural or legal person, competent authorities should in particular take into consideration the total turnover of the responsible legal person or the annual income and net assets of the responsible natural person.

Finally, reference should be made to Recital 36, which states:

> competent authorities should closely coordinate their supervision and ensure consistent decisions, especially in the event of infringements of this Regulation. Where such an infringement concerns an incorrect or misleading notification, the competent authority identifying that infringement should also inform the ESAs and the relevant competent authorities of the Member States concerned. In the event of disagreement between the competent authorities, ESMA, and, where appropriate, the Joint Committee of the European Supervisory Authorities, should exercise their binding mediation powers.

This copious reference to Recitals underlines the concept of cooperation that should exist between the authorities concerned in an STS securitisation. It is, by definition, a transnational transaction and its actors are transnational. Given these elements, therefore, the regulation does not refer to an authority with exclusive national competence, but to an authority with transactional competence.

If the competence had been "universal," providing that one imagines the EU as a legal universe – for example in terms of relations with the arranger – the EU itself would have become competent to supervise all the subjects and stages of securitisation. This would avoid the risk of misinformed supervision due to incorrect communication of the lack thereof. If the solution adopted had been to centralise the National Supervisory Authority, this would have facilitated the establishment of a strong power inclusive of disciplinary power. The risk would have been to induce operators to choose their preferred supervisor through the transfer of the registered office of the institution or banking group that securitises in a country with a friendly Authority.

The supervision of STS securitisations and of the parties that take part in them is regulated by Art. 29 "Designation of competent authorities."[113] According to it, the competent authorities in each area

> shall be supervised by the following competent authorities in accordance with the powers granted by the relevant legal acts: (a) for insurance and reinsurance undertakings, the competent authority designated in accordance with point (10) of Article 13 of Directive 2009/138/EC; (b) for alternative investment fund managers, the competent authority responsible designated in accordance with Article 44 of Directive 2011/61/EU; (c) for UCITS and UCITS management companies, the competent authority designated in accordance with Article 97 of Directive 2009/65/EC; (d) for institutions for occupational retirement provision, the competent authority designated in accordance with point (g) of Article 6 of Directive 2003/41/EC of the European Parliament and of the Council (1); (e) for credit institutions or investments firms, the competent authority designated in accordance with Article 4 of Directive 2013/36/EU, including the ECB with regard to specific tasks conferred on it by Regulation (EU) No 1024/2013.[114]

Art. 9(3) stipulates that:

> where originators, original lenders and SSPEs are supervised entities in accordance with Directives 2003/41/EC, 2009/138/EC, 2009/65/EC, 2011/61/EU and 2013/36/EU and Regulation (EU) No 1024/2013, the relevant competent authorities designated according to those acts, including the ECB with regard to specific tasks conferred on it by Regulation (EU) No

113 Broadly speaking, the theme of the supervision of securitisations and securitised products has been occurring in the literature for some time. G. Usher, 'EU Securitisation Regulation Heralds Simple, Transparent and Standardised Securitisation' (2015/2016) *Finance & Credit Law*, Dec/Jan, 4–6; P. Dorin, M. Vojtko, 'Simple, Transparent and Standardised Synthetic Securitisations – The Next Step Ahead?' (2017) *Journal of International Banking Law and Regulation* 32(7), 299–306; R. Ambery, S. Bowmer, 'The Use of Limited Partnership Special Purpose Entities in Property Securitisations' (2001) *Journal of International Banking Law* 16(6), 153–156; H. von Reden, 'Regulation of Securitised Products Post the Financial Crisis' (2013) UCL *Journal of Law and Jurisprudence* 2(1), 112–140; M.C. Nwogugu, 'Economic Policy and the Constitutionality of Asset Securitisation' (2009) *International Company and Commercial Law Review* 20(7), 245–254; J. Woolfe, 'Securitisation: Upgrade Essential, but "Moribund"' (2017) *Global Risk Regulator* 15(4), 7–8.

114 Art. 29(1).

> 1024/2013, shall supervise compliance with the obligations set out in Articles 6, 7, 8 and 9 of this Regulation.[115]

It is also provided that Member States shall designate one or more competent authorities to supervise the compliance of originators, sponsors and SSPEs with Articles 18 to 27, and the compliance of third parties with Article 28 (Art. 29(5)). This is a legal provision which clearly refers to the concept of simple, transparent and standardised securitisation. Likewise, the same legal provision stipulates that "Member States shall inform the Commission and ESMA of the designation of competent authorities pursuant to this paragraph by 18 January 2019."[116] In this area, therefore, ESMA takes on a very significant role: it is not just a regulator, but in fact a supervisor.[117]

This confirms that the approach adopted by the European legislator to securitisation has no universal connotations. It follows, therefore, that there is a competition between different national authorities in relation to the parties involved and at the stage of securitisation in which they intervene. For the sake of transparency it is prescribed by Art. 29(8) that "ESMA shall publish and keep up-to-date on its website a list of the competent authorities referred to in this Article."

Given the multiplicity of supervisors involved in the supervisory system, Art. 30, heading "Powers of the competent authorities," stipulates that each Member State "shall ensure that the competent authority designated in accordance with Article 29(1) to (5) has the supervisory, investigatory and sanctioning powers necessary to fulfil its duties under this Regulation." As a result of this, Art. 30(1) encompasses legal provisions consistent with the previous provisions, examined above. In a nutshell, the underpinning philosophy is the emphasis placed on an effective, rather than formal, supervisory power given to what is defined as the Designated Authority.

Specifically, this means the power/duty of the Supervisory Authority to periodically review "the arrangements, processes and mechanisms that originators,

115 It is the responsibility of the different countries to inform the Commission and ESMA about the choice of competent authorities. This is a requirement that does not apply to entities that only sell exposures under an ACBP programme or other transaction or other securitisation scheme and that do not actively create exposures for purposes to securitise them regularly.

116 Paragraph 6 specifies that "paragraph 5 of this Article shall not apply with regard to those entities that are merely selling exposures under an ABCP programme or other securitisation transaction or scheme and are not actively originating exposures for the primary purpose of securitising them on a regular basis. In such a case, the originator or sponsor shall verify that those entities fulfil the relevant obligations set out in Articles 18 to 27."

117 It is recalled that ESMA already acts as a supervisor for credit rating agency activities and operations. Specifically, pursuant to Art. 29(7), it "shall ensure the consistent application and enforcement of the obligations set out in Articles 18 to 27 of this Regulation in accordance with the tasks and powers set out in Regulation (EU) No 1095/2010. ESMA shall monitor the Union securitisation market in accordance with Article 39 of Regulation (EU) No 600/2014 of the European Parliament and the Council (1) and apply, where appropriate, its temporary intervention powers in accordance with Article 40 of Regulation (EU) No 600/2014."

sponsors, SSPEs and original lenders have implemented in order to comply with this Regulation."[118] Furthermore, pursuant to Art. 30(3), "competent authorities shall require that risks arising from securitisation transactions, including reputational risks, are evaluated and addressed through appropriate policies and procedures of originators, sponsors, SSPEs and original lenders." In force of the further paragraph, there is a duty of the competent authority to control

> the specific effects that the participation in the securitisation market has on the stability of the financial institution that operates as original lender, originator, sponsor or investor as part of its prudential supervision in the field of securitisation, taking into account, without prejudice to stricter sectoral regulation: (a) the size of capital buffers; (b) the size of the liquidity buffers; and (c) the liquidity risk for investors due to a maturity mismatch between their funding and investments.[119]

One of the limits of the legislation that was in force before the 2007–2008 financial crisis was to place excessive pressure on operators. The main objective of the transition from micro-prudential to macro-prudential supervision is to prevent systemic risks. This preventive activity is also carried out through the assignment of macro-prudential supervisory functions to the ESRB, always within the limits of its mandate.[120]

118 This further verification to be carried out includes the analysis of a number of key elements and stages of the securitisation transaction that is being implemented. In particular "the review referred to in the first subparagraph shall include: (a) the processes and mechanisms to correctly measure and retain the material net economic interest on an ongoing basis, the gathering and timely disclosure of all information to be made available in accordance with Article 7 and the credit-granting criteria in accordance with Article 9; (b) for STS securitisations which are not securitisations within an ABCP programme, the processes and mechanisms to ensure compliance with Article 20(7) to (12), Article 21(7), and Article 22; and (c) for STS securitisations which are securitisations within an ABCP programme, the processes and mechanisms to ensure, with regard to ABCP transactions, compliance with Article 24 and, with regard to ABCP programmes, compliance with Article 26(7) and (8)" (Art. 30(2)).

119 The last part of the paragraph states that "in cases where the competent authority identifies a material risk to financial stability of a financial institution or the financial system as a whole, irrespective of its obligations under Article 36, it shall take action to mitigate those risks, report its findings to the designated authority competent for macroprudential instruments under Regulation (EU) No 575/2013 and the ESRB."

120 This has been set out in Art. 31(2): "in order to contribute to the prevention or mitigation of systemic risks to financial stability in the Union that arise from developments within the financial system and taking into account macroeconomic developments, so as to avoid periods of widespread financial distress, the ESRB shall continuously monitor developments in the securitisation markets. Where the ESRB considers it necessary, or at least every 3 years, in order to highlight financial stability risks, the ESRB shall, in collaboration with the EBA, publish a report on the financial stability implications of the securitisation market. If material risks are observed, the ESRB shall provide warnings and, where appropriate, issue recommendations for remedial action in response to those risks pursuant to Article 16 of Regulation (EU) No 1092/2010, including on the appropriateness of modifying the risk-retention levels, or the taking of other macroprudential

3.10 Criminal and administrative law matters

The analysis of the sanctioning system, from both a criminal and administrative perspective, has always been a topic that engages scholars in their reasoning and interpretation.

In this respect, the Securitisation Regulation gives food for thought, as it contains an *ad hoc* definition of the sanctioning system, specifically addressed to securitisations, not simply the STS ones. Internationally, it has been observed that the set-up of a wide range of sanctions expands the regulator's ability to respond effectively, promptly and seriously to the violations committed.[121] From a normative point of view, the penalties which can be inflicted by the supervisory authorities are both administrative and criminal.

In this regard, the Securitisation Regulation specifically distinguishes those conducts falling within the realm of criminal offences, also by arranging for the activation of instruments of protection relating to an offence.[122]

More theoretically, it should be added that, as far as the financial matter is concerned, it is difficult to distinguish between sanctions that shall be regarded as criminal and sanctions without *coloration pénale*. In relation to the Securitisation Regulation, this conundrum does not seem to be difficult to solve: the presence, within the same piece of legislation, of a microsystem specifically called criminal – and to which the administrative system is linked – makes the interpretation a comparatively easy process.[123]

measures, to the Commission, the ESAs and to the Member States. The Commission, the ESAs and the Member States shall, in accordance with Article 17 of Regulation (EU) No 1092/2010, communicate to the ESRB, the European Parliament and the Council the actions undertaken in response to the recommendation and shall provide adequate justification for any inaction within three months of the date of transmission of the recommendation to the addressees."

121 I. MacNeil, *Enforcement and Sanctioning*, in N. Moloney, E. Ferran, J. Payne (eds), *The Oxford Handbook of Financial Regulation*, Oxford University Press, Oxford, 2015, 296. About the concept of *misconduct*, see A.A. Rasti, *In-Depth Analysis: Fine for Misconduct in the Banking Sector – What Is the Situation in the EU?* (2017) *European Parliament*, March.

122 As scholars maintain, criminalisation within the banking supervision is not always the correct answer in the hypothesis in which rule-breaking is episodic, repetitive or continuous. I. MacNeil, *Enforcement and Sanctioning* (n. 122), 297.

123 Administrative sanctions are aimed at compensating the damage caused by the offender, while criminal sanctions have, as their objective, punishment of the offender. In the legal system, as well as jargon, of the European Union and, more specifically, in the legislative framework of the European Convention on Human Rights, the difference between administrative and criminal penalties is of fundamental importance in assessing whether the European Court of Human Rights has jurisdiction. The criteria that are adopted to distinguish between these different sanctions are based on *the ratio decidendi* established by few *dicta* of the European Court of Human Rights and the Court of Justice. The reference goes to: *Engel v Netherlands* (1979–80), European Court of Human Rights, 23 November 1976 (1977) 1 EHRR 706; *Zolotukhin v Russia* (14939/03), European Court of Human Rights, 10 February 2009 (2012) 54 EHRR 16.

The *coloration pénale* usually requires that the applicable safeguards are even more stringent: the reference goes to principles[124] that are applied for the benefit of both the natural person and the legal person.[125]

Specifically, as far as STS securitisations are concerned, the framework provides, *de minimis* – therefore without the possibility for Member States to derogate, *in peius*[126] – sanctions pursuant to Articles 32 and 33 of the Rules of Procedure. The first legal provision (Art. 32) stipulates that, notwithstanding Member States being entitled to increase the harshness of this system, Member States:

> shall lay down rules establishing appropriate administrative sanctions, in the case of negligence or intentional infringement, and remedial measures, applicable at least to situations where: (a) an originator, sponsor or original lender has failed to meet the requirements provided for in Article 6;[127] (b) an originator, sponsor or SSPE has failed to meet the requirements provided for in Article 7;[128] (c) an originator, sponsor or original lender has failed to meet the criteria provided for in Article 9;[129] (d) an originator, sponsor or

124 This is the principle of non-culpability, of *ne bis in idem*, the right not to speak, the principle of reviewing the correctness of the application of the sanction, the principle of separation between investigative and decision-making functions. F. Lefevre, S. Loosveld, 'The Influence of European Law on the Powers of Financial Supervisors' (2010) *Journal of International Banking Law and Regulation*, 49–52.

125 The reference is to the rulings of both the Court of Justice of the EU, specifically to *Hoffmann-La Roche & Co. AG v Commission of the European Communities*, 13 February 1979 (Case 85/76), and the European Court of Human Rights (*Dubus v France*, 11 June 2009). Among scholars (A. De Moor-van Vugt, *Administrative Sanctions in EU Law*, 31 March 2012, online), it is maintained that the main characteristic of EU law is to bring about the principle that "the protection of the individuals extends to legal persons (companies) as well. This is not self-evident, since the ECHR was originally drafted for natural persons, and the CJ has tried to follow that Convention when developing specific guarantees in EU law."

126 Therefore, in this case, the Securitisation Regulation works as a "normative floor."

127 Art. 6 deals with "Risk retention." The main underpinning principle spelled out in this legal provision is that the originator, sponsor or original lender of a securitisation "shall retain on an ongoing basis a material net economic interest in the securitisation of not less than 5%. That interest shall be measured at the origination and shall be determined by the notional value for off-balance-sheet items. Where the originator, sponsor or original lender have not agreed between them who will retain the material net economic interest, the originator shall retain the material net economic interest. There shall be no multiple applications of the retention requirements for any given securitisation. The material net economic interest shall not be split amongst different types of retainers and not be subject to any credit-risk mitigation or hedging."

128 Art. 7 is headed "Transparency requirements for originators, sponsors and SPEs."

129 Art. 9 refers to "Criteria for credit granting." In more detail: "Originators, sponsors and original lenders shall apply to exposures to be securitised the same sound and well-defined criteria for credit-granting which they apply to non-securitised exposures. To that end, the same clearly established processes for approving and, where relevant, amending, renewing and refinancing credits shall be applied. Originators, sponsors and original lenders shall have effective systems in place to apply those criteria and processes in order to ensure that credit-granting is based on a thorough assessment of the obligor's creditworthiness taking appropriate account of factors relevant to verifying the prospect of the obligor meeting his obligations under the credit agreement."

> SSPE has failed to meet the requirements provided for in Article 18;[130] (e) a securitisation is designated as STS and an originator, sponsor or SSPE of that securitisation has failed to meet the requirements provided for in Articles 19 to 22 or Articles 23 to 26;[131] (f) an originator or sponsor makes a misleading notification pursuant to Article 27(1);[132] (g) an originator or sponsor has failed to meet the requirements provided for in Article 27(4);[133] or (h) a third party authorised pursuant to Article 28 has failed to notify material changes to the information provided in accordance with Article 28(1), or any other changes that could reasonably be considered to affect the assessment of its competent authority.[134]

Fundamentally, penalties are linked with simple, transparent and standardised securitisations and, particularly, the circumstance that the operator, mainly the sponsor, has used this "label" even in the absence of the required requirements. However, a further set of penalties is provided for, including where the simplicity, transparency and standardisation criteria pertain to ABCP securitisations.

On such grounds, responsibility lies on each Member State to ensure that administrative sanctions and/or further measures are effectively implemented and that "those sanctions and measures shall be effective, proportionate and dissuasive." The degree of the penalties which, in relation to administrative infringements, may be applied is left to the discretion of the Member State. If this is true, it is also right to point out that the objective of the European Union legislature is to avoid too limited a range of sanctions. This means that each Member State must

130 Art. 18 is headed "Use of designation simple, transparent and standardised securitisation." More specifically: "Originators, sponsors and SSPEs may use the designation 'STS' or 'simple, transparent and standardised,' or a designation that refers directly or indirectly to those terms for their securitisation, only where: (a) the securitisation meets all the requirements of Section 1 or Section 2 of this Chapter, and ESMA has been notified pursuant to Article 27(1); and (b) the securitisation is included in the list referred to in Article 27(5). The originator, sponsor and SSPE involved in a securitisation considered STS shall be established in the Union."

131 The heading of Art. 26 is "Programme-level requirements," relating to ABCP securitisation.

132 "STS notification requirements" is the heading of Art. 27 of the Securitisation Regulation. Art. 27(1) stipulates the following:

1. Originators and sponsors shall jointly notify ESMA by means of the template referred to in paragraph 7 of this Article where a securitisation meets the requirements of Articles 19 to 22 or Articles 23 to 26 ('STS notification'). In the case of an ABCP programme, only the sponsor shall be responsible for the notification of that programme and, within that programme, of the ABCP transactions complying with Article 24. The STS notification shall include an explanation by the originator and sponsor of how each of the STS criteria set out in Articles 20 to 22 or Articles 24 to 26 has been complied with. ESMA shall publish the STS notification on its official website pursuant to paragraph 5. Originators and sponsors of a securitisation shall inform their competent authorities of the STS notification and designate amongst themselves one entity to be the first contact point for investors and competent authorities."

133 Pursuant to this specific legal provision (Art. 27(4)), the originator and sponsor "shall immediately notify ESMA and inform their competent authority when a securitisation no longer meets the requirements of either Articles 19 to 22 or Articles 23 to 26."

134 Art. 32(1) of the Securitisation Regulation.

legislate for each minimum level of sanctions, while there is not any potential fetter as far as their harshness is concerned.

The minimum level of sanctions is represented by the reprimand, injunction or professional ban. In this way, Art. 32(2)[135] stipulates that each Member State is entitled to issue a reprimand, that is to say a statement indicating the identity of the natural or legal person and the nature of the infringement; an injunction; or a professional ban. If the violation stems from a missing notification, or from the STS quality of a securitisation, the temporary injunction is the favourite option. It is worth noting that legal arrangements are made for penalties of a purely financial nature to be drawn up by Member States.

Administrative penalties shall be inflicted in practice, subject to the condition that, in cases where the benefit resulting from the infringement of the sanction can be determined, the pecuniary administrative penalties are at least twice such a benefit.

From a general perspective, it can be argued that the sanctioning framework established by the EU legislature is very broad and somehow implies a Member State's entitlement to rule the matter in detail, despite the fact that a level playing field is fixed *ex ante*.

135 "Member States shall confer on competent authorities the power to apply at least the following sanctions and measures in the event of the infringements referred to in paragraph 1: (a) a public statement which indicates the identity of the natural or legal person and the nature of the infringement in accordance with Article 37; (b) an order requiring the natural or legal person to cease the conduct and to desist from a repetition of that conduct; (c) a temporary ban preventing any member of the originator's, sponsor's or SSPE's management body or any other natural person held responsible for the infringement from exercising management functions in such undertakings; (d) in the case of an infringement as referred to in point (e) or (f) of the first subparagraph of paragraph 1 of this Article a temporary ban preventing the originator and sponsor from notifying under Article 27(1) that a securitisation meets the requirements set out in Articles 19 to 22 or Articles 23 to 26; (e) in the case of a natural person, maximum administrative pecuniary sanctions of at least EUR 5 000 000 or, in the Member States whose currency is not the euro, the corresponding value in the national currency on 17 January 2018; (f) in the case of a legal person, maximum administrative pecuniary sanctions of at least EUR 5 000 000, or in the Member States whose currency is not the euro, the corresponding value in the national currency on 17 January 2018 or of up to 10 % of the total annual net turnover of the legal person according to the last available accounts approved by the management body; where the legal person is a parent undertaking or a subsidiary of the parent undertaking which has to prepare consolidated financial accounts in accordance with Directive 2013/34/EU of the European Parliament and of the Council (1), the relevant total annual net turnover shall be the total net annual turnover or the corresponding type of income in accordance with the relevant accounting legislative acts according to the last available consolidated accounts approved by the management body of the ultimate parent undertaking; (g) maximum administrative pecuniary sanctions of at least twice the amount of the benefit derived from the infringement where that benefit can be determined, even if that exceeds the maximum amounts in points (e) and (f); (h) in the case of an infringement as referred to in point (h) of the first subparagraph of paragraph 1 of this Article, a temporary withdrawal of the authorisation referred to in Article 28 for the third party authorised to check the compliance of a securitisation with Articles 19 to 22 or Articles 23 to 26."

Implementing rules shall take into account the specific activities carried out by legal persons. Therefore, it is stipulated that, where

> the provisions referred to in the first paragraph apply to legal persons, Member States shall confer on competent authorities the power to apply the administrative sanctions and remedial measures set out in paragraph 2, subject to the conditions provided for in national law, to members of the management body, and to other individuals who under national law are responsible for the infringement.[136]

The legal principle above has raised understandable doubts and perplexities among scholars. It should be noted that in legal systems[137] which have implemented the concept of the administrative responsibility of entities, administrative sanctions will be applied without this giving rise to any uncertainty. Conversely, the States which have not provided for or do not have clear legislation in this field, from a strictly theoretical point of view, may not be allowed to inflict sanctions of such a nature.

Nevertheless, the *modus operandi* of the European Union legislator, when it allows legal entities – in countries that do not clearly recognise the concept of administrative responsibility of the institution – to not apply these administrative sanctions, may drive a coach and horses through the same concept of the level playing field. Upon closer inspection, though, this outcome is not consistent with the EU regulatory philosophy, because the EU, as a "quasi" legal system, should ontologically avoid a similar situation.

These doubts are confirmed by the legal provisions of Art. 34 ("Criminal sanctions"), which states that Member States "may decide not to lay down rules for administrative sanctions or remedial measures for infringements which are subject to criminal sanctions under their national law." In other words, it is possible for a particular Member State not to implement the administrative system encompassed within the Securitisation Regulation provided that the national criminal system is both considered and assessed as adequate. However, in recalling the general principles, particularly the fact that the quantum of administrative sanctions under the Securitisation Regulation, that is up to €5,000, is very high, it is not possible to rule out that these administrative sanctions can already possess, even for a legal person, a criminal connotation. Therefore, the possibility for a Member State to exclude them seems to highlight a contradiction within the Securitisation Regulation.

Beyond what has been stated above, it is added in the following paragraph that, in cases where Member States

136 Art. 32(3).
137 Italy is one of them.

> have chosen, in accordance with paragraph 1 of this Article, to lay down criminal sanctions for the infringement referred to in Article 32(1), they shall ensure that appropriate measures are in place so that competent authorities have all the necessary powers to liaise with judicial, prosecuting, or criminal justice authorities within their jurisdiction to receive specific information related to criminal investigations or proceedings commenced for the infringements referred to in Article 32(1), and to provide the same information to other competent authorities as well as ESMA, the EBA and EIOPA to fulfil their obligation to cooperate for the purposes of this Regulation. (Art. 34(2))

As regards the actual exercise of the power to impose administrative sanctions, Art. 33 steps up to the plate. It stipulates that competent authorities "shall exercise the powers to impose administrative sanctions and remedial measures referred to in Article 32 in accordance with their national legal frameworks," pursuant to the appropriate legislative mechanism. Therefore, for the authority to be competent according to the Securitisation Regulation it is possible to exercise this power "directly." A further option is the collaboration of the competent authority with other authorities already existing in that Member State. A third option is the responsibility of the competent authority albeit with a delegation conferred on other authorities. Finally, the application can be given by a Member State to the competent judicial authorities. Overall, the four options contemplated leave room to say that harmonisation in this area is more a slightly fictitious statement; it is not tantamount to a real scenario.

Beyond this aspect, which may certainly translate into an issue, it is added (Art. 33(2)) that the competent authorities of each Member State,[138] "when determining the type and level of an administrative sanction or remedial measure imposed under Article 32, shall take into account the extent to which the infringement is intentional or results from negligence and all other relevant circumstances." Therefore, the first criterion to be adopted is the subjective one, where, needless to say, the intention of the infringement is more consistent with a more stringent penalty. The fact that the EU legislature, in this area, picks up from the shelves traditional legal concepts (intention versus negligence), which translate into each legal system of the EU with a variety of shades, may be a reason for not justifying the judicial option (one of the four options) contemplated by the Securitisation Regulation. On the other hand, the judicial assessment as regards the sanctioning power of the authority, which may raise a concern about the speed of the process, may be justified in cases of small Member States. To elaborate, the slower pace of the judiciary, in small countries, is more than compensated by the limited volume of securitisations taking place in those Member States.

Other factors to be taken into account in assessing the sanction are – if appropriate, therefore pursuant to a discretionary power of the authority – the additional following seven.

138 Therefore, the judicial authority could be one of them, according to the legislative options.

The first set (all under lett. a) consist of the "materiality, gravity and the duration of the infringement," where materiality shall be construed as the seriousness of the conduct, gravity as the impact on the public and duration its period of time.

The second set (under lett. b) relate to the degree of liability[139] of the natural or legal person responsible for the infringement. In this respect, this criterion shall be helpful in order to apportion the liability among different people and/or entities, should the conduct arise from more than one individual working for the organisation.

A further criterion (lett. c), focused on the "financial strength of the responsible natural or legal person," potentially allows the authority to increase the quantum of the sanction, for those –mainly legal persons, although the individuals are also, theoretically, subject to the legal provision – who may be the "big fish" in the pond of the illegal conduct under the scrutiny of the authority.

The additional criterion (lett. d) of "the importance of profits gained or losses avoided by the responsible natural or legal person" will be pegged on the conduct of the culprit. The higher the profit gained or the lower the loss avoided as a result of the relevant conduct, the more serious the sanction. The caveat therein, specifically "insofar as they can be determined," means that the authority will not act as a "witch-hunter," therefore these elements (either the gain or the loss) being impossible to assess will mean an exemption from the sanction.

In the Securitisation Regulation, particular attention is paid to a new feature (lett. e): the losses for third parties caused by the infringement. The third parties seem to be, first and foremost, the investors, although the authority will be in a position, given the broad tenor of the legal provision, to find further people (and/or legal entities), so long as there is a causation link between the conduct under the spotlight and the damage suffered by the affected "third parties." In this case too, "the damage shall be determined."

The penultimate feature (lett. f) is represented by "the level of cooperation of the responsible natural or legal person with the competent authority, without prejudice to the need to ensure disgorgement of profits gained or losses avoided by that person," whereas the last feature (lett. g) is connected with "relapse," i.e. the previous infringements which the responsible natural or legal person may have already committed: this is in connection with conduct under the Securitisation Regulation, it should be added.

In the light of the above, the law – having regard to both the administrative and criminal sanctions – seems to be consistent with – and ontologically adjacent to – the principles laid down by the legislature, pursuant to the principles of the Securitisation Regulation. In this regard, it is worth mentioning Art. 35 ("Notification duties"), i.e. the need for cooperation among authorities and the imposition of sanctions. According to the latter, Member States "shall notify the laws, regulations and administrative provisions implementing this chapter, including any relevant criminal legal provisions, to the Commission, ESMA, the EBA

139 The Securitisation Regulation mentions, probably incorrectly, the concept of responsibility.

and EIOPA by 18 January 2019. Member States shall notify the Commission, ESMA, the EBA and EIOPA without undue delay of any subsequent amendments thereto."

In this respect, it is possible to maintain that cooperation can be defined as the new pillar of the regime of new securitisations and, with this assumption, the focus seems to be Art. 36 of the Rules of Procedure.

The first paragraph, in fact, provides that "the competent authorities referred to in Article 29 and ESMA, the EBA and EIOPA shall cooperate closely with each other and exchange information to carry out their duties pursuant to Article 30 to 34."

The second paragraph of Art. 36 (Art. 36(2)) additionally stipulates that the cooperation is informed by regulatory purposes, because the coordination aims to identify and remedy "infringements of this Regulation, develop and promote best practices, facilitate collaboration, foster consistency of interpretation and provide cross-jurisdictional assessments in the event of any disagreements."

Of particular interest is the establishment of a "specific securitisation committee" within the "framework of the Joint Committee of the European Supervisory Authorities." It is assumed that with this, the wish of the Community legislator is that "competent authorities shall closely cooperate, in order to carry out their duties pursuant to Articles 30 to 34" (Art. 36(3)).

The next paragraph (Art. 36(4)) stipulates that:

> where a competent authority finds that one or more of the requirements under Articles 6 to 27 have been infringed or has reason to believe so, it shall inform the competent authority of the entity or entities suspected of such infringement of its findings in a sufficiently detailed manner. The competent authorities concerned shall closely coordinate their supervision in order to ensure consistent decisions.

Art. 36(5) states that:

> where the infringement referred to in paragraph 4 of this Article concerns, in particular, an incorrect or misleading notification pursuant to Article 27(1), the competent authority finding that infringement shall notify without delay the competent authority of the entity designated as the first contact point under Article 27(1) of its findings. The competent authority of the entity designated as the first contact point under Article 27(1) shall in turn inform ESMA, the EBA and EIOPA and shall follow the procedure provided for in paragraph 6 of this Article.

For example, if the Authority detecting the infringement is the one of the country where the vehicle issuing the securitised securities is located, as the originator and the sponsor have made a misleading disclosure regarding the securitisation portfolio, the first authority will notify the other two authorities. These are the authority of the place in which the originator is located and the authority of the place in which the sponsor is located. The competent authority of the person designated as the first contact person, which in our example is that of both the sponsor and the originator, will notify ESMA, EBA and finally EIOPA, all in accordance with Art. 27(1)(6).

The reaction time of the competent authority to the conduct of the person suspected of the infringement is very rapid, based on European Union predictions.[140] The competent authority must take the necessary measures within 15 working days to rectify the breach detected and notify all other competent authorities concerned. From this a "ping-pong" between the different authorities concerned should derive. Should the dispute not be resolved within three months of the date of notification to all the competent authorities concerned, the matter will be referred to ESMA pursuant to Art. 19 and, if applicable, Art. 20 of Regulation (EU) No. 1095/2010.[141]

The role assumed by ESMA, in this case, will be supplementary: in the case of failure to reach an agreement between competent authorities, ESMA will adopt the decision pursuant to Art. 19(3) of EU Regulation No. 1095/2010 within one month. During this procedure, a securitisation that should be on the list published by ESMA shall continue to be considered as STS and shall be kept on that list. There is also a norm which suggests a reform that, prospectively, the securitisation players under discussion can make. In the event that the violation by these

140 Pursuant to Art. 36(6) "Upon receipt of the information referred to in paragraph 4, the competent authority of the entity suspected of the infringement shall take within 15 working days any necessary action to address the infringement identified and notify the other competent authorities involved, in particular those of the originator, sponsor and SSPE and the competent authorities of the holder of a securitisation position, when known. When a competent authority disagrees with another competent authority regarding the procedure or content of its action or inaction, it shall notify all other competent authorities involved about its disagreement without undue delay. If that disagreement is not resolved within three months of the date on which all competent authorities involved are notified, the matter shall be referred to ESMA in accordance with Article 19 and, where applicable, Article 20 of Regulation (EU) No 1095/2010. The conciliation period referred to in Article 19(2) of Regulation (EU) No 1095/2010 shall be one month. Where the competent authorities concerned fail to reach an agreement within the conciliation phase referred to in the first subparagraph, ESMA shall take the decision referred to in Article 19(3) of Regulation (EU) No 1095/2010 within one month. During the procedure set out in this Article, a securitisation appearing on the list maintained by ESMA pursuant to Article 27 of this Regulation shall continue to be considered as STS pursuant to Chapter 4 of this Regulation and shall be kept on such list. Where the competent authorities concerned agree that the infringement is related to non-compliance with Article 18 in good faith, they may decide to grant the originator, sponsor and SSPE a period of up to three months to remedy the identified infringement, starting from the day the originator, sponsor and SSPE were informed of the infringement by the competent authority. During this period, a securitisation appearing on the list maintained by ESMA pursuant to Article 27 shall continue to be considered as STS pursuant to Chapter 4 and shall be kept on such list. Where one or more of the competent authorities involved is of the opinion that the infringement is not appropriately remedied within the period set out in third subparagraph, first subparagraph shall apply."

141 The conciliation period provided for by Art. 19(2) of Regulation (EU) No. 1095/2010 is one month.

subjects is determined by a breach in good faith pursuant to Art. 18, the competent authorities may decide to grant up to three months to the originator, the sponsor and the SSPE to correct the breach detected. This period shall begin on the day on which the competent authority informs those entities. During this period, a securitisation that appears in the list published by ESMA pursuant to Art. 27 continues to be considered an STS and is kept on that list.

Finally, Art. 27 states that "ESMA, in close cooperation with the EBA and EIOPA, shall develop draft regulatory technical standards specifying the information that the originator, sponsor and SSPE are required to provide in order to comply with the obligations referred to in paragraph 1." The last two legal provisions take operational connotations that prescribe, firstly, that "The Commission is empowered to supplement this Regulation by adopting the regulatory technical standards referred to in this paragraph in accordance with Articles 10 to 14 of Regulation (EU) No 1095/2010." Secondly, it is stipulated that ESMA, in close cooperation with EBA and EIOPA, shall develop draft regulatory technical standards to clarify the general obligation of cooperation.

In conclusion, attention should be paid, albeit briefly, to the issue of the publication of administrative penalties. It is one of the most important issues and is regulated by Art. 37 of the Securitisation Regulation. According to paragraph 1

> Member States shall ensure that competent authorities publish on their official websites, without undue delay and as a minimum, any decision imposing an administrative sanction against which there is no appeal and which is imposed for infringement of Article 6, 7, 9 or 27(1) after the addressee of the sanction has been notified of that decision.

This procedure must take place only after notification to the recipient.

The content of this publication should include a set of essential information on "the type and nature of the infringement and the identity of the persons responsible and the sanctions imposed" (Art. 27(2)). Publication, in particular, fulfils a deterrent criterion which should, therefore, deter operators from infringing the above-mentioned norm, as they would otherwise incur a serious reputational damage.

Art. 37(3) contains an exception to the rule that could be defined as general. In this regard it is stated that:

> where the publication of the identity, in the case of legal persons, or of the identity and personal data, in the case of natural persons is considered by the competent authority to be disproportionate following a case-by-case assessment, or where the competent authority considers that the publication jeopardises the stability of financial markets or an ongoing criminal investigation, or where the publication would cause, insofar as it can be determined, disproportionate damages to the person involved, Member States shall ensure that competent authorities either: (a) defer the publication of the decision imposing the administrative sanction until the moment where the reasons for non-publication cease to exist; (b) publish the decision imposing the

> administrative sanction on an anonymous basis, in accordance with national law; or (c) not publish at all the decision to impose the administrative sanction in the event that the options set out in points (a) and (b) are considered to be insufficient to ensure: (i) that the stability of financial markets would not be put in jeopardy; or (ii) the proportionality of the publication of such decisions with regard to measures which are deemed to be of a minor nature.

The function of deterrence, otherwise definable as moral persuasion, is confirmed by Art. 37(5):

> competent authorities shall ensure that any publication referred to in paragraphs 1 to 4 shall remain on their official website for at least five years after its publication. Personal data contained in the publication shall only be kept on the official website of the competent authority for the period which is necessary in accordance with the applicable data protection rules.

The last part of Article 37, namely paragraph 6, provides that ESMA shall be informed by the competent authorities of "all administrative sanctions imposed, including, where appropriate, any appeal in relation thereto and the outcome thereof."

The sanction framework may be considered complete with the indication that ESMA maintains a central database which keeps all the administrative penalties notified. Only the European financial and banking regulatory authorities (ESMA, EBA, EIOPA) and the competent authorities can access it.[142]

3.11 The UK STS legislative framework after Brexit

In simply glancing at the succession of events during which the passing of the Securitisation Regulation has unfolded, it is obvious that a question will soon arise as to the legacy of the legislation in the UK, in the light of the Brexit process unleashed in June 2016 with a controversial referendum and the majority of votes in favour of leaving the Union.

In the wake of those events, the UK formally left the European Union at 11:00 pm on 31 January 2020; until 11:00 pm on 31 December 2020, there was a transitional period (the "Brexit Transition Period"), during which the UK was regarded as a Member State of the Union, albeit departing. Before 31 December 2020, the EU legislation that was directly applicable in the UK up to that date was transposed into "retained EU law." This was possible due to the European

142 Art. 37(7): "ESMA shall maintain a central database of administrative sanctions communicated to it. That database shall be only accessible to ESMA, the EBA, EIOPA and the competent authorities and shall be updated on the basis of the information provided by the competent authorities in accordance with paragraph 6."

Union (Withdrawal) Act 2018, as amended by the European Union (Withdrawal Agreement) Act 2020 (as so amended, the "EUWA").

What happened to the EU Securitisation Regulation[143] is no different from the other pieces of legislation that originated from Brussels. This piece of legislation has been retained by the UK, and, when it formally left the EU (31 December 2020), each law was then amended by hundreds of pieces of secondary legislation, each of which now mirrors, at a domestic level, what used to be part of the body of law coming from the European Union.

The end of the Brexit Transition Period meant that a parallel regime for securitisation in the UK was implemented. This regime is similar to the one existing in the Union, although some adaptations were required.

> These amendments are encompassed within an *ad hoc* piece of UK legislation.

Some changes are merely "cosmetic" and due to the fact that the UK is no longer a Member State of the EU. The very terms "Member States" or "the Union" have now been replaced with, fundamentally, "the United Kingdom." Likewise, the reference to ESMA, EBA and EIOPA (the EU financial supervisory authorities) has been replaced with the FCA, the Financial Conduct Authority, and/or the PRA, the Prudential Regulation Authority, i.e. the UK supervisory authorities.

Other changes, though, are less formal and may be discussed in depth, because they could be instrumental in further and more substantial changes to the UK legislation.

In this chapter emphasis has been placed on the concept of "sponsor:" it is the credit institution or investment firm which, for the purposes of the STS label, is eligible to retain a risk in the vehicle.

The UK definition of a sponsor does not need clarifications when it deals with a credit institution, as it is clearly stipulated that the sponsor can be headquartered even outside the EU. By contrast, in referring to an investment firm, it appears – as inferable from the literal interpretation of the relevant legal provisions – that it is an investment firm pursuant to the EU definition: this would rule out any eligibility of non-EU investment firms. If this asymmetry could be justified from an EU point of view, this may not be the case in the UK and with the underpinning philosophy of the UK Securitisation Regulation: an investment firm shall be in a position to act as a sponsor even if it is located in a third country, therefore outside the EU too.

A further demarcation line to be drawn between the UK and the EU Securitisation Regulation lies in the day-to-day delegation of the portfolio management by the sponsor. While this delegation is possible in the Union in accordance with the applicable EU Directive (the CRRD),[144] the UK definition

143 From a financial point of view, see A. Kara, N. Karimow, A.P. Nguyen, 'Brexit Referendum and the UK Securitization Market' (2021) *Applied Economics Letter* 13, 1092–1097.

144 Therefore, such an entity shall be headquartered in the EU.

of "sponsor" stipulates that active portfolio management can be delegated to an asset manager, broadly considered, with a very *laisser-faire* approach. Therefore, so long as the asset manager is located in a jurisdiction and it is regarded as such, the delegation will be possible. For the purposes of STS securitisations, the EU Securitisation Regulation acknowledges the role of an originator, sponsor and securitisation special purpose entity so long as they are established in the EU. The UK Securitisation Regulation is not characterised by the same level of rigour: for a non-ABCP securitisation, the SSPE does not need to be in the UK for the same to be regarded as STS. For the UK STS securitisation, particularly for ABCP programmes, only the sponsor needs to be in the UK.[145]

A further area in which differences between the Securitisation Regulations in the UK and in the EU are obvious is due diligence. As mentioned in this chapter, institutional investors must verify compliance with certain requirements before investing in a securitisation position pursuant to the EU Securitisation Regulation. There are separate yet similar requirements with respect to risk retention and credit granting, depending on whether the originator or another relevant entity is established in the EU or a third country. However, the requirements in relation to verifying compliance with transparency have been amended in the UK Securitisation Regulation.

The focus should now be shifted towards Art. 5(1)(e), in both the EU and the UK version. As to the former, Art. 5(1)(e) of the EU Securitisation Regulation stipulates that institutional investors must verify that "the originator, sponsor or SSPE has, where applicable, made available the information required by Article 7 in accordance with the frequency and modalities provided for in that Article."[146] Still in the EU legal framework, in the case of non-EU entities, they should not be directly subject to Article 7. Given the uncertainty of the matter, a possible interpretation of Art. 5(1)(e) is that, given the expression "where applicable," EU investors should not be required to comply with Article 5(1)(e) in the case of

145 In addition, the UK Securitisation Regulation contains grandfathering provisions in relation to STS with the effect that any securitisations which have met the EU STS requirements, which have been notified to ESMA prior to the end of the Brexit Transition Period or within two years thereafter and which have been included in ESMA's list of STS securitisations, can continue to be considered to be STS for UK purposes. However, there is currently no reciprocal provision under the EU regime (although this may be considered in the future) and so transactions where the originator, sponsor and/or SSPE is not in the EU will no longer be capable of being EU STS.

146 Article 7 sets out detailed disclosure requirements, requiring originators, sponsors and SSPEs to make available certain information to holders of a securitisation position, competent authorities and, upon request, potential investors. This includes any prospectus, all transaction documents which are essential in order to understand the transaction, a transaction summary in the event that there is no prospectus, any STS notification, reports on the underlying exposures and investor reports and notification of any inside information and significant events. Regulatory technical standards setting out the information to be provided (the "EU Disclosure RTS"), and implementing technical standards setting out the format and the required forms of reporting templates for making available such information (the "EU Disclosure ITS"), came into force in September 2020. For further information please see previous Legal Update "Disclosure Technical Standards and Templates Published in Relation to the EU Securitisation Regulation."

securitisations where the originator, sponsor and SSPE are not established in the EU.[147] An opposite interpretation is possible as well: an EU investor would be required to obtain such disclosure because of the underpinning philosophy of the Securitisation Regulation. Because in several instances non-EU originators were not inclined to complete detailed reporting templates, investors shall now be better protected.[148]

In June 2020 a report was published by the High Level Forum on Capital Markets Union, which was established by the European Commission ("the Commission"), setting out a number of recommendations with a view to scaling up the EU securitisation market and recognising the key role that securitisation has in funding the real economy. The report recommended that it should be clarified that Article 5(1)(e) does not apply with respect to securitisations where the originator, sponsor or SSPE are not established in the EU. Instead, an EU investor would need to receive sufficient information to meet the due diligence requirements proportionate to the risk profile of the securitisation exposure. This wording has generally been seen as helpful, but if implemented in this form there is still some uncertainty as to exactly what this means in practice. In addition, it does not resolve the issue for transactions where asset-level data is not required or provided for a particular type of transaction or asset class in a third country. At this stage the wording is simply a recommendation and market participants are awaiting further clarifications.

In the case of the UK Securitisation Regulation, the wording of Article 5(1)(e) has been amended so that it applies in the case of originators, sponsors and SSPEs which are established in the UK. In addition, a new Article 5(1)(f) has been added, which states that the investor must verify that an originator, sponsor or SSPE which is established in a third country

> has, where applicable, (i) made available information which is substantially the same as that which it would have made available in accordance with point (e) if it had been established in the UK; and (ii) has done so with such frequency and modalities as are substantially the same as those with which it

147 Art. 7 does not apply to such non-EU entities.

148 Some scholars have qualified the UK as a "third country" from a capital market perspective. Hence, it is affirmed that "Brexit will drive wider change to the third country regime." N. Moloney, 'Reflections on the EU Third Country Regime for Capital Markets in the Shadow of Brexit' (2020) *European Company and Financial Law Review* 1, 36. However, this is merely a hypothesis, still missing empirical evidence, given the fact that the evolution of capital markets in the "love–hate relationship" between the Union and the UK is not clear yet. As far as the new "mosaic" of the European capital market is concerned, see E. Howell, 'Post-"Brexit" Financial Governance: Which Dispute Settlement Framework Should Be Utilised' (2020) *Modern Law Review* 23, 128; H. Berger, N. Badenhoop, 'Financial Services and Brexit: Navigating Towards Future Market Access' (2018) *European Business Organisation Law Review* 19, 679; E. Ferran, 'The UK as a Third Country in EU Financial Services Regulation' (2017) *Journal of Financial Regulation* 3, 40.

> would have made information available in accordance with point (e) if it had been so established.[149]

As a result of the uncertainty as to how both Art. 5(1)(e) of the EU Securitisation Regulation and Art. 5(1)(f)[150] of the UK Securitisation Regulation should be interpreted, it is not yet clear to what extent the two will be aligned and whether the standard will be different for EU and UK investors. The view that the UK legal framework seems to be more observant and compliant with the need for protecting its own domestic investors is certainly corroborated.

Another area of analysis and discussion is concerned with technical standards, risk retention, disclosure and the power of the FCA.

As far as the first issue is concerned, in the case of EU Regulation technical standards that have not been put in place yet with respect to the EU Securitisation Regulation (and also with respect to certain related aspects of the Capital Requirements Regulation), the onshoring process will no longer apply, and new UK technical standards will need to be developed. In Art. 18 ("The Securitisation (Amendment) (EU Exit) Regulations 2019") on the use of the label "simple, transparent and standardised securitisation," the existing text of the first paragraph will now become paragraph 1; ESMA will be substituted with the FCA.

Regarding Art. 18(2), originators and sponsors involved in a securitisation that is not an ABCP programme or an ABCP transaction and is considered STS "must be established in the United Kingdom. The sponsor involved in an ABCP programme considered STS must be established in the United Kingdom. The sponsor involved in an ABCP programme which is not considered STS must be established in the United Kingdom if an ABCP transaction within that programme is considered STS."

For the new legislative framework, "relevant securitisation" means

> a securitisation (a) which meets all the requirements of Section 1 or Section 2 of this chapter, and of which ESMA was notified pursuant to Article 27(1) before exit day, or is notified pursuant to Article 27(1) after exit day but

149 It is unclear what the words "substantially the same" are intended to mean. It is possible that the UK regulators will be minded to interpret this to mean that UK investors do not have to obtain the specified reporting templates when investing in third country securitisations. However, it is likely that UK investors will interpret this wording to the effect that they will want to receive detailed reporting. The extent to which information will need to be in line with the UK requirements, and whether this needs to be asset-level data, remains to be seen, and as for EU investors, this could be particularly challenging for UK investors where asset-level reporting is not required or is not provided in that third country.

150 The amendments are not extensive and this will be welcomed by UK reporting entities. In the case of UK investors in transactions with originators, sponsors and/or SSPEs (all based in the EU), the fact that the UK requirements will be similar also means that it seems likely that UK investors will be able to accept reporting in the form of the required EU templates as being "substantially the same" for the purposes of Article 5(1)(f) of the UK Securitisation Regulation.

> before the expiry of a period of two years beginning with exit day; and (b) which is included in the list referred to in Article 27(5).[151]

Regarding the "original" Art. 19 of EU Securitisation Regulation, only paragraph 2 shall be omitted in the EU Exit Regulation.

About the element of risk retention, both Securitisation Regulations impose a direct obligation on the originator, sponsor or original lender of a securitisation to retain a material net economic interest in the securitisation of not less than 5%. This is understood to apply directly to originators, sponsors and original lenders established in the EU, or the UK, as applicable. However, as a result of the investor due diligence requirements under Article 5 of each of the Securitisation Regulations, EU and UK investors will not be able to invest in securitisations with originators, sponsors and original lenders which are not established in the EU, or the UK, as applicable, unless the risk retention requirements have been complied with. Provided that the transaction is risk retention compliant for the purposes of the EU regime, it is now likely that it proves to be risk retention compliant for the purposes of the UK regime as well, and vice versa. However, entities that are not directly subject to the risk retention requirements may want to consider limiting the extent of their compliance to the requirements as at the closing date of the transaction, given the possibility of future changes to the two regimes.

Under the Securitisation Regulations, technical standards are required to be put in place in order to set out the more detailed aspects of the risk retention requirements. Because the new risk retention regulatory technical standards did not come into force before the end of the Brexit Transition Period, new UK technical standards will have to be developed. While the UK regulators had previously been considering and consulting with market participants on the EBA Draft RTS, it is possible that there will be some differences between the final EU and UK regulatory technical standards in relation to risk retention.

Based on this, Art. 6 of the Securitisation Regulation has changed in the following way. Paragraph 4 now reads as follows:

> Where – (a) a mixed financial holding company, (b) a UK parent institution, (c) a financial holding company established in the United Kingdom, or (d) a subsidiary of such a company or institution, as an originator or sponsor, securitises exposures from one or more credit institutions, investment firms or other financial institutions which are included in the scope of supervision on a consolidated basis, the requirements set out in paragraph 1 may be satisfied

151 Art. 18(3). The second part of this paragraph states that "In this paragraph a reference to Section 1 or Section 2 of this Chapter or to Article 27 is a reference to that Section or Article as it had or has effect in relation to an EEA State at any time on and after the date of the notification and before the end of the period referred to in the second subparagraph."

> on the basis of the consolidated situation of the mixed financial holding company, UK parent institution or financial holding company concerned.[152]

A further change is the replacement of the words "and to the Union" in the following way: "and, if the originator or sponsor is a subsidiary, to the mixed financial holding company, UK parent institution or financial holding company which is the parent undertaking of the subsidiary."[153]

In order to facilitate the transition from the EU Securitisation Regulation regime to that under the UK Securitisation Regulation, UK lawmakers have put in place various transitional norms under temporary transitional powers granted to them by the UK Treasury for a limited period until 31 March 2022 (the so-called "TTP Period"). This means that in many cases, UK regulated entities can continue to comply with the previous requirements under the EU Securitisation Regulation instead of the UK Securitisation Regulation, while they prepare to comply with the new UK regime. In particular, UK originators, sponsors and SSPEs may use the EU disclosure templates rather than the UK disclosure templates during the TTP Period.

For the future development of the securitisation market between the EU and the UK, the amendments to the EU Securitisation Regulation and the CRR are close to being finalised in order to introduce an STS regime for on-balance-sheet synthetic securitisations and to make certain adjustments with respect to non-performing exposures. The inclusion of an STS framework for on-balance-sheet synthetic securitisation also had to be considered under the EU Securitisation Regulation, and has been the subject of reports by the EBA and the Commission. This development has been broadly welcomed by the securitisation industry. However, is not yet clear whether any similar amendments will be considered in the context of the UK Securitisation Regulation.

Under the EU Securitisation Regulation, the Joint Committee of the European Supervisory Authorities is required to prepare a report on certain matters with respect to the EU Securitisation Regulation. This was due by 1 January 2021,[154] although the final report was eventually issued on 17 May 2021.[155] The aim of the report, as clarified from the outset,[156] was to identify

> the status of the application of the Securitisation Regulation (Regulation (EU) 2017/24021) (SECR) as well as some initial inconsistencies and challenges that occurred in the first years of implementation of the SECR and which may affect the overall efficiency and consistency of the new securitisation regime.

152 Art. 8(3), lett. a), EU Exit Regulation 2019.

153 Art. 8(3), lett. b), EU Exit Regulation 2019. It is highlighted that any reference to "Member State" shall be regarded as omitted (Art. 8(4), EU Exit Regulation 2019).

154 Art. 44 of the EU Securitisation Regulation.

155 Joint Committee Report on the Implementation and Functioning of the Securitisation Regulation (Article 44), Final report, JC 2021 31, retrieved online.

156 Paragraph 1 of the Executive Summary of the Report.

> Based on evidence collected from market participants and competent authorities, the report also identifies possible solutions, recommendations and key messages to address them. However, it should be noted that, due to the late adoption of the level 2 implementing measures, the report is based on a limited experience with regards to the status of application of the SECR.

Worthy of analysis are the recommendations of the Joint Committee, mostly based on the role of Third Parties Verifiers (henceforth also "TPV"), whose role is to verify STS compliance. As emphasised in paragraph 145 of the Report:

> In order to help facilitate the entrance of new TPVs in the market and to provide more guidance to securitising parties and institutional investors in performing their own assessments of compliance with the STS criteria, it is recommended that further guidance and Q&As on compliance with the STS criteria could be published by competent authorities.

Additionally, the same Paragraph 145 of the Report clarifies that

> more transparency from TPVs on how they apply the criteria to perform the STS assessment could be of benefit to securitising parties in carrying out their own assessment and for competent authorities in their supervision of compliance with the STS requirements. This will result in more consistency and transparency across the securitisation market.

Based on the report, the burden is apparently shifted onto the TPV on whether the STS criteria, throughout the lifetime of a securitisation, are met. Specifically, the competent authorities shall "withdraw the authorisation of a TPV in accordance with Article 28(1) of the Securitisation Regulation if it considers that the TPV is no longer compliant with the authorisation conditions."[157]

Additionally, the Commission was required by 1 January 2022 to prepare a report considering the findings of the "Joint Committee" and assessing certain aspects of the EU Securitisation Regulation and to present the report to the

157 Paragraph 145 of the Report. Such a Report still stresses that, in order to ensure sufficient investor protection, "it is recommended that clarifications should be provided by the European Commission in the level 1 text that whilst the TPV may verify the compliance of a securitisation with the STS criteria at issuance, the securitising parties are under an ongoing obligation to check compliance with the STS requirements throughout the lifetime of the securitisation. This will further highlight that securitising parties should not solely rely on a TPVs assessment at issuance and continue to fulfil its obligations throughout the lifetime of a securitisation." A further recommendation (heading "Supervision of TPV authorisation conditions") spells out the principle that the need for competent authorities "to develop a consistent approach to ongoing supervision of authorisation conditions for TPVs should be further analysed. Such analysis could be carried out by the JCSC. If deemed necessary, guidance could be provided by the ESAs JC to work on a common approach to supervising ongoing monitoring of authorisation conditions, focussing on a common understanding of robust methodologies for assessing STS criteria" (*ibidem*).

European Parliament and the Council of the European Union. Furthermore, a legislative proposal was to accompany this report. Based on our investigations, these documents are still missing.

Under the UK Securitisation Regulation (henceforth the "UK SR"), the UK Treasury must review the functioning of the UK Securitisation Regulation and submit a report to Parliament by 1 January 2022. It is possible that the two regimes will diverge further following those reports and any resulting legislative changes.[158]

It should be observed that the UK SR mentions the "publication and notification of decisions."[159] In this respect, the FCA does provide the list of securitisations – the ones approved – on its website, in accordance with Art. 12 of the UK SR. Eventually

> withdrawal of registration under Article 13a takes effect: (a) immediately upon the adoption of the decision if the notice states that is the case; (b) on such date as may be specified in that notice; or (c) if no date is specified in the notice, when the matter to which the notice relates is no longer open to review.[160]

Another duty of the FCA is to give a repository written notice about securitisation.[161] The written notice, in accordance with paragraph 6, must:

> (a) give details of the decision made by the FCA; (b) state the FCA's reasons for the decision; (c) state when the decision takes effect; (d) inform the securitisation repository that it may either: (i) request a review of the decision by the FCA, and make written representations for the purpose of the review, within such period as may be specified in the notice; or (ii) refer the matter to the Upper Tribunal ('the Tribunal') within such period as may be specified in the notice; and (e) indicate the procedure on a reference to the Tribunal.[162]

The FCA must review its own original decision and provide written notice of its new decision, if the application comes to a securitisation repository.[163] This legal provision is concerned with a particular kind of FCA decision, that is to say:

> a decision –

158 Any amendments to the EU Securitisation Regulation or any related EU technical standards, or any new EU technical standards, will not form part of UK law, and as time goes by, the two regimes may start to look more different.

159 Art. 15, EU Exit Regulation 2019. This legal provision substitutes the text from Art. 13 to Art. 15 of the EU Securitisation Regulation.

160 Art. 15(4), EU Exit Regulation 2019. The decision of the FCA to withdraw registration "may be expressed to take effect immediately (or on a specified date) only if the FCA, having regard to the ground on which it is exercising its power reasonably, considers that it is necessary for the withdrawal or direction to take effect immediately (or on that date)" (paragraph 5).

161 Last part of paragraph 6.

162 Art. 15(7).

163 Art. 15(8)(10).

(a) to maintain a decision to refuse an application for registration, made under Article 12;
(b) to refuse to revoke a decision made under paragraph 1 or 2 of Article 13a to withdraw the registration of the securitisation repository on the FCA's own initiative; or
(c) to maintain a decision to refuse an application from a securitisation repository under paragraph 3 of Article 13a to withdraw the registration of the securitisation repository.[164]

This written notice must:

(a) give details of the new decision made by the FCA;
(b) state the FCA's reasons for the new decision;
(c) state whether the decision takes effect immediately or on such date as may be specified in the notice;
(d) inform the securitisation repository that it may, within such period as may be specified in the notice, refer the new decision to the Tribunal; and
(e) indicate the procedure on a reference to the Tribunal.[165]

The FCA could, by own initiative, withdraw the registration of a securitisation repository in the case that the latter:

(a) expressly renounces the registration or has provided no services for the preceding 6 months;
(b) obtained the registration by making false statements or by any other irregular means; or
(c) no longer meets the conditions for registration.[166]

The FCA's decision may be examined by the Tribunal if:

(a) refuses to register the securitisation repository under Article 12;
(b) exercises its power under paragraph 1 or 2 of Article 13a to withdraw the registration of a securitisation repository; or
(c) refuses the securitisation repository's application under paragraph 3 of Article 13a to withdraw its registration.[167]

While the UK Securitisation Regulation regime undoubtedly looks very similar to the one under the EU Securitisation Regulation – and so it will be very familiar

164 Art. 15(11).
165 Art. 15(12). By virtue of this amendment, this is the new Art. 13.
166 This is the new Art. 13(lett. A), "Withdrawal of registration." Paragraph stipulates that the "FCA may also, on its own initiative, withdraw the registration of a securitisation repository where it is desirable to do so to advance one or more of its operational objectives set out in section 1B(3) of the 2000 Act."
167 "Where there is a review under paragraph 8 of Article 13, paragraph 1 applies only in relation to the FCA's decision in response to that review."

to parties who have been dealing with those requirements since 1 January 2019 – there are some differences which need to be kept in mind. In addition, it will be important to monitor developments closely in order to consider the impact for market participants of any future changes with respect to the Securitisation Regulations and the related legislation.

There are a number of points to consider in terms of the practical impact of the separate EU and UK securitisation regimes. Firstly, in each transaction it is important to consider to what extent there will need to be compliance with each regime by entities which are directly subject to it.[168]

Transaction parties will also need to consider whether the transactions will be targeted at or be funded (initially or at a later time) by EU and/or UK investors. The related wording in prospectuses and other offering documents, transaction documents and documents such as risk retention memos will need to be drafted accordingly, and we are currently seeing a range of different approaches in the market, depending on the degree of compliance required under the directly applicable requirements of the Securitisation Regulations, or contractually agreed to by non-EU or non-UK entities.

A stress point is the interpretation of Article 5(1)(e) under the EU Securitisation Regulation, and the different wording with respect to verifying the disclosure of the relevant information as set out in Article 5(1)(f) of the UK Securitisation Regulation (which also still needs to be clarified). The information required by EU and UK investors may be different, depending on the information provided in the context of the relevant transaction.

More generally, the changes can be summarised as follows: a) ESMA became the FCA; b) the reference to "Member State" changes to "the UK."

A further important aspect relates to the new role of the UK in securitisation markets.[169] After the 2007–2008 economic and financial crisis, during which securitisations and their governance were held liable for the collapse of the financial markets, alongside derivatives, the EU and UK walked abreast. Since then, the actions of these two "Unions" have been aligned and a series of coordinated actions have been carried out at both the domestic and international level.[170]

At the time of the crisis, in fact, more stringent rules of securitisation were implemented by the British authorities. At a further stage, more specifically in

168 Where, for example, one of the parties is located in the EU and another party is located in the UK, there will need to be compliance with the relevant aspects of the two regimes, and this will need to be considered carefully.

169 "The UK has been a leading member of the market-making coalition. Over the financial crisis, the UK advocated for greater national discretion under the pivotal 2013 Capital Requirements Directive IV/Capital Requirements Regulation (CRD IV/CRR) – which provides the spine of the EU's banking rulebook and implements the Basel III Accord – particularly with respect to the domestic application of capital and other supervisory tools to local risks to financial stability." N. Moloney, 'Brexit and EU Financial Governance: Business as Usual or Institutional Change?' (2017) *European Law Review* 1, 112–118.

170 More specifically, the attention is to the alliance between the Bank of England and the ECB with the support of the EBA and European Commission.

2013, the Governor of the Bank of England kickstarted his plan to re-launch securitisations.[171] In other words, as far as the EU economy is concerned, the UK can be considered both an ally and an opponent.

For a forecast about the UK's position, the UK is not constrained by the need for conforming to the agreed EU position, "and does not need to reconcile its preferences with those of the EU [...] when negotiating in international financial *fora*."[172] Ultimately, the UK and the US are likely to better cooperate with each other, so long as their preferences are aligned. Nevertheless, the EU and the UK might have similar preferences on certain issues too. According to this line of reasoning, not only is a UK–EU alliance possible, but it is also likely to occur, although opposition from the US, particularly of a political nature, may completely alter the scenario.

171 "A well-functioning securitisation market means more efficient balance sheets for the financial sector as a whole which frees up capacity, which then can have a knock-on effect." Reuters, "Highlights – Bank of England Governor Carney speaks," 2016, online.

172 L. Quaglia, 'It Takes Two to Tango: The European Union and the International Governance of Securitisation in Finance' (2021) *Journal of Common Market Studies* 6, 1377.

4 The securitisation process from due diligence to ESG factors

4.1 The financial regulation on securitisations

In other parts of this work a theory has been corroborated that the concept of shadow banking, albeit "fashionable" in the law and economics literature, falls short of a definition shared in a unanimous way.[1] Thus, scholars, in somehow battening down the hatches, resort to a simple definition which, without totally clarifying the matter, at least avoids any blatant mistakes. According to this line of reasoning, then, the term "shadow banking" encompasses financial activities which intermediaries are authorised to carry out, because they are not prohibited, even though the applicable rules are vague or even non-existent. It is, therefore, possible to conclude that "shadow banking" refers to activities carried out in areas where regulation, albeit in place, is unconventional.

1 Some scholars maintain the different view that the expression "shadow banking" refers to the activity of intermediation that is carried out by conduit that cannot rely on the network of public protection. By contrast, it is contended, from a different quarter, that traditional intermediaries, namely banks, are not necessarily able to protect depositors in the event of a crisis affecting the entire banking system, particularly in circumstances like the EU, where the third pillar of the European Banking Union has not been implemented yet.

As far as shadow banking is concerned, reference can be made to E.F. Gerding, 'Code, Crash, and Open Source: The Outsourcing of Financial. Regulation to Risk Models and the Global Financial Crisis' (2009) *Washington Law Review* 84, 127; E.F. Gerding, 'The Next Epidemic: Bubbles and the Growth and Decay of Securities Regulation' (2006) *Connecticut Law Review* 38, 393; E.F. Gerding, *Law, Bubbles, and Financial Regulation*, Routledge, London and New York, 2013; E.F. Gerding, 'The Subprime Crisis and the Link between Consumer Financial Protection and Systemic Risk' (2009) *FIU Law Review* 5, 93 (2009); E.F. Gerding, 'The Dialectics of Bank Capital: Regulation and Regulatory Capital. Arbitrage' (2016) *Washburn Law Journal* 55, 357; E.F. Gerding, 'Contract as Pattern Language' (2013) *Washington Law Review* 88, 1323; E.F. Gerding, 'Remutualization' (2020) *Cornell Law Review* 105, 797; E.F. Gerding, 'Bank Regulation and Securitization: How the Law Improved. Transmission Lines between Real Estate and Banking Crises' (2015) *Georgia Law Review* 50, 89; D. Reiss, 'Consumer Protection out of the Shadows of Shadow Banking: The Role of the Consumer Financial Protection Bureau' (2012) *Brooklyn Journal of Corporate Finance & Commercial Law* 7, 131; E.F. Gerding, 'Credit Derivatives, Leverage, and Financial Regulation's Missing Macroeconomic Dimension' (2011) *Berkeley Business Law Journal* 8, 29.

DOI: 10.4324/9780429293436-4

Securitisations, until 2008, were not subject to regulation; the focus turned to them after the 2007–2008 financial crisis, during a time in which, during summary trials chaired by judges-turned-academics, these transactions were held liable for causing the "mayhem and carnage" of the insolvency of major credit institutions across the globe. At present, also as a result of a completely different approach to the matter, they benefit from very stringent regulation which, at an EU level, and to a certain extent in the UK too, is fully harmonised.

It can be stated, to further elaborate, that securitisations will continue to be the subject matter of an increasingly rigorous *ad hoc* and unified regulation. As far as the EU is concerned, the aim of the legislative intervention from Brussels (in 2017 and, following the COVID-19 pandemic crisis, in 2021) is to formalise a process, developed over the last decade, aimed at making the market of securitised financial instruments simple, transparent and standardised, and, in the latest developments of the legislation, sustainable too, because green assets to be securitised are viewed in a preferential way.[2]

The requirements that are prescribed for STS securitisation are addressed to two particular categories of securitisations: short term and long term.

Specifically, the regulatory criteria required and prescribed for these two categories shall be implemented on the basis of the EBA recommendation and in the light of the parameters set forth by the Basel Committee on Banking Supervision and the IOSCO.

Bearing in mind the definition of shadow banking, it is not unproblematic to infer that regulated financial transactions can be traced back to this category. Within a harmonised regulatory environment in which supervised entities – i.e. those in charge of these transactions – are subject to heavy burdens limiting the entitlement to purchase structured products, it would be even speculative to merely conceive the "shadow" nature of these financial transactions.[3] The same inference can be made for SPVs, vehicles which, now disguised as "SPPEs," in the Securitisation Regulation, are likewise in the mirror of the EU supervisors.

Due diligence – one of the pillars of the EU piece of legislation on STS securitisations – is the legal notion that, in merger and acquisition (M&A) transactions, is perceived and defined as a legal process directed to protecting the buyer against both legal and accounting risks associated with an acquisition transaction.[4] In this respect, the Securitisation Regulation turns due diligence

2 This has been dissected in other parts of this work.

3 Chapter 2 of this work mentions the potential excessive regulation or overregulation or hyperregulation of the banking financial market and the costs entailed in this phenomenon.

4 The legal literature on the M&A transactions is very limited, in the light of the major economic implications of the phenomenon. See R. Tromans, 'Formula One M&A' (2007) *European Lawyer* 69, 53–56; K.S. Reddy, 'Regulatory Framework of Mergers and Acquisitions: A Review of Indian Statutory Compliances and Policy Recommendations' (2016) *International Journal of Law and Management* 58(2), 197–215; A. Bingel, 'Ad Hoc Disclosure of German Listed Target Companies in M&A Transactions' (2013) *Banking Law and Regulation* 28(5), 181–187; K. Tully, 'The Mechanics of M&A in Europe' (2001) *Corporate Finance* 204 (Supp: Focusing Strengths through M&A),

into an essential condition that must be met in order to purchase any securitised instrument.[5]

17–20; R. Gillespie, S. Gore, 'The Evolution of European Mergers and Acquisitions Activity' (1997) *International Company and Commercial Law Review* 8(12), 417–422; A. Echarri, C. Vazquez, 'PE vs M&A' (2005) *European Lawyer* 49, 68–69; R. Parnham, 'M&A Related Litigation on the Increase' (2002) *European Lawyer* 22, 8; S.M. Banker, 'The Regulatory Response to the Internationalisation of Mergers and Acquisitions' (1991) *International Company and Commercial Law Review* 2(5), 155–159.

5 The reference is to Art. 5 of the Securitisation Regulation, headed "Due-diligence requirements for institutional investors."

"1. Prior to holding a securitisation position, an institutional investor, other than the originator, sponsor or original lender, shall verify that: (a) where the originator or original lender established in the Union is not a credit institution or an investment firm as defined in points (1) and (2) of Article 4(1) of Regulation (EU) No 575/2013, the originator or original lender grants all the credits giving rise to the underlying exposures on the basis of sound and well-defined criteria and clearly established processes for approving, amending, renewing and financing those credits and has effective systems in place to apply those criteria and processes in accordance with Article 9(1) of this Regulation; (b) where the originator or original lender is established in a third country, the originator or original lender grants all the credits giving rise to the underlying exposures on the basis of sound and well-defined criteria and clearly established processes for approving, amending, renewing and financing those credits and has effective systems in place to apply those criteria and processes to ensure that credit-granting is based on a thorough assessment of the obligor's creditworthiness; (c) if established in the Union, the originator, sponsor or original lender retains on an ongoing basis a material net economic interest in accordance with Article 6 and the risk retention is disclosed to the institutional investor in accordance with Article 7; (d) if established in a third country, the originator, sponsor or original lender retains on an ongoing basis a material net economic interest which, in any event, shall not be less than 5 %, determined in accordance with Article 6, and discloses the risk retention to institutional investors; (e) the originator, sponsor or SSPE has, where applicable, made available the information required by Article 7 in accordance with the frequency and modalities provided for in that Article;

2. By derogation from paragraph 1, as regards fully supported ABCP transactions, the requirement specified in point (a) of paragraph 1 shall apply to the sponsor. In such cases, the sponsor shall verify that the originator or original lender which is not a credit institution or an investment firm grants all the credits giving rise to the underlying exposures on the basis of sound and well-defined criteria and clearly established processes for approving, amending, renewing and financing those credits and has effective systems in place to apply those criteria and processes in accordance with Article 9(1).

3. Prior to holding a securitisation position, an institutional investor, other than the originator, sponsor or original lender, shall carry out a due-diligence assessment which enables it to assess the risks involved. That assessment shall consider at least all of the following: (a) the risk characteristics of the individual securitisation position and of the underlying exposures; (b) all the structural features of the securitisation that can materially impact the performance of the securitisation position, including the contractual priorities of payment and priority of payment-related triggers, credit enhancements, liquidity enhancements, market value triggers, and transaction-specific definitions of default (c) with regard to a securitisation notified as STS in accordance with Article 27, the compliance of that securitisation with the requirements provided for in Articles 19 to 22 or in Articles 23 to 26, and Article 27. Institutional investors may rely to an appropriate extent on the STS notification pursuant to Article 27(1) and on the information disclosed by the originator, sponsor and SSPE on the compliance with the STS requirements, without solely or mechanistically relying on that notification or information. Notwithstanding points (a) and (b) of the first subparagraph, in the case of a fully supported ABCP programme, institutional investors in the commercial paper

A further pillar laid down by the Securitisation Regulation is the retention requirement. Following the financial crisis of 2007–2008, requirements were introduced into the legislation as a remedy to address some anomalies in the securitisation system. Retention requirements relate to an obligation imposed on the originator/arranger, alternatively between each other, to keep a net economic interest in the securitisation they are involved with. This "floor" must be at least 5%, to avoid any possible risk of divergence of interest with investors. This is an obligation that was identified, for the first time, by the G20 and immediately incorporated into legislation to protect the principle of transparency in financial

---

issued by that ABCP programme shall consider the features of the ABCP programme and the full liquidity support.

4. An institutional investor, other than the originator, sponsor or original lender, holding a securitisation position, shall at least: (a) establish appropriate written procedures that are proportionate to the risk profile of the securitisation position and, where relevant, to the institutional investor's trading and non-trading book, in order to monitor, on an ongoing basis, compliance with paragraphs 1 and 3 and the performance of the securitisation position and of the underlying exposures. Where relevant with respect to the securitisation and the underlying exposures, those written procedures shall include monitoring of the exposure type, the percentage of loans more than 30, 60 and 90 days past due, default rates, prepayment rates, loans in foreclosure, recovery rates, repurchases, loan modifications, payment holidays, collateral type and occupancy, and frequency distribution of credit scores or other measures of credit worthiness across underlying exposures, industry and geographical diversification, frequency distribution of loan to value ratios with band widths that facilitate adequate sensitivity analysis. Where the underlying exposures are themselves securitisation positions, as permitted under Article 8, institutional investors shall also monitor the exposures underlying those positions; (b) in the case of a securitisation other than a fully supported ABCP programme, regularly perform stress tests on the cash flows and collateral values supporting the underlying exposures or, in the absence of sufficient data on cash flows and collateral values, stress tests on loss assumptions, having regard to the nature, scale and complexity of the risk of the securitisation position; (c) in the case of fully supported ABCP programme, regularly perform stress tests on the solvency and liquidity of the sponsor; (d) ensure internal reporting to its management body so that the management body is aware of the material risks arising from the securitisation position and so that those risks are adequately managed; (e) be able to demonstrate to its competent authorities, upon request, that it has a comprehensive and thorough understanding of the securitisation position and its underlying exposures and that it has implemented written policies and procedures for the risk management of the securitisation position and for maintaining records of the verifications and due diligence in accordance with paragraphs 1 and 2 and of any other relevant information; and (f) in the case of exposures to a fully supported ABCP programme, be able to demonstrate to its competent authorities, upon request, that it has a comprehensive and thorough understanding of the credit quality of the sponsor and of the terms of the liquidity facility provided.

5. Without prejudice to paragraphs 1 to 4 of this Article, where an institutional investor has given another institutional investor authority to make investment management decisions that might expose it to a securitisation, the institutional investor may instruct that managing party to fulfil its obligations under this Article in respect of any exposure to a securitisation arising from those decisions. Member States shall ensure that, where an institutional investor is instructed under this paragraph to fulfil the obligations of another institutional investor and fails to do so, any sanction under Articles 32 and 33 may be imposed on the managing party and not on the institutional investor who is exposed to the securitisation."

markets.[6] Nevertheless, negative aspects may arise from this legislative provision. One of these concerns is the provision to make retention requirements mandatory only for arrangers but not for originators. The rationale of this exclusion concerns the need to ensure that the originator's interest does not prejudice certain principles such as, for example, true sale and bankruptcy remoteness.

Before going into the details of the concept of due diligence, which is the subject matter of the following section, it is necessary to mention the private law implications of the legal opinion, this being a document requested by the arranger to the legal counsel before the conclusion of the securitisation. It can be anticipated that both the legal opinion and the due diligence are intertwined with each other, given the fact that, for the purposes of protection of the market, particularly those who are willing to invest in STS securitised products, a legal opinion duly provided upon completion of the transaction is required. Otherwise, the STS label would be at risk of being stripped off if already given, or declined if the request of authorisation is lodged.

4.2 Due diligence

Securitisation transactions are usually carried out by market participants without having full awareness of the risk of the investment.[7] This is an aspect that connotes shadow banking and specifically the securitisation market in which investors often have to refer to obscure mathematical models or rough approximations.[8]

Although no definition of diligence is provided, the concept at stake needs to be interpreted through the lenses of both transparency and standardisation. In other words, it is a required condition for investors, particularly qualified investors, to be able to make informed investment decisions that are consistent with the regulations of a particular country.

In order to limit the area of risks, specific legal provisions were adopted following the 2007–2008 financial crisis and before the adoption of the Securitisation Regulation. The obligations contained therein were applicable to any exposure transferred risk covered by securitisation. These obligations were laid down: a) by the CRR for credit institutions and investment firms; b) by the Delegated Regulation (EU) No 231/2013 for AIFM; c) by Regulation (EU) no. 35/2015 for insurance and reinsurance undertakings until 31 December 2018.

Structured product financial market participants[9] can be divided into three categories: a) financial institutions and investment firms; b) insurance companies and pension funds; c) alternative investment fund managers. Prior to the date of the

6 P. de Gioia Carabellese, *Securitisations*, in I.H-Y. Chiu, I. MacNeil (eds), *Research Handbook on Shadow Banking: Legal and Regulatory Aspects. Edward Elgar's Series*, Edward Elgar, Cheltenham and Northampton (MA), 2018, 117–170.

7 S.L. Schwarcz, 'Regulating Shadow Banking' (2012) *Review of Banking & Financial Law*, 634.

8 J.D. Coval, J. Jurek, E. Stafford, *The Economics of Structured Finance*, Working Paper No. 09-070, Harvard Business School, Cambridge (MA), 2008.

9 These are normally legal entities and, more specifically, financial entities.

EU Regulation there was a misalignment for each category. Within institutional entities, transferable collective investment undertakings,[10] such as occupational pension schemes,[11] were not required to comply with the requirement of due diligence.[12]

Art. 5 of the Securitisation Regulation, headed "Due-diligence requirements for institutional investors," stipulates that the institutional investor, at a time prior to the realisation of the investment transaction, must verify a number of elements if this institutional investor is different from the originator, promoter or original supplier. These are pre-investment verification and diligence requirements, to be linked with the obligations encompassed in the Securitisation Regulation itself.

A distinction can be made between pre-investment due diligence and post-investment due diligence.

The most important aspects of the due diligence requirements preceding the investment are concerned with the need to verify that: a) the exposures subject to securitisation stem from the originator, namely in the course of the ordinary business of the latter; b) that the original originator or supplier has fulfilled the retention obligation, at a rate of not less than 5%, as already mentioned.[13] The institutional investor shall also verify all risks associated with the transaction, taking as a reference the factors relating to the quality of the securitised assets and the way in which the transaction is structured.[14]

As regards the post-investment due diligence requirements, the institutional investor is required to verify the performance of the securitised position and provide verification safeguards, the purpose being to monitor the risk position.[15]

In M&A transactions, due diligence is a legal process aimed at protecting the buyer from legal and accounting risks that may unfold during an acquisition

10 EU Directive No. 2009/65/CE, in particular Art. 2(1), lett. b).

11 EU Directive No. 2016/2341/UE.

12 Due diligence is not a new feature of European regulation. The European Banking Authority, in the Final Report on EBA Draft Guidelines on outsourcing arrangements, 25 February 2019 stipulates that due diligence before a bank outsourcing contract is entered into by a banking intermediary. This is an indication of the sensitivity of the European legislator with regard to this issue. Due diligence is, at present, the *sine qua non condition* for entrusting the task to the service provider. It should be added that due diligence may be a useful parameter in favour of the injured party, to which the claim for damages may be anchored. It should be noted that the discipline described has increased the costs of the banking market, which has seen a reduction in profit margins.

13 The originator, promoter or the special purpose vehicle, in the event that the obligation is applicable, makes available the information contained in Art. 7 of the Securitisation Regulation.

14 These are qualitative and structural requirements respectively.

15 The assessment of the risk profile of the transaction can be defined as the stress test to be carried out by the investor. If it relates to a fully guaranteed securitisation, it concerns the solvency and liquidity of the sponsor as they may constitute risk elements. If the securitisation is not fully collateralised, the test will cover both cash flows and collateral values provided in support of the underlying positions. The results of these tests must be reported to the management body on a regular basis or if a deterioration of the data is to be achieved. The Securitisation Regulation requires the supervised entity to provide accurate reporting of the investment transaction and the risks associated with it.

process, ultimately a sale and purchase agreement. Both the business practice and scholarly works refer to the concept of due diligence in connection with the acquisition of shareholdings in corporate entities. Due diligence, though, becomes vital and crucial in the pre-acquisition process, therefore prior to the acquisition of the shareholding,[16] in other words in a moment preceding the conclusion of the contract, the purchase of the shares and/or quotas.[17] This concept of due diligence, first and foremost of an accounting nature, should be combined with the concept of legal due diligence, which is related to legal risks potentially affecting the target company, such as pending disputes, tax issues, environmental issues and, in general, all risks concerning the company to be acquired.

Given that, from a historical perspective, the due diligence process is one of the areas where the autonomy of the contracting parties is strong, the European Union legislator has not left this micro-area of law untouched. Hence, the activities that may define its perimeter, in an unequivocal way, have been pencilled by Brussels. In this scenario, the securitisation due diligence is the subject matter of the intervention by the EU legislator too, especially with regard to the acquisition of securitised financial instruments issued by an SPV. The European Union requirements make both the elements mandatory, if and when the assets should be purchased.

In the Securitisation Regulation, due diligence is a key element of investment in securitised products and applies irrespective of the STS requirement. In other words, any institutional investor who wants to invest in securitised securities must comply with the rules and procedures laid down in Art. 5.

The strategic role played by the concept of due diligence is set out in Art. 1 of the Securitisation Regulation ("Subject matter and scope").[18] Not only does it define the concept of securitisation, but also it establishes the *ratio essendi* of a series of legal obligations: due diligence; risk maintenance and transparency incumbent on the parties; the criteria for granting credit; the requirements to sell securitisations to retail customers; the prohibition of resecuritisation; the requirements for SSPs; and finally the conditions and procedures for securitisation data. Ultimately, it

16 The due diligence referred to in this requirement is functional to overcoming the existence of an information asymmetry. The buyer, in fact, is an extraneous subject to the company to be acquired and, consequently, does not know the related characteristics. The absence of prior verifications would result in the buyer being exposed to a different scenario than the one assumed with losses related to the company.

17 The due diligence described above seems to be instrumental in making a perusal of non-obvious liabilities which the target company may be affected by. As a result, it appears to be accounting due diligence.

18 "This Regulation lays down a general framework for securitisation. It defines securitisation and establishes due diligence, risk-retention and transparency requirements for parties involved in securitisations, criteria for credit granting, requirements for selling securitisations to retail clients, a ban on re-securitisation, requirements for SSPEs as well as conditions and procedures for securitisation repositories. It also creates a specific framework for simple, transparent and standardised ('STS') securitisation. 2. This Regulation applies to institutional investors and to originators, sponsors, original lenders and securitisation special purpose entities."

can be affirmed that there is an attempt to mould a specific framework for STS securitisations. Among all these elements, one shared fundamental feature for an STS transaction is the due diligence obligation.

The objective of the due diligence requirement can be derived from Recital 9,[19] which seems to enshrine the principle of the public relevance of this negotiation process, considered to be extremely significant for the market. It is therefore possible to affirm that the concept of due diligence has lost its pure private law "soul".

Another legal provision referring to the concept of due diligence is Recital 12 which seems to indicate a correlation between due diligence and the effectiveness of due diligence. The Securitisation Regulation also seems to refer to the conduct of the originator in the event of omissions, including the circumstance in which relevant pieces of data are hidden in the data room.

Recital 13 stipulates that

> the main purpose of the general obligation for the originator, sponsor and the SSPE to make available information on securitisations via the securitisation repository is to provide the investors with a single and supervised source of the data necessary for performing their due diligence.

The Recital continues by saying that, whilst private securitisations are often bespoke, they

> are important because they allow parties to enter into securitisation transactions without disclosing sensitive commercial information on the transaction (e.g. disclosing that a certain company needs funding to expand production or that an investment firm is entering a new market as part of its strategy) and/or related to the underlying assets (e.g. on the type of trade receivable generated by an industrial firm) to the market and competitors.[20]

19 "Investments in or exposures to securitisations not only expose the investor to credit risks of the underlying loans or exposures, but the structuring process of securitisations could also lead to other risks such as agency risk, model risk, legal and operational risk, counterparty risk, servicing risk, liquidity risk and concentration risk. Therefore, it is essential that institutional investors be subject to proportionate due-diligence requirements ensuring that they properly assess the risks arising from all types of securitisations, to the benefit of end investors. Due diligence can thus also enhance confidence in the market and between individual originators, sponsors and investors. It is necessary that investors also exercise appropriate due diligence with regard to STS securitisations. They can inform themselves with the information disclosed by the securitising parties, in particular the STS notification and the related information disclosed in this context, which should provide investors with all the relevant information on the way STS criteria are met. Institutional investors should be able to place appropriate reliance on the STS notification and the information disclosed by the originator, sponsor and securitisation special purpose entity (SSPE) on whether a securitisation meets the STS requirements. However, they should not rely solely and mechanistically on such a notification and such information."

20 *Ibidem*.

In bespoke securitisation, since investors are in direct contact with the structured finance transaction players, and because, as a result of this, they "receive the information necessary to perform their due diligence directly from them," "it is appropriate to exempt private securitisations from the requirement to notify the transaction information to a securitisation repository."[21]

The concept of a single and controlled source useful for the purposes of due diligence could strengthen the interpretation of due diligence as an operation to be carried out jointly by the obliged and main operators[22] with a possible responsibility for all players.[23]

Recital 33 of the Securitisation Regulation specifies that investors "should perform their own due diligence on investments commensurate with the risks involved but they should be able to rely on the STS notification and on the information disclosed by the originator, sponsor and SSPE on whether a securitisation meets the STS requirements. However, they should not rely solely and mechanistically on such notifications and information." Although this provision is not difficult to interpret, some doubts arise as to the expression "their own" related to "due diligence." This approach opens up the possibility that the activity contemplated can also be carried out through different subjects such as, for example, legal advisors. Given that due diligence is usually carried out by lawyers and technicians it seems that the concept of "their own" can take on a non-technical meaning. It could refer to the investor's top management bodies that have to carry it out and that have powers within the purchasing company to be defined in advance and with the exclusion of entities that operate without taking real responsibility.

Finally, Recital 49 contains a transitional legal provision, according to which the "due-diligence requirements that are applied in accordance with existing Union law before the date of application of this Regulation should continue to apply to securitisations issued on or after 1 January 2011, and to securitisations issued before 1 January 2011 where new underlying exposures have been added or substituted after 31 December 2014."[24]

21 *Ibidem.*

22 That is transferor, promoter, vehicle.

23 The reference is to Recital 27 where it is stipulated that "to ensure that investors perform robust due diligence and to facilitate the assessment of underlying risks, it is important that securitisation transactions are backed by pools of exposures that are homogenous in asset type, such as pools of residential loans, or pools of corporate loans, business property loans, leases and credit facilities to undertakings of the same category, or pools of auto loans and leases, or pools of credit facilities to individuals for personal, family or household consumption purposes. The underlying exposures should not include transferable securities, as defined in point (44) of Article 4(1) of EU Directive 2014/65/EU. To cater for those Member States where it is common practice for credit institutions to use bonds instead of loan agreements to provide credit to nonfinancial corporations, it should be possible to include such bonds, provided that they are not listed on a trading venue."

24 This legal provision is compounded by the one encompassed with the same Recital at stake: "The relevant provisions of Commission Delegated Regulation (EU) No 625/2014 (1) that specify the risk-retention requirements for credit institutions and investments firms within the meaning of

Art. 5(1), heading "Due-diligence requirements for institutional investors," does not belong, strictly speaking, to the subject area of due diligence, as it deals with the requirements pursuant to which the buyer, who is an institutional investor,[25] must verify the "quality" of the target asset before acquiring an interest in asset-backed securities.[26] The lack of one of these factors, as mentioned in Art. 5(1) of the Securitisation Regulation, makes it impossible for the institutional investor to purchase the securitised financial instruments.

The first requirement is that the original originator or lender, albeit established within the EU but not a credit institution, "grants all the credits giving rise to the underlying exposures on the basis of sound and well-defined criteria and clearly established processes." This legal provision is limited to the acquisition of non-bank securitisations and is justified by the fact that compliance with strict criteria in granting credit is not applicable to entities that do not belong to the group of supervised banking entities. Consequently, if the originator is an insurance

Regulation (EU) No 575/2013 of the European Parliament and of the Council (2) should remain applicable until the moment that the regulatory technical standards on risk retention pursuant to this Regulation apply. For reasons of legal certainty, credit institutions or investment firms, insurance undertakings, reinsurance undertakings and alternative investment fund managers should, for securitisation positions outstanding as of the date of application of this Regulation, continue to be subject to Article 405 of Regulation (EU) No 575/2013 and to Chapters I, II and III and Article 22 of Delegated Regulation (EU) No 625/2014, Articles 254 and 255 of Delegated Regulation (EU) 2015/35 and Article 51 of Commission Delegated Regulation (EU) No 231/2013 (3) respectively. In order to ensure that originators, sponsors and SSPEs comply with their transparency obligations, until the regulatory technical standards to be adopted by the Commission pursuant to this Regulation apply, the information referred to in Annexes I to VIII of Commission Delegated Regulation (EU) 2015/3 (1) should be made publicly available."

25 Institutional investors other than the originator, sponsor or original lender are exempt from verification.

26 "1. Prior to holding a securitisation position, an institutional investor, other than the originator, sponsor or original lender, shall verify that: (a) where the originator or original lender established in the Union is not a credit institution or an investment firm as defined in points (1) and (2) of Article 4(1) of Regulation (EU) No 575/2013, the originator or original lender grants all the credits giving rise to the underlying exposures on the basis of sound and well-defined criteria and clearly established processes for approving, amending, renewing and financing those credits and has effective systems in place to apply those criteria and processes in accordance with Article 9(1) of this Regulation; (b) where the originator or original lender is established in a third country, the originator or original lender grants all the credits giving rise to the underlying exposures on the basis of sound and well-defined criteria and clearly established processes for approving, amending, renewing and financing those credits and has effective systems in place to apply those criteria and processes to ensure that credit-granting is based on a thorough assessment of the obligor's creditworthiness; (c) if established in the Union, the originator, sponsor or original lender retains on an ongoing basis a material net economic interest in accordance with Article 6 and the risk retention is disclosed to the institutional investor in accordance with Article 7; (d) if established in a third country, the originator, sponsor or original lender retains on an ongoing basis a material net economic interest which, in any event, shall not be less than 5 %, determined in accordance with Article 6, and discloses the risk retention to institutional investors; (e) the originator, sponsor or SSPE has, where applicable, made available the information required by Article 7 in accordance with the frequency and modalities provided for in that Article."

company, which is supervised but not a credit institution, then this entity, albeit headquartered in EU territory, will be subject to the obligation to verify the subsistence of the requirement.

Regardless of whether the originator is supervised, in the event that the registered office and the headquarters[27] are not established in the territory of the EU, an essential requirement of due diligence is the verification of the criterion laid down in lett. b):

> the originator or original lender grants all the credits giving rise to the underlying exposures on the basis of sound and well-defined criteria and clearly established processes for approving, amending, renewing and financing those credits and has effective systems in place to apply those criteria and processes to ensure that credit-granting is based on a thorough assessment of the obligor's creditworthiness.

In other words, institutional investors established in the EU cannot invest in high-risk securitised products.

Another element to be assessed, within the due diligence process, is the one contained in lett. c):

> if established in the Union, the originator, sponsor or original lender retains on an ongoing basis a material net economic interest in accordance with Article 6 and the risk retention is disclosed to the institutional investor in accordance with Article 7.

Closely related to this legal provision is the following one encapsulated in lett. d), according to which the original originator, promoter or supplier established in a third country "retains on an ongoing basis a material net economic interest which, in any event, shall not be less than 5 %, determined in accordance with Article 6, and discloses the risk retention to institutional investors."

Continuing this analysis, lett. e) establishes the duty of the originator, sponsor or vehicle to make available "the information required by Article 7 in accordance with the frequency and modalities provided for in that Article." More generally, this is a transparency legal provision that, at first glance, appears to be extremely useful to ensure that the disclosures by the vehicle are rigorous and accurate. Tentatively, the norm at stake applies to activities that follow up on the conclusion of the acquisition contract by the institutional investor in securitised instruments. In the light of this, it can be affirmed that this is a legal provision to be related to *ex post* obligations, rather than purely due diligence duties: the latter encumbrances, in fact, include, by definition, activities to be carried out prior to the conclusion of the acquisition contract. Further conundrums relate to the "geographical" magnitude of the legal provision of lett. e), as well as the existence of a sanction

27 The "Directorate-General" in the red-tape jargon of the EU legislature.

and/or penalty, in cases where this norm was circumvented. In other words, it is not clear what consequences the securitisation players face in cases where the disclosure was not complied with. The question ultimately relates to whether the acquisition can be invalidated or whether the enforcement mechanism provided for in the regulation may be applied in these circumstances too.

The exact definition of due diligence before acquiring a stake in a securitised security is referred to in Art. 5(3). According to this provision "Prior to holding a securitisation position, an institutional investor, other than the originator, sponsor or original lender, shall carry out a due-diligence assessment which enables it to assess the risks involved."[28] Given that this is an activity that must be carried out prior to holding a securitisation position, it is considered that the activities mentioned in the following lett. a) and lett. c) can be traced back to the scope of due diligence.

Firstly, it is necessary to realise the extent of "the risk characteristics of the individual securitisation position and of the underlying exposures." The risk entailed to a securitisation transaction is dual, given the fact that securitisations are by definition "structured" operations. The scrutiny of the underlying security risk is vital in order to assess the appropriateness of the investment.

In the same sense, the requirement of lett. b) needs some interpretation. In following this legal provision, the institutional investor shall have to evaluate

> all the structural features of the securitisation that can materially impact the performance of the securitisation position, including the contractual priorities of payment and priority of payment-related triggers, credit enhancements, liquidity enhancements, market value triggers, and transaction-specific definitions of default.

The institutional investor will then assess that the securitisation is in accordance with both the characteristics contained in Art. 19–22 for the STS securitisation and those enshrined in Art. 23–26 on the subject of ABCP.

The investor-buyer can rely, as regards compliance, on notifications that are made pursuant to Art. 27. Reliance on that notification for the purpose of verifying compliance with it does not exempt the acquiring investor from carrying out a verification which could be defined as internal. It should be aimed at verifying that the simplicity, transparency and standardisation requirement is met. The choice made by the European legislator could be defined as penalising and contradictory. If the objective is to create a public register of STS transactions, and provided that this register is truly public, and if the inclusion in the register is subject, in turn, to accurate regulatory checks, it could become a duplication. This would be a double assessment required of the institutional investor as regards its own assessment.

28 The obligation, even in this case, is on the institutional investor who is not the originator, the promoter or the original lender.

The standard could also lead to operational problems. The reference goes to the hypothesis in which an STS securitisation does not respect the simplicity, transparency and standardisation requirements despite having been notified to the register and factually verified by the institutional investor. According to the legislation under analysis, this state of the art is likely to hinder the institutional investor in any purchase. From a theoretical point of view, this investor would be entitled to activate a liability proceeding against the public body for having previously and superficially registered the programme in the special register (Art. 27).[29]

The use of new and technical terminology referred to in the Rules of Procedure does not make any exception to the main characteristic of European Union legislation. The reference goes to the expression contained in Art. 5(4) of the Securitisation Regulation, i.e. "shall at least," an expression referring to the institutional investor, once it has made the investment in securitised securities.

It is not possible to deal with due diligence from a legal perspective without considering, from an empirical perspective, that this legal concept defines the *ex ante* activities that a buyer puts in place before the acquisition of an asset.

At the first stage, lett. a) of Art. 5(4) states that an institutional investor other than the originator, sponsor or original lender shall:

> establish appropriate written procedures that are proportionate to the risk profile of the securitisation position and, where relevant, to the institutional investor's trading and non-trading book, in order to monitor, on an ongoing basis, compliance with paragraphs 1 and 3 and the performance of the securitisation position and of the underlying exposures. Where relevant with respect to the securitisation and the underlying exposures, those written procedures shall include monitoring of the exposure type, the percentage of loans more than 30, 60 and 90 days past due, default rates, prepayment rates, loans in foreclosure, recovery rates, repurchases, loan modifications, payment holidays, collateral type and occupancy, and frequency distribution of credit scores or other measures of credit worthiness across underlying exposures, industry and geographical diversification, frequency distribution of loan to value ratios with band widths that facilitate adequate sensitivity analysis. Where the underlying exposures are themselves securitisation positions, as permitted under Article 8, institutional investors shall also monitor the exposures underlying those positions.

29 It is possible that in providing for this additional burden on the buyer, the provision pursued the objective of protecting the same authority from a possible legal risk. The reference is to the creation of a trust relating to the subsistence of the requirement of simplicity, transparency and standardisation.

The following letter states that, if the securitisation is different from a fully guaranteed ABCP programme, the institutional investor must implement, on regular basis,

> stress tests on the cash flows and collateral values supporting the underlying exposures or, in the absence of sufficient data on cash flows and collateral values, stress tests on loss assumptions, having regard to the nature, scale and complexity of the risk of the securitisation position.[30]

Regardless of whether the securitisation transaction is guaranteed, the Securitisation Regulation seems to prompt the implementation of a corporate governance regime under which the top-level structures of the institutional investor, which is often a bank, are not kept in the dark about the securitisation transaction itself. In this regard, the institutional investor, pursuant to lett. d), ensures "internal reporting to its management body so that the management body is aware of the material risks arising from the securitisation position and so that those risks are adequately managed." This is a legal provision to be included in the "field" of that banking and financial regulation whose objective is to remove the information barriers existing between the institution's top-level bodies and, on the other hand, the operational bodies, such as the finance office.[31]

The establishment of two maintenance requirements is set forth by letter e) with the difference that it is addressed to the Supervisory Authority. Namely, it is established that the institutional investor should:

> be able to demonstrate to its competent authorities, upon request, that it has a comprehensive and thorough understanding of the securitisation position and its underlying exposures and that it has implemented written policies and procedures for the risk management of the securitisation position and for maintaining records of the verifications and due diligence in accordance with paragraphs 1 and 2 and of any other relevant information.

It should be added that securitisation and, specifically, investment in securitised securities, should not become an opportunity for the investor and its board to move away from the supervisory activity typical of a supervised entity.

Within the supervisory powers,[32] the institution in its different operational structures, therefore from the top bodies to the bottom of the operational offices,

30 It is clear that the charges provided for in lett. b) are less burdensome than those required by lett. a).

31 In the experience that preceded the crisis of 2007–2008, it was found that both in terms of derivatives and structured finance transactions, the operating offices were overly burdened by technical operations. This had provoked an alienation of the managerial organs with respect to the operative reality. The obligation introduced by the Rules of Procedure would prevent this risk. As a result of the new regulation, the Body has both a right and a duty to be informed about all the operations of its institutional investor concerning its structured finance exposures.

32 The powers of disclosure, regulation and inspection.

should be able to provide information to the Supervisory Authority about the investment in securitised instruments. In accordance with lett. f) in the case of exposures to a fully supported ABCP programme, be able to demonstrate to its competent authorities, upon request, that it has a comprehensive and thorough understanding of the credit quality of the sponsor and of the terms of the liquidity facility provided. It is therefore necessary to recall the definition of institutional investor offered by the Securitisation Regulation, namely Art. 2. Within the scope of this provision:

> institutional investor means an investor which is one of the following: (a) an insurance undertaking as defined in point (1) of Article 13 of Directive 2009/138/EC; (b) a reinsurance undertaking as defined in point (4) of Article 13 of Directive 2009/138/EC; (c) an institution for occupational retirement provision falling within the scope of Directive (EU) 2016/2341 of the European Parliament and of the Council (1) in accordance with Article 2 thereof, unless a Member State has chosen not to apply that Directive in whole or in parts to that institution in accordance with Article 5 of that Directive; or an investment manager or an authorised entity appointed by an institution for occupational retirement provision pursuant to Article 32 of Directive (EU) 2016/2341; (d) an alternative investment fund manager (AIFM) as defined in point (b) of Article 4(1) of Directive 2011/61/EU that manages and/or markets alternative investment funds in the Union; (e) an undertaking for the collective investment in transferable securities (UCITS) management company, as defined in point (b) of Article 2(1) of Directive 2009/65/EC; (f) an internally managed UCITS, which is an investment company authorised in accordance with Directive 2009/65/EC and which has not designated a management company authorised under that Directive for its management; (g) a credit institution as defined in point (1) of Article 4(1) of Regulation (EU) No 575/2013 for the purposes of that Regulation or an investment firm as defined in point (2) of Article 4(1) of that Regulation.

Essentially, the definition of an institutional investor as a supervised entity that is subject to extremely strict regulation is somehow inferable from the wording. An indication of this is that a simple acquisition of securities is not channelled through the "motorways" of contract law, rather it is subject to more stringent regulation that forces the prospective buyer to carry out effective checks. If a violation of the regulation occurs, not only will this affect the validity of the acquisition, but it also may jeopardise the possibility that the supervised entity and its representatives are subject to the sanctions and, more generally, the enforcement provided for in the specific area of the Securitisation Regulation.[33]

33 The exception to the above is that the supervisory authority will order the sale if the risk remains.

4.3 The legal opinion

An "antidote" against the re-characterisation of a securitisation transaction – hence the empowerment of a Court to hold that it is not a true sale – is the legal opinion (henceforth also the "LO"). From a conceptual point of view, the closing legal opinion, which is issued at the time of signing the documentation, encompasses and at the same time constitutes the examination of both the operation and the relevant documentation.[34]

The LO should be issued by a qualified lawyer authorised in the jurisdiction or jurisdictions in which the securitisation transaction takes place or in which the same transaction will be effective. However, considering the fact that structured finance transactions are effective across different jurisdictions, there is never correspondence between the place where the lawyer issuing the LO is qualified and all the jurisdictions where the different contracts of the securitisation will be effective. Apparently, the only exception would be a very "domestic" securitisation, where the whole process from the origination to the vehicle takes place in the same country and the same jurisdictions.

Nevertheless, even in the usual cases in which the securitisation is transnational, it often happens that arrangers are satisfied with the legal opinion provided by an international law firm whose lawyers involved with the transaction are qualified in one jurisdiction, e.g. the one where the originator is located, although these lawyers are not necessarily qualified in other jurisdictions where some contracts of the transaction will be effective. Generally speaking, the market regards an LO of this kind, albeit "partial," satisfactory, since it relates to a set of documents, but not all, giving a broad picture of the transaction. This conclusion seems to be corroborated by the "real world," where the international standing of a law firm may exude an "allure" that allows the relevant legal opinion to go beyond the strictly formal requirement.

This is not a *modus operandi* that comes without criticism. In fact, it is contrary to the principles of trust and truth that should exist between the arranger and the markets. It should also be added that, despite the Securitisation Regulation, the

34 Lexis PSL Banking & Finance (Editorial), 'Legal Opinions: What Should they Cover?' (2014) *Butterworths Journal of International Banking & Financial Law* 29(6), 418–419; A. Dodds, E. Macleod, 'There Are as Many Opinions as There Are Experts: Issues to Consider When Drafting Reasoned Legal Opinions' (2020) *Butterworths Journal of International Banking & Financial Law* 35(3), 179–181; A.N. Field, 'Legal Opinions: A Defence of the Section on Business Law's Response to the ABA Opinion Accord' (1993) *International Business Lawyer* 21(7), 321–323; G. Yeowart, 'Updated Guide to English Opinion Letters in Financial Transactions' (2021) *Butterworths Journal of International Banking & Financial Law* 2021, 36(3), 202–208; M. Whalley, 'Cannes Report: Legal Opinions, Conflicting Interests and Loyalties' (1993) *International Business Lawyer* 21(2), 57–58; S.M. Alter, 'The Case for Seeking Legal Advice' (2004) *Managing Intellectual Property* 143, 20–23. The real conundrum, in dealing with legal opinions, is to ascertain (1) the goal of such a documentation and what they should be concerned about; (2) the perimeter of those who, taking part in the transaction, are interested in receiving authority opinions; (3) the matters covered by enforceability opinions; and (4) the way they can be used in cross-border transactions.

common practices unfolded so far have not changed. On the other hand, lawyers often insert numerous qualifications in their LO, as far as their own jurisdiction is concerned, to the point that the LO turns out to be not really effective or protective, to say the least. By way of example, reference can be made to the tendency to sign a legal opinion without assuming any responsibility for jurisdictions in which the securitisation will be effective, if they do not belong to the jurisdiction of the same lawyer signing the legal opinion. In light of this, the burning question is whether the LO is really suitable to play the role of protecting the market. The signs that it is window-dressing, rather than a serious commitment, are right there.

Furthermore, as far as the subject matter of the LO is concerned, this is based on specific circumstances and documents, in turn often based on assumptions and circumstances of a technical nature.[35] In light of this, the LO can be defined as the point of view of a lawyer, essential for the transaction, because the release of this "package" is to be considered a condition precedent for the granting of the credit or the issuance of securities.

As to more practical aspects, the legal opinion will be issued by a lawyer appointed by the bank or a consortium of credit institutions acting as arranger: with the LO they aim to ensure that the specific issues related to the transaction, with particular attention to re-characterisation, are excluded. From this point of view, therefore, the LO should rely exclusively on the persons to whom it is addressed, usually to the bank that organises the operation. The latter receives assurances that the securitised securities and the issuing entity, the SPV, are bankruptcy remote entities. Consequently, given that this is a genuine sale, the bankruptcy of the originator is not capable of affecting the institution's ability to repay the securities.

A further complex question is whether the subscribers of the securitised products, namely the investors, may really trust the LO. This uncertainty stems from the fact that lawyers who issue LOs usually include a disclaimer under their expert opinion. A common wording is the following: "this opinion is given only to the persons to whom it is addressed and may not be relied upon by any other person. It may not be disclosed to third parties without a prior written consent."[36]

In common law jurisdictions, it is very unlikely that an investor will successfully take a liability action on the basis of an incorrect LO.[37] The relevant legal case is *Hedley Byrne & Co. Ltd v Heller & Partners Ltd*[38] which, to this day, continues to be regarded as a stone that cannot be moved.

35 R. McCormick, *Legal Risk in the Financial Markets*, 2nd ed., Oxford University Press, Oxford, 2010, 419.

36 P.R. Wood, *International Loans, Bonds, Guarantees, Legal Opinions: The Law and Practice of International Finance Series*, Sweet & Maxwell, London, 2007, 423. This limited liability is also corroborated by the *dictum Allied Finance & Investments Ltd v Haddow & Co* (1983) NZLR 22 CA.

37 P.R. Wood, *International Loans, Bonds, Guarantees, Legal Opinions* (n. 32), 424.

38 *Hedley Byrne & Co. Ltd v Heller & Partners Ltd* (1964) AC 465. In August 1958, Hedleys wanted a banker's report relating to a company which then had an account with the bank. In November

Whilst this is the common law approach, different legal stances may come from Brussels. The European Union legislation, especially in the area of capital markets and structured finance, could theoretically push towards a contractual liability of lawyers who sign the LO. This new form of liability could become a possible legislative step of the European Union legislation, whose laws may in the future arrange for a strict liability regime of lawyers who issue the LO.

More generally, de-recognition of claims – i.e. the removal, for accounting purposes, of the type of claims from the assets of the vehicle – is allowed only if it can be assumed that the originator continues to maintain effective control over the exposure of the transferred credit risk. This scenario fundamentally happens either if the assignor is in a position to purchase back from the buyer the exposure previously transferred in order to make the relevant profit, or if the seller has an obligation to keep the risk of the transferred exposure. Nevertheless, the appointment of the originator as a servicer does not represent, *per se*, a criterion

---

1957, Hedleys had already received a report about the company, although it had been given by another bank, though not by direct communication. Hedleys banked at a Piccadilly branch of National Provincial Bank, Ltd. Hedleys asked that a report concerning Easipower Ltd should be obtained. The Piccadilly branch communicated with the City office of their bank, the National Provincial. The National Provincial City office telephoned the bank on 18 August 1958, and it is common knowledge that the representative of the National Provincial said that "they wanted to know in confidence" and "without responsibility" on the part of the bank as to the respectability and standing of Easipower Ltd and whether Easipower Ltd "would be good for an advertising contract for £8/9,000." To that oral inquiry the bank then gave an oral answer. In due course the answer then given was communicated by the Piccadilly branch of the National Provincial to Hedleys. It was communicated orally and a letter of confirmation from that branch (dated 21 August 1958) was sent to Hedleys. The latter had the headings "Confidential" and "For your private use and without responsibility on the part of this bank or the manager." The oral answer which the bank had given to the City office of the National Provincial was passed on with the prefatory words – "In reply to your telephoned inquiry of 18 August bankers say:–" There was a later inquiry. On 4 November 1958, in a letter to the Piccadilly branch of the National Provincial, Hedleys wrote: "I have been requested by the Directors to again ask you to check the financial structure and status of Easipower Limited." Hedleys made some particular references and concluded their letter with the words: "I would be appreciative if you could make your check as [1963] 2 All ER 575 at 588 exhaustive as you reasonably can." In a letter dated 7 November and headed "Private and Confidential" the City office of the National Provincial asked the bank for their "opinion in confidence as to the respectability and standing of Easipower, Ltd" and asked the bank to state whether they considered Easipower Ltd "trustworthy, in the way of business, to the extent of £100,000 per annum, advertising contract." The bank replied in a letter dated 11 November and sent to the City office of the National Provincial. The letter had the headings "Confidential" and "For your private use and without responsibility on the part of this Bank or its officials." On 14 November the Piccadilly branch of the National Provincial wrote to Hedleys (heading their letter "Confidential. For your private use and without responsibility on the part of this Bank or the Manager") with the prefatory words: "In reply to your inquiry letter of 4 November Bankers say," and passed on what the bank had stated in their letter to the City office of the National Provincial (see Lord Hodson's statements at paragraph 504).

based on which the control on the transferred exposures can be inferred.[39] As far as this aspect is concerned, two observations are necessary.

First, it is required that the originator does not hold any liability for the assets that are transferred to the vehicle. The originator, therefore, cannot have any contractual obligation to repurchase in the event of losses, nor can it guarantee the repayment of either interest or capital to those who invest in securities issued by the SPV. From a practical point of view, what has just been described could be achieved with the use of a side letter with which the originator and arranger agree that the former undertakes to buy the credits again in the event of a default. The above would be an operation capable of raising issues that go beyond the civil sphere.

Secondly, it is considered essential that the SPV be allowed to exercise sole control over the assets and adopt any form of protection that a normal owner is allowed to exercise. The SPV should become the true owner to whom all rights should be granted, such as the right to sell, pledge and, more generally, guarantee (including assets) and manage the securitised assets. Finally, the assets must be isolated from the originator in the event of bankruptcy since this ensures that the SPV is bankruptcy remote.[40]

4.4 Due diligence and the legal opinion: between a rock and a hard place

The underpinning philosophy of due diligence, as well as the "body of law" enshrined in Art. 28 of the Securitisation Regulation, is to prevent different types of risks: not only private threats, i.e. the unexpected losses which private investors may incur, but also public hazards, i.e. the stability of the financial market that may be potentially jeopardised by a reckless investment in securitised products. By contrast, Art. 5 is aimed at preventing the nonchalant acquisition of securitised financial instruments.

Bearing this in mind, not only can the two norms be considered inconsistent with each other, but they can also reveal an overlap of regulation.

As far as the first element is concerned, the potential issue relates to the literal meaning of the two legal provisions at stake: Art. 5 fundamentally pursues an objective: to "establish appropriate written procedures that are proportionate to the risk profile of the securitisation position and, where relevant, to the institutional investor's trading and non-trading book, in order to monitor, on an ongoing basis, compliance with paragraphs 1 and 3 and the performance of the securitisation position and of the underlying exposures."[41] Accordingly, scholars highlight that

39 S. Gleeson, *International Regulation of Banking*, 2nd ed., Oxford University Press, Oxford, 2012, 286.

40 It is an objective that is achieved in a purely contractual way in common law systems, while it is strengthened by legislation in civil law systems.

41 Art. 5(4), lett. a.

the first paragraph of Art. 5 does not seem to refer to due diligence, because it merely hints at the requirements that an institutional investor needs to stick to in order to purchase an interest in securitised products. More precisely, the legal opinion that the investor needs to obtain should be made before "holding a securitisation position" and "shall carry out a due-diligence assessment which enables it to assess the risks involved."[42]

As regards the second element, Art. 28 prescribes that the activity carried out by the "third party verifying" is the compliance with the STS criteria provided for in Art. 19–22 or Art. 23–26.[43]

In the light of the above, the two norms encompassed in Art. 5 and Art. 28 apparently correspond with each other, whereas the reality may be quite different.

This outcome is supported by a further consideration relating to the definition of the entity which is subject to the two duties at stake. In detail, the third party verifying, in force of Art. 27(2), is the one used by "the originator, sponsor or SSPE," "to check whether a securitisation complies," and to the extent that this third party is authorised according to Art. 27(2). By contrast, Art. 5 mentions merely an "institutional investor, other than the originator, sponsor or original lender."

Based on the consideration above, the potential question as to whether the two parties, the one under Art. 5 and the other one under Art. 28, can be the same may be answered in the affirmative, on the condition that the party is a "party authorised." However, based on black letter law, apparently the two parties do not have to be different from a formal point of view. The element that differentiates the two is the substantial aspect.

Based on this intermediate conclusion, should the two parties coincide, it would spark off a potential conflict of interest. It is still difficult to say whether this is a European Union legislator's blunder or a deliberate choice. Beyond the literal interpretation of the specific legal provisions, and in looking at the broader picture, including the assessment of the purposes of the entire piece of legislation, it is by contrast possible to suggest that the two parties will be different, as they will never coincide.

The lesson that can be learnt from this apparent gap is that even extensive and widespread regulation can leave gaps to fill in. The answer, on the other hand, is to both peruse and identify the ultimate meaning of a given statute. The legal framework of the supervision on compliance with the STS label still remains a very complex area and it requires the intervention of different levels of control: the problematic aspect is that, from a literal and formal point of view, the existence of a void cannot be denied.

42 Art. 5(3).
43 Art. 28(1).

4.5 Investors and market protection

The entities who buy bonds from an SPV are often institutional investors and are defined by Art. 2(1)(12) of the Securitisation Regulation. The definition of institutional investor is instrumental to the identification of a due diligence obligation that is defined by Art. 5 of the Securitisation Regulation. This legal provision stipulates that, before acquiring the securities issued by the vehicle, the institutional investors perform due diligence, that is, they make checks both on the originator and the risks associated with the securitisation in question.

From the perusal of Art. 5 of the Securitisation Regulation, it becomes obvious that the attention of the European Union legislator is turned to the originators who belong to third-party countries. The rationale behind this is self-explanatory. Given that these entities do not have to comply with the stricter and stricter criteria imposed by the EU, the quality of the assigned claims becomes more important and the ensuing focus of the legislation will be broader. The risk appears to be greater[44] if the originator is not established in the EU and is not a credit institution either. In this case, the criteria of solidity, as well as the procedures to put in place, shall be verified more carefully. In essence, in these circumstances, the Securitisation Regulation reminds us that the originator or original lender

> grants all the credits giving rise to the underlying exposures on the basis of sound and well-defined criteria and clearly established processes for approving, amending, renewing and financing those credits and has effective systems in place to apply those criteria and processes to ensure that credit-granting is based on a thorough assessment of the obligor's creditworthiness.[45]

The existence of a link between the originator and the EU requires that the institutional investor should verify that the originator maintains a significant net economic interest on an ongoing basis, in other words the maintenance of a risk within the meaning of Art. 6 of the Rules of Procedure.[46] Strictly speaking, the verification by the institutional investor relates to the fact that the originator continuously maintains a material net economic interest of not less than 5%[47] and communicates the maintenance of risk to institutional investors.

The activities that must be carried out by an institutional investor are the focus of Art. 5(3) of the Securitisation Regulation. First, an assessment is required as concerns "the risk characteristics of the individual securitisation position and of the underlying exposures" (lett. a). The potential acquisition of real estate securitised securities should take into account the risk of the development of that market. Second, the evaluation must take into consideration

44 Consequently, more caution is required.

45 Art. 5(1), lett. b).

46 There is therefore an ancillary obligation to inform institutional investors of any changes.

47 It is determined in accordance with Art. 6.

all the structural features of the securitisation that can materially impact the performance of the securitisation position, including the contractual priorities of payment and priority of payment-related triggers, credit enhancements, liquidity enhancements, market value triggers, and transaction-specific definitions of default (lett. b).

Finally, if the acquisition by the institutional investor in a securitised security complies with STS securitisation, it must verify that the securitisation also complies with the relevant requirements.[48]

A violation of due diligence obligations impacts the activity of certain entities and bodies, to which some consequent rights and duties are assigned in order to activate specific safeguards. The first bodies are those in charge of supervising the institutional investor. The supervisory responsibility translates into the entitlement of the public body to begin the investigation, with the ensuing enforcement of sanctions in the event that the investigations unveiled a violation.[49]

The sale of securitisations to retail customers requires compliance with the body of law of Art. 3. This provision prohibits retail sales unless certain conditions are met. For example, "the seller of the securitisation position has performed a suitability test in accordance with Article 25(2) of Directive 2014/65/EU."[50] It is also required that the seller of the securitised asset has assessed that such an exposure can be considered suitable for a particular retail consumer.[51] Finally, it is provided that "the seller of the securitisation position immediately communicates in a report to the retail client the outcome of the suitability test."[52]

With the securitisation, investors with different "palates" of risk can be satisfied more transparently, because bonds are issued in two classes: senior bonds and junior bonds. Junior bonds are subordinate to seniors. Mention has already been made of the fact that the distinction between different bond classes is called tranching.

The risk that the SPV is not able to repay the principal sum and interest on the securities is qualified as a credit risk for investors; this can be mitigated by the use of different instruments. Thanks to tranching, junior notes, in being subordinated to senior notes, absorb the first losses, and therefore the credit risk on notes with higher seniority is reduced, although not neutralised.

48 "With regard to a securitisation notified as STS in accordance with Article 27, the compliance of that securitisation with the requirements provided for in Articles 19 to 22 or in Articles 23 to 26, and Article 27. Institutional investors may rely to an appropriate extent on the STS notification pursuant to Article 27(1) and on the information disclosed by the originator, sponsor and SSPE on the compliance with the STS requirements, without solely or mechanistically relying on that notification or information."

49 Liability can also have a civil nature in the event that non-compliance with the rules of due diligence has resulted in a concrete damage to the stakeholder.

50 Art. 3(1), lett. a), of the Securitisation Regulation.

51 "The seller of the securitisation position is satisfied, on the basis of the test referred to in point (a), that the securitisation position is suitable for that retail client" (following lett. b).

52 See final lett. c) of Art. 3(1) of the Securitisation Regulation.

Second, overcollateralisation can be used as a means of mitigating the SPV risk. The originator transfers more receivables to the SPV than investors really need. The interest that the SPV receives on receivables from debtors is higher than what the SPV has to pay to investors. Any resulting surplus will be credited to the "Reserve Account."

Third, the structure of securitisations is arranged in such a way that investors can exercise a recourse action on assets by collateralising the originator's debtors.[53] Should the SPV default on the fulfilment of its obligations towards investors, the latter could enforce these guarantees through the trustee.

A fourth way to mitigate credit risk on the SPV is to create a subordinated loan from the originator to the SPV (equity piece). This is a loan that has to be repaid, only if, with the SPV becoming insolvent, all investor claims, including junior bonds, have been satisfied.

Finally, a liquidity facility can be concluded between the SPV and a liquidity provider, which is usually another bank (different from the arranger), which allows the SPV to have cash to pay the bond holders. In the same way as in a syndicated loan context, a securitisation transaction requires a trustee that acts for the full range of bond holders, similarly to what the trustee does for the lender in a syndicated loan. Specifically, the security trustee is mandated by a contract to enforce the security rights against the SPV and debtors on behalf of investors.[54]

Security rights protecting claims must be transferred to the security trustee in order to allow it to execute such security rights. As a result of the transfer, investors will be able to claim security rights in the event of a non-payment of the SPV. The SPV is also entitled to purchase credits from the originator through the issuance of bonds and can pay the principal and interest on bonds with the relevant revenues from credits that the originator has transferred to the SPV.

The interest rate to be paid by the vehicle to the bond holders is usually variable. In contrast, the interest rate that the SPV receives from the debtors on the transferred claims is usually fixed. To mitigate this interest rate/mismatch risk, the SPV usually enters into a swap contract with a swap counterparty. Under this derivative contract, the counterparty accepts variable interest flows and provides fixed feedback flows. As a result, the SPV receives a fixed interest rate to be paid to bondholders. Mismatch may also occur for reasons other than misalignment between receivables revenues and bond costs. For example, first, a surplus can be realised when debtors pay out their loans prematurely; second, it can be realised in the event that debtors default. In the event of a surplus, the SPV and an account provider may enter into an investment contract that allows the SPV, in the event

53 In a "classic" securitisation, collateral would consist of mortgages that the borrowers have granted on the property financed by the loan from which the receivables originate.

54 M. Haentjens, P. de Gioia Carabellese, *European Banking and Financial Law*, 2nd ed., Routledge, London and New York, 2020, 189–214.

of an incidental credit surplus, to invest the surplus temporarily. In the event of a temporary credit deficit, the conclusion of a liquidity facility between the SPV and a liquidity provider may provide cash. In this way the SPV would be allowed to always pay the bond holders.

4.6 ESG factors and sustainable securitisations

The unique aspect of the latest pieces of legislation in the financial area is mainly concerned with a new, increased sensibility to the environment.[55] Thus, the banking regulation, which may now fill in the "green banking" box too, is considered essential for the ecological transition.

Also in connection with this postulation, most scholars underline that shadow banking may increase the quality of sustainability, in addition to being an opportunity for "actors" (such as banks and, more generally, businesses) to play an active role in the process of sustainability: the final stage of this "Grand Tour" is an economic system where the major themes of sustainable development may be viewed as the main stage of financial and economic development.

Traditionally, the *modus operandi* of the banking business has led to an increase in polluting emissions.[56] Also in view of this, speculative financial transactions have so far been hardly considered environmentally conscious. By contrast, the new underpinning idea of future financial markets is that there is a strong relationship between the banking system and the ecosystem; as a result of this, the regulation, broadly considered, is expected to act as a thread between these different areas.

In the EU legal environment, reference shall be made to Regulation (EU) 2019/2088:[57] the latter requires banks and businesses to apply a duty of transparency in connection with the ESG nature of financial products. The measurement of sustainability shall be clear, concrete, transparent and quantifiable. Therefore, the ultimate objective is a possible prospective reconciliation between environmental and financial factors, a far cry from the oxymoron which in the past used to be associated with them.

The body of law existing in the financial sector is now adamant that its aims and objectives include those relating to both the environment and environmental risk. Hence, the banking legislation has coined the – linguistically new – expressions "sustainable finance" or "green finance." Not only does this happen as a

55 Among the others, see I.Y-Y. Chiu, L. Lin, D. Rouch, 'Law and Sustainable Finance' (2022) *European Business Organisation Law Review* 23(1), 1–7.

56 A. Pettifor, *The Case for the Green New Deal*, Verso Publisher, London and New York, 2019, 31 ff.

57 In full: "Regulation (EU) 2019/2088 of the European Parliament and of the Council of 27 November 2019 on sustainability-related disclosures in the financial services sector" (OJEU, 22 June 2020 L 198/13).

need for improving the sustainability profile of banking activity, but this is also an opportunity to let actors play an active role in the ecological transition process. The final point is to move toward an economic system able to address the major issues of sustainable development.

The ultimate idea within the European Union is to implement "A new strategic agenda 2019–2024"[58] of the European Council which is focused on several missions: a) protecting citizens and freedoms; b) developing a strong and vibrant economic base; c) building a climate-neutral, green, fair and social Europe; d) promoting European interests and values on the global stage. More specifically, this agenda was subsequently outlined in the "New Green Deal" project by the European Commission and, at the last stage, was endorsed by the European Parliament with "Agenda 21" and "Agenda 2030." As a result of these agendas, the financial sector has undergone a revolutionary metamorphosis: banking and financial activity is interpreted not only as a means of achieving an income, but also as a new and alternative way to produce a result with a social purpose.

The concept of a sustainable bank, which is ontologically coupled with sustainable finance, has been the subject matter of different interpretations. First and foremost, it is linked with sustainable projects that may generate profits in the short term. Second, it refers to financial products in a position to generate long-term returns. Finally, there is a possible interpretation leaving room for affirming that the financial policy of recent times has been conceived to shape investments that could generate an economic surplus as well as social profits, in order to positively benefit the environmental system. For these reasons, sustainable finance

58 www.consiliumeuropa.ue.

operations differ from traditional operations.[59] Not coincidentally, the concept of sustainable finance implies the clarification of a sustainable transaction:[60]

> Sustainability transition in conventional reception is associated with the process of multi-level transformation of the economic and socio-technological system intended to increase its environmental sustainability and social fairness. This particular concept is typically evoked in the context of transition to green economy of low emission and resource efficiency, based on clean technologies and other solutions generally referred to as eco-innovation. The sustainability transition influence profoundly financial sector.[61]

As far as the European Union is concerned, and its (quasi) legal system, reference shall be made to a few pieces of legislation, specifically:

1. Commission Delegated Regulation (EU) 2021/1253 of 21 April 2021 amending Delegated Regulation (EU) 2017/565 as regards the integration of

59 See M. La Torre, A. Trotta, H. Chiappini, A. Rizzello, 'Business Models for Sustainable Finance: The Case Study of Social Impact Bonds' (2019) *Sustainability* 11, 1–23; H. Ahlström, D. Monciardini, 'The Regulatory Dynamics of Sustainable Finance: Paradoxical Success and Limitations of EU Reforms' (2021) *Journal of Business Ethics*, 24 February, online; M.A. Urban, D. Wójcik, 'Dirty Banking: Probing the Gap in Sustainable Finance' (2019) *Sustainability* 11, 1–23; H. Liang, L. Renneboog, *Corporate Social Responsibility and Sustainable Finance: A Review of the Literature, ECGI Working Paper Series in Finance Working Paper*, no. 701, September 2020; D. Schoenmaker, *Investing for the Common Good: A Sustainable Finance Framework*, Bruegel Essay and Lecture Series, Bruegel, 2017. It is arduous to define the concept of sustainable finance. In looking at the matter from an EU point of view, and taking into account the literature on this point – see D. Claringbould, M. Koch, P. Owen, 'Sustainable Finance: The European Union's Approach to Increasing Sustainable Investments and Growth – Opportunities and Challenges' (2019) *Vierteljahrshefte zur Wirtschaftsforschung* 88(2), 11–27) – it is worth recollecting the following:

"Sustainable finance is understood by the European Commission as finance having a strong green, environmental and social component, to support economic growth while reducing pressures on the environment, addressing greenhouse gas emissions and tackling pollution, minimising waste and improving efficiency in the use of natural resources. Sustainable finance also encompasses increasing awareness of and transparency on risks which may impact on the sustainability of the financial system and the management of such risks by financial and corporate actors through appropriate governance. This conceptual approach of sustainable finance has been further specified by the European Commission in setting out its Action Plan on financing sustainable growth of March 2018. This approach is based on the understanding that climate change, environmental and social issues are often closely intertwined and can have spill-over effects.

Sustainable finance includes three main components when used in the current EU policy context, which are (1) mobilising finance for investments which help address climate change, or have a positive environmental impact or support sustainable development (2) taking into account environmental and social aspects and potential risks when making investment and finance decisions and (3) reflecting on longer-term time horizons and impact of economic and financial market activities."

60 B. Ryszawska, 'Sustainability Transition Needs Sustainable Finance' (2016) *Copernican Journal of Finance & Accounting* 5(1), 185–194.

61 *Ibidem*.

sustainability factors, sustainability risks and sustainability preferences in certain organisational requirements and operating conditions of investment firms.

2. Commission Delegated Regulation (EU) 2021/1255 of 21 April 2021 amending Delegated Regulation (EU) No 231/2013 as regards sustainability risks and sustainability factors to be taken into account by AIFM.
3. Commission Delegated Regulation (EU) 2021/1256 of 21 April 2021 amending Delegated Regulation (EU) 2015/35 as regards the integration of sustainability risks into the governance of insurance and reinsurance undertakings.
4. Commission Delegated Regulation (EU) 2021/1257 of 21 April 2021 amending Delegated Regulations (EU) 2017/2358 and (EU) 2017/2359 as regards the integration of sustainability factors, sustainability risks and sustainability preferences in the control and product governance requirements for insurance companies and insurance distributors and in the conduct of business rules and investment advice for insurance investment products.
5. Commission Delegated Directive (EU) 2021/1269 of 21 April 2021 amending Delegated Directive (EU) 2017/593 as regards the integration of sustainability factors into product governance obligations.
6. Commission Delegated Directive (EU) 2021/1270 of 21 April 2021 amending Directive 2010/43/EU as regards sustainability risks and sustainability factors to be taken into account for undertakings for collective investment in transferable securities (UCITS).

All these measures are to be transposed or implemented by 2 August 2022, with the exception of Delegated Directive (EU) 2021/1269, whose transposition deadline has been fixed for 22 November 2022.

With regard to the ESG securitisation matter, some scholars[62] may be sceptical as to how securitisations may qualify as ESG-tainted or, better, ESG-driven. In particular, the gist for investors as well as issuers is to grasp the real nature of marketable products – securitisations – and determine if a financial instrument can be considered suitable for the final users (the investors, by definition). Another point is the difficulty in qualifying a securitisation as green: in other words, it is not clear how sustainability criteria could be identified for a securitisation seeking to be qualified as green.

4.6.1 ESG structured finance within the EU framework

Quite unexpectedly, the ESG-securitisation concept was crystallised in the legislative securitisation framework long before the adoption of the "European Green Deal" and the "Action Plan on Financing Sustainable Growth" mentioned

62 There still is a dearth of official scholarly works on this subject. However, the relevant question seems to be reasonable.

above. On such grounds, reference is made to Regulation (EU) 2017/2402 (the "Securitisation Regulation"). More specifically, Recital 30 stipulates as follows:

> Where data on the environmental impact of assets underlying securitisations are available, the originator and sponsor of such securitisations should publish them. Therefore, the originator, the sponsor and the SSPE of an STS securitisation where the underlying exposures are residential loans or auto loans or leases should publish the available information related to the environmental performance of the assets financed by such residential loans or auto loans or leases.

Based on the tenor of Recital 30, it is possible to say that there is a flavour of sustainability within the Securitisation Regulation, rather than a driver. In 2017 and in the preceding years of discussion of this piece of legislation, sustainability was merely an opportunity entailed to the securitisation, whereas in the latest developments sustainability is becoming a major of goal of the financial market.[63] Nevertheless, from a legal point of view, the concept of ESG securitisation is still very nebulous, given the fact that "the EU taxonomy does not apply to securitisation transactions." Additionally, financial instruments, when issued by SPV, are not tantamount to "financial products," pursuant to the "SFDR," therefore the Regulation (EU) 2019/2088 (the "Sustainable Finance Disclosure Regulation").

Another indicator of an initial degree of sustainability is Art. 22(4): "In the case of a securitisation where the underlying exposures are residential loans or auto loans or leases, the originator and sponsor shall publish the available information related to the environmental performance of the assets financed by such residential loans or auto loans or leases, as part of the information disclosed pursuant to point (a) of the first subparagraph of Article 7(1)."

Since the Securitisation Regulation came into force, many regulations and provisions that, directly or indirectly, embody the concept of securitisation have been adopted. The most important ones are:

1. Regulation (EU) 2019/2088, (the "SFDR"), came into force on 10 March 2022. It applies to financial market participants but not to the bank.[64]
2. The combined framework of Regulation (EU) 2020/852, "EU Taxonomy Regulation" and Directive 2013/34/EU, "EU Non-Financial Reporting Directive."[65] This piece of legislation points to the criteria to adopt in order to regard certain business activities as "environmentally sustainable."

63 More recently, the same EBA, in its Report (EBA, *EBA Report on Developing a Framework for Sustainable Securitisation*, online), highlights that the market of sustainable structured finance transactions is becoming egregious.

64 Reference to this piece of EU legislation is made in other parts of this work.

65 In full: "Regulation (EU) 2020/852 of the European Parliament and of the Council of 18 June 2020 on the establishment of a framework to facilitate sustainable investment, and amending Regulation (EU) 2019/2088" (OJEU, 22 June 2020, L 198/13).

3. The Commission Delegated Regulation (C/2021/2800), headed "Taxonomy Climate Delegated Act," and the proposal for a regulation on "European Green Bonds".[66] This shall be aligned with the WU Taxonomy Regulation (European Green Bonds), which in its turn has to comply with the transparency and reporting standards, and has to be audited and registered with ESMA.[67]
4. The provisions set forth in the proposal of Art. 449 lett. a) "a description of their securitisation and resecuritisation activities, including their risk management and investment objectives in connection with those activities, their role in securitisation and resecuritisation transactions, whether they use the simple, transparent and standardised securitisation (STS) as defined in point (10) of Article 242, and the extent to which they use securitisation transactions to transfer the credit risk of the securitised exposures to third parties with, where applicable, a separate description of their synthetic securitisation risk transfer policy."

In Regulation (EU) 2021/557,[68] it is prescribed that, in order to integrate sustainability-related transparency requirements in Regulation (EU) 2017/2402, EBA, in conjunction with the other EU financial Authorities,[69]

> should be mandated to publish a report on developing a specific sustainable securitisation framework. That report should duly assess, in particular, the introduction of sustainability factors, the implementation of proportionate disclosure and due diligence requirements, the content, methodologies and presentation of information in relation to environmental, social and governance-related adverse impacts, and any potential effects on financial stability and on the scaling up of the Union securitisation market and of bank lending capacity. Based on that report, the Commission should submit a report to the European Parliament and to the Council on the creation of

66 In full, in its provisional version: "Commission Delegated Regulation (EU) [...] supplementing Regulation (EU) 2020/852 of the European Parliament and of the Council by establishing the technical screening criteria for determining the conditions under which an economic activity qualifies as contributing substantially to climate change mitigation or climate change adaptation and for determining whether that economic activity causes no significant harm to any of the other environmental objectives" (Document C(2021)2800).

67 In full: "Regulation (EU) 2020/852 of the European Parliament and of the council of 18 June 2020 on the establishment of a framework to facilitate sustainable investment, and amending Regulation (EU) 2019/2088" (OJEU, 22 June 2020, L 198/13).

68 In full: "Regulation (EU) 2021/557 of the European Parliament and of the Council of 31 March 2021 amending Regulation (EU) 2017/2402 laying down a general framework for securitisation and creating a specific framework for simple, transparent and standardised securitisation to help the recovery from the COVID-19 crisis" (OJEU, 6 April 2021, L 116/1).

69 Literally, the piece of legislation stipulates: "in close cooperation with the European Supervisory Authority (European Securities and Markets Authority) (ESMA), established by Regulation (EU) No 1095/2010 of the European Parliament and of the Council, and the European Supervisory Authority (European Insurance and Occupational Pensions Authority) (EIOPA), established by Regulation (EU) No 1094/2010 of the European Parliament and of the Council."

> a specific sustainable securitisation framework, together with a legislative proposal, if appropriate.[70]

Art. 1(1), par. 30, of Regulation (EU) 2021/557, refers to Art. 2(24) Regulation (EU) 2019/2088[71] for a definition of "sustainability factors," i.e. "environmental, social and employee matters, respect for human rights, anti-corruption and anti-bribery matters." In this way, the European Regulation 2021/557 highlights that, in order to complement the transparency requirements relating to sustainability, the ESBA in agreement with the EMA should be responsible for publishing a report on the development of a specific framework for sustainable securitisations. The report

> should duly assess, in particular, the introduction of sustainability factors, the implementation of proportionate disclosure and due diligence requirements, the content, methodologies and presentation of information in relation to environmental, social and governance-related adverse impacts, and any potential effects on financial stability and on the scaling up of the Union securitisation market and of bank lending capacity. Based on that report, the Commission should submit a report to the European Parliament and to the Council on the creation of a specific sustainable securitisation framework, together with a legislative proposal, if appropriate.[72]

The crucial aspect is the consideration that the disclosures to investors of both the integration of sustainability risks and the consideration of adverse sustainability

70 Recital 28 of the Securitisation Regulation. The subsequent Recital stipulates as follows: "Disclosures of the integration of sustainability risks and the consideration of adverse sustainability impacts on investment decision-making to investors are insufficiently developed because such disclosures are not yet subject to harmonised requirements. Pursuant to Regulation (EU) 2019/2088 of the European Parliament and of the Council, manufacturers of financial products and financial advisers to end-investors are obliged to consider the principal adverse impacts of investment decisions on sustainability factors, and to disclose how their due diligence policies take those principal adverse impacts into account. The disclosures of adverse sustainability impacts are accompanied by regulatory technical standards, which are jointly developed by EBA, ESMA and EIOPA (collectively, the 'European Supervisory Authorities') on the content, methodologies and presentation of the relevant information to be disclosed under Regulation (EU) 2019/2088. Originators of STS securitisations should also have the option to disclose specific information regarding the consideration of adverse impacts on sustainability factors, giving particular attention to climate and other environmental, social and governance-related impacts. To harmonise information disclosure and to ensure consistency between Regulation (EU) 2019/2088 and Regulation (EU) 2017/2402, the Joint Committee of the European Supervisory Authorities should develop regulatory technical standards, building as much as possible on their work in the context of Regulation (EU) 2019/2088 and adapting it, where necessary and relevant, to the specificities of securitisations."

71 "Regulation (EU) 2019/2088 of the European Parliament and of The Council of 27 November 2019 on sustainability-related disclosures in the financial services sector" (OJEU, 22 June 2020 L 198/13).

72 Recital 28.

impacts on investment decision-making "are insufficiently developed because such disclosures are not yet subject to harmonised requirements."[73]

Regulation (EU) 2021/557 involves the introduction of a new legal provision, that is Art. 45-*bis*, entitled "Development of a sustainable securitisation framework." The new legal provision stipulates as follows:

> By 1 November 2021, EBA, in close cooperation with ESMA and EIOPA, shall publish a report on developing a specific sustainable securitisation framework for the purpose of integrating sustainability-related transparency requirements into this Regulation. That report shall duly assess in particular: (a) the implementation of proportionate disclosure and due diligence requirements relating to potential positive and adverse impacts of the assets financed by the underlying exposures on sustainability factors; (b) the content, methodologies and presentation of information in respect of sustainability factors in relation to positive and adverse impacts on environmental, social and governance-related matters; (c) how to establish a specific sustainable securitisation framework that mirrors or draws upon financial products covered under Articles 8 and 9 of Regulation (EU) 2019/2088 and takes into account, where appropriate, Regulation (EU) 2020/852 of the European Parliament and of the Council; (d) possible effects of a sustainable securitisation framework on financial stability, the scaling up of the Union securitisation market and of bank lending capacity.[74]

The starting point of ESMA's report is the awareness that the current mosaic at "national" level on sustainable finance is heterogeneous. While work has been done in the field of non-financial information reported by listed companies as well as in relation to elements related to governance on product selling as part of ESMA's advice to the European Commission on integrating sustainability risks and factors in MiFID II, other areas have not been addressed yet. There are different starting points and ambitions at national level, as well as different levels of law with different possibilities of enforcement. In this context, there is the opportunity, as well as the imperative, to proactively build a common supervisory culture.[75]

73 Recital 29.

74 It is also specified (2): "In drafting the report referred to in paragraph 1 of this Article, EBA shall where relevant, mirror or draw upon the transparency requirements set out in Articles 3, 4, 7, 8 and 9 of Regulation (EU) 2019/2088 and seek input from the European Environment Agency and the Joint Research Centre of the European Commission. 3. In conjunction with the review report under Article 46, the Commission shall, based on the EBA report referred to in paragraph 1 of this Article, submit a report to the European Parliament and to the Council on the creation of a specific sustainable securitisation framework. The Commission's report shall, where appropriate, be accompanied by a legislative proposal."

75 ESMA, *Strategy on Sustainable Finance*, 6 February 2020 par. 3 Supervisory Convergence No. 9, p. 6.

To pursue the stated objective, ESMA highlighted the methodology that it will follow, namely:

> a. Developing a mapping of local supervisory practices and requirements relating to ESG factors; b. Building awareness amongst NCAs around the impact of ESG factors; c. Promoting the discussion of cases studies and supervisory practices regarding ESG factors; d. Developing tools to foster supervisory convergence of EU law in the ESG area.[76]

In the report being analysed, ESMA itself defined sustainable finance as "a new topic" which "requires a specific expertise mix that has not traditionally been found in financial market regulators. Equally, it is a transversal topic that cuts across all ESMA's existing activities. Communication on Sustainable Finance therefore needs to be a two-way exchange, with ESMA and the CNS seeking external expertise, as well as communicating on its planned work."[77]

Again, these norms do not explicitly contain any overall sustainability precepts, but rather an encouragement to make more explicit some sustainable implications of the investment in structured finance products. Therefore, STS securitisations and green securitisations cater for different goals, since the STS label "has been primarily designed to differentiate transparent and simple products from more opaque and complex securitisation products to make it easier for investors to understand and assess the risks of investing in securitisation."[78] By contrast, the purpose of a green securitisation is not different "from any other type of securitisation in terms of its structure."[79]

Despite the differences, some regulatory aspects of STS securitisations may be helpful to develop a more efficient ESG securitisation: the origination process; the servicing process; the standardisation of the documentation. In the light of this, to put it in the EBA view, although it is very likely that two different legislative frameworks will be put in place for STS (already existing) and green securitisations, "the process of obtaining an STS label and a potential green securitisation label could be streamlined for securitisations seeking both labels."[80]

76 From this perspective, the focus is on "mitigating risks of greenwashing, preventing mis-selling practices or misrepresentations and fostering transparency and reliability in the reporting of non-financial information: the objective is to develop guidelines or supervisory briefings to harmonise the supervisory practices of NCAs both when: (i) selecting the market participants, transactions and risks that are relevant from an ESG perspective; and (ii) when putting in place examination procedures aiming at identifying any areas of lack of compliance. The development of these tools is not necessarily intended to occur as a standalone exercise, but it may occur by incorporating considerations relating specifically to ESG aspects when updating existing supervisory convergence tools." ESMA, *Strategy on Sustainable Finance*, 6 February 2020, par. 3 Supervisory Convergence No. 11, 6–7.

77 ESMA, *Strategy on Sustainable Finance*, 6 February 2020 par. 6 Outreach/Communication, 11.

78 EBA, *EBA Report on Developing a Framework for Sustainable Securitisation*, online.

79 *ibidem*.

80 *ibidem*.

4.6.2 UK Securitisation Regulation and "unsustainable" finance

The UK onshored the EU Securitisation Regulation with effect from 1 January 2021 with a few minor changes. The same requirements of the EU Securitisation Regulation apply through the UK Securitisation Regulation.

At present, the UK legislative framework on securitisation does not refer to sustainability technical standards. Even so, on 24 June 2021, the HM Treasury issued a call for evidence to make a review of the securitisation legislation body in the UK. In this way, the UK government established the GTAG (Green Technical Advisory Group) set up for an initial period of two years in order to oversee the government's delivery of the UK green taxonomy framework. The ultimate goal is to develop criteria to be used to define investments as ESG.

The government's strategy aims to make the financial system green: the basic concept is mobilising finance for clean and resilient growth, and capturing the resulting opportunities for UK firms.

An important aspect to analyse involves the challenges that UK market-based finance must face. In the first stage, there are many difficulties in connection with mapping climate exposures due to voluntary disclosure and the subjective ESG approach. At the second level, the goal of cross-border activities may pave the way for the possibility of green avoidance and green evasion. In this way, in the absence of a Green Public Taxonomy or a credible and serious attitude to manage the investments, UK institutional investors suffer significant exposure to greenwashing.[81] The economies of scale existing between the Securitisation Regulation and the emerging ESG Securitisation are confirmed by due diligence: no additional investor due diligence requirements are necessary for securitisations specifically. As the Securitisation Regulation is already hinged upon due diligence requirements, it is very likely that the sustainability-related disclosures for securitisation, among the major aspects, "will enhance transparency regarding the ESG credentials of securitisation products and should therefore facilitate ESG due diligence assessment."[82]

4.6.3 Oxymorons and convergences between EU securitisations and regulation

Even in the absence of a specific regulation, ESG offerings have recently taken place in the synthetic securitisation market. In January 2020, West Bank and NatWest Markets arranged a £1.1 billion synthetic securitisation which referenced a pool of loans relating to offshore wind, solar, smart-meters, energy-from-waste and biomass power. A third-party provider verified the loans as being green.

81 D. Gabor, Y. Dafermos, M. Nikolaidi, P. Rice, F. van Lerven, R. Kerlslake, A. Pettifor, M. Jacobs, *Finance and Climate Change: A Progressive Green Finance Strategy for the UK. Report of the Independent Panel Commissioned by Shadow Chancellor of the Exchequer John McDonnell MP*, HMSO, London, 2019, 37 ff.

82 EBA, *EBA Report on Developing a Framework for Sustainable Securitisation*, online.

The following year, in February, Glennmont Partners completed a €1.3 billion synthetic risk transaction backed by a portfolio of project finance loans for solar, wind and bio-energy plants owned by Intesa SanPaolo.

The above examples show that, even in the absence of *ad hoc* regulation, structured green finance transactions can be carried out. The idea is that, if the end turns out be worthy of a positive assessment, it is possible to lay down adequate guidelines that allow investors to concretely carry out a green securitisation.

An empirical approach, from which regulation could take its cue, could be to carry out securitisation transactions not only for the construction of more sustainable housing but also for the construction of infrastructure.[83]

Sustainable credits could also arise from the purchase of new technology, such as SAPR mechanisms, to be used in the production chain. The reference goes to transport services in a broad sense, precision agriculture, but also surveillance of territories.

As in the wake of the financial crisis of 2007–2008, it can be seen that the securitisation phenomenon is taking place in unregulated legal territory. Based on the assumption that the rationale of securitisations is to create liquidity, overregulation of the phenomenon could make them less attractive. In this sense, therefore, the risk is that a parallel, alternative and more accessible market may be created to execute financial transactions.

In view of this, therefore, a less than stringent framework for ESG securitisations could only have positive aspects. According to this line of reasoning, a possibility would be to encourage the creation of liquidity[84] aimed at supporting the pursuit of sustainability and social solidarity objectives.

83 A.N. Zhilkina, O.N. Zhilkin, V.K. Krylov (2020) *Financial and Economic and Information Aspects of Smart City – AI at Citizens' Service*, in E. Popkova, B. Sergi (eds), *Artificial Intelligence: Anthropogenic Nature vs. Social Origin*, ISC Conference, Volgograd, 2020, Springer; I. Antenucci, 'Infrastructures of Extraction in the Smart City Zones, Finance, and Platforms in New Town Kolkata' (2021) *International Journal of Communication* 15, 2652–2668. In Italian, see P. de Gioia Carabellese, C. Della Giustina, 'Smart City: Innovazione, Infrastrutture e Smart Finance. Un Nuovo Parametro di Costituzione e di Digital Regulation' (2021) *Diritto e Politica dei Trasporti*, 68–87.

84 Some scholars point out that securitisation, as an economic-contractual technique, "often takes the form of a tranching process, with the successive tranches having different levels of risk and premiums, typically in a cash flow waterfall. This helps making the new issued securities more attractive to a wider array of private investors according to their risk-return profile. Overall, green securitisations may facilitate more efficient financing arrangements, by reducing transaction costs, increasing green project portfolios to a sufficient scale and attracting bondholders into the green market throughout a gamut of bespoke protection levels against insolvency risk and of diversified green projects." R. Agliardi, 'Green Securitisation' (2021) *Journal of Sustainable Finance & Investment*, 14–15.

4.7 From ESG factors to automated vehicles

The development of financial markets is closely related to the development of primary business activities. This has already been highlighted above,[85] where a description is provided of mortgages granted for plantations.[86]

From this concept arises the theory, unequivocally speculative, that securitisations could be potentially viewed as transactions connected with automated vehicles or drones.[87] This existence of this link is corroborated by a purposive "green" interpretation of the Securitisation Regulation. In a nutshell, the AV, which is currently regarded as the new paradigm of sustainability in multifarious business areas, could be transposed in the future into the urban environment, in order to be ultimately amalgamated in the broader concept of the smart city.[88]

The potential of AVs is concerned with various aspects: delivery; logistics; farm work; transport and so on. As far as farming is concerned,[89] AVs, either as aeroplanes or ground machines, should be further implemented in the management of 4.0 farms. Thus, the technology of UAVs (Unmanned Aerial Vehicles), cameras, including thermal cameras, already allow one to measure the

85 See Chapter 1.

86 J. Riley, *International Government Finance and the Amsterdam Capital Market 1740–1815*, Cambridge University Press, Cambridge, 1980; K.G. Rouwenhorst, *The Origins of Mutual Funds*, in W.N. Goetzmann, K. Geert Rouwenhorst, (eds), *Origins of Value*, Yale University Press, Yale, 2005. A similar position holds that financial innovation must be interpreted as a process of evolution, growth and improvement, the creation of which coincides with the establishment of the same market. In a historical perspective, it is recalled that the first derivatives were exchanged at the time of the Mesopotamian civilisation as a support for the exchange of agricultural goods and to insure against the risks of disasters that would starve the population. Added to this is that the first futures on wheat were the subject of exchange at the Temple and those who secure the success of the operation to be concluded were the religious representatives. C. Orlandi, 'I Derivati nella Politica Fiscale: una Time Bomb' (2005) *Rivista di Diritto Finanziario* 3, 340 ff.

87 Drone does bear a well-known literal meaning. Nevertheless, there is somehow a connection between the incubation (of the "original" drone) and the technological side of the "drone," i.e. the unmanned vehicles. This is why the two terms (automated machines and drones) are synonyms in this field of law.

88 V.S. Kenk, J. Krizaj, V. Struc, S. Dobrisek, 'Smart Surveillance Technologies in Border Control' (2013), *European Journal of Law and Technology*, 4.

89 P. Lottes, R. Khanna, J. Pfeifer, R. Siegwart, C. Stachniss, 'UAV-Based Crop and Weed Classification for Smart Farming' (2017) *IEEE International Conference on Robotics and Automation (ICRA)*, 3024–3031; A.D. Boursianis, M.S. Papadopoulou, P. Diamantoulakis, A. Liopa-Tsakalidi, P. Barouchas, G. Salahas, G. Karagiannidis, S. Wan, S.K. Goudos, 'Internet of Things (IoT) and Agricultural Unmanned Aerial Vehicles (UAVs) in Smart Farming: A Comprehensive Review' (2020) *Internet of Things*, 1–17; P.K.R. Maddikunta, S. Hakak, M. Alazab, S. Bhattacharya, T.R. Gadekallu, W.Z. Khan, Q.-Viet Pham, 'Unmanned Aerial Vehicles in Smart Agriculture: Applications, Requirements, and Challenges' (2021) *EEE Sensors Journal* 16, 17608–17619; G. Idoje, T. Dagiuklas, M. Iqbal, 'Survey for Smart Farming Technologies: Challenges and Issues' (2021) *Computers & Electrical Engineering*, 92, 1–14. As far as the UK is concerned, see M. Jaman, J. Vesey, P. Febre, *White Paper, UAVs for UK Agriculture: Creating an Invisible Precision Farming Technology*, 20 July 2016, 1–33.

temperature in the air as well as on the ground. Additionally, they are equipped with sensors of various types. Based on this, not only can one detect fumes and dust, but also it is possible, thanks to UAVs, to optimise natural resources through a constant monitoring and analysis system. All these features are instrumental in measuring the response to fertilisation and irrigation, even in connection with the impact that climate change may have on cultivations.[90]

In other words, thanks to the use of UAV mechanisms, it is possible to better manage any site-specific cultivation. In turn, this allows one to pursue not only a sustainable– thanks to the fact that it is carried out and implemented respecting the environment – but also a profitable activity.[91] This leads, on the one hand, to improved work efficiency, and on the other, to increased income for farmers. An empirical implementation relating to the potential "osmosis" and connection between sustainability and finance is the vertical farm.[92] To such an end, the vertical farm can be regarded as the epitome of hydroponic agriculture carried out in an artificial and supervised environment.[93] Vertical farms have several strengths, particularly taking into account that recurrent financial and environmental crises engender an issue of scarcity of resources.[94]

90 The literature on climate change is too vast to be compressed into a footnote. Nevertheless, reference can be made to K.R. Gray, R. Tarasofsky, C. Carlarne (eds), *The Oxford Handbook of International Climate Change Law*, Oxford University Press, Oxford, 2016; L. Rajamani, J. Peel (eds), *The Oxford Handbook of International Environmental Law*, 2nd ed., Oxford University Press, Oxford, 2021.

91 This is doable since the specific and timely needs of cultivations are detected by this new technology.

92 Although the vertical farm is a new concept, it is possible to define it as: "A multilayer indoor plant production system in which all growth factors, such as light, temperature, humidity, carbon dioxide concentration, water, and nutrients, are accurately controlled to produce high quantities of high-quality fresh produce year-round, completely independent of solar light and other outdoor conditions." See M. Sharath Kumar, E. Heuvelink, L.F.M. Marcelis, 'Vertical Farming: Moving from Genetic to Environmental Modification' (2020) *Trends in Plant Science*25(8), 724–727. More generally, vertical farms are divided according to size and purpose of use: 1) plant factory with artificial lighting (PFAL), an industrial-scale vertical farm located in a devoted building; 2) container farm, a modular vertical farm contained in a shipping container; 3) in-store farm, a vertical farm located at the place of consumption or purchase (i.e. retail and restaurants); 4) appliance farm, a vertical farm appliance integrated into a home or office (M. Butturini, L.F.M. Marcelis, *Vertical Farming in Europe*. In T. Kozai, G. Niu, M. Takagaki (eds), *Plant Factory*, Elsevier, Amsterdam, 2020, 77–91.

93 This definition has been conceived by Professor G.E. Bailey. This is recalled by K. Al-Kodmany, 'The Vertical Farm: A Review of Developments and Implications for the Vertical City' (2018) *Buildings* 24(8), 2 ff.

94 On the issue of the scarcity of resources, see P. Rozin, 'The Selection of Foods by Rats, Humans, and Other Animals' (1976) *Advances in the Study of Behavior*, online. In general, regarding the vertical farm, see K. Bohn, A. Viljoen, 'The Edible City: Envisioning the Continuous Productive Urban Landscape (CPUL)' (2012) *Field Journal* 1, 149 ff.; J. de Anda, H. Shear, 'Potential of Vertical Hydroponic Agriculture in Mexico' (2017) *Sustainability* 1, 1 ff.; D. Despommier, *The Vertical Farm: Feeding the World in the 21st Century*, Macmillan, London, 2011; D. Despommier, *Vertical Farms in Horticulture*, in P.B. Thompson, D.M. Kaplan (eds), *Encyclopedia of Food and Agricultural Ethics*, Springer, Dordrecht, 2014, 1783 ff.; S. Walters, K. Stoelzle Midden, 'Sustain-

In view of this, the vertical farm concept may cater for an opportunity, if not a solution. First, vertical farms make it possible to tackle the risk of malnutrition, or even of starvation, because healthy food is produced with an increased output of resources and, on top of that, sustainably. In essence, via vertical farming the uncertainties connected with nature and its biological circles are minimised. Likewise, the historical issue of the scarcity of soil is more than compensated by this new agricultural technology, which is possible to define as "agri-tech." Within the broader theme of the scarcity of resources, the adjacent issue of the scarcity of water is likewise addressed. In essence, this saves the water that, in normal conditions and following a traditional system, would be used both for irrigation and during the ensuing phase of crop washing.[95]

Second, these structures rely on a huge quantity of energy, because they are based on LED lighting and, more generally, a techno-engineering system which is propelled by traditional, then over-consuming, sources of energy.[96] Hence, it is necessary to ensure that the functioning of such a structure is guaranteed via renewable sources of energy. To such an end, entrepreneurs would be interested in having access to liquidity, therefore financial sources. The ultimate purpose of this would be to lay down the foundations of a real sustainable green business.[97] It is clear, in this scenario, that entailed in this new business are profitable "flows" of future money – receivables in the legal language of finance – and these flows/receivables may certainly lend themselves to the purposes of securitisations.[98]

---

ability of Urban Agriculture: Vegetable Production on Green Roofs' (2018) *Agriculture* 11, 1 ff.; S. Shekhar Solankey, S. Akhtar, A.I.L. Maldonado, H. Rodriguez-Fuentes, J.A. Vidales Contreras, J.M. Márquez Reyes, *Urban Horticulture*, IntechOpen, 2021.

95 This is because they are ready to eat.

96 In a possibly near future, the management of these resources would originate from artificial beings, or artificial agents, managed on remote basis via Wi-Fi or, more generally, in a remote way. In the most futuristic scenario, the delivery of goods via "drones" may be conceived, also in order to reduce pollution.

97 Nowadays, there are still uncertainties as to whether the produce of this new concept of farming is genuine and whether, from a different perspective, other issues, at the moment not visible, may be unleashed by this new concept of farming.

98 The possible *file rouge* between ecology and securitisation is given by the Danish market and pieces of research carried out in Denmark (D. Despoina Avgoustaki and G. Xydis, 'Indoor Vertical Farming in the Urban Nexus Context: Business Growth and Resource Savings' (2020) *Nature*, 12, online). According to OECD statistics, Denmark emitted approximately 51,620 tons of GH gases in 2016. In fact, according to a WWF report (2014) (WWF Report, WWF: Denmark Has World's Fourth Largest Ecological Footprint. Available online: http://cphpost.dk/news/international/wwf-denmark-has-worlds-fourth-largest-ecological-footprint.html (accessed on 15 November 2019)), Denmark's ecological footprint per capita is the fourth largest in the world after Qatar, Kuwait, and the United Arabs Emirates. In 2014, Gitte Seeberg, the Secretary General of WWF Denmark, stated in a newspaper that the Danish nation consists of roads, cities and wheat fields, but one of the main problems is the lack of biodiversity in Denmark. Adding to this, the Danes' high meat consumption is one of the biggest reasons for its large ecological footprint. Finally, Global Footprint Network has calculated that Denmark has a bio-capacity per person of 4.4 global hectares (gha) and an ecological footprint of 6.7 gha per person. Furthermore, it states that until 2014, the ecological footprint versus the bio-capacity in Denmark was 40,246,094 gha. Clearly, there is

The application of UAVs[99] to the farming world, therefore, makes the concept of sustainability highly valuable. Pursuant to Recital 1, heading "Proposal for a Directive of the European Parliament and of the Council on Corporate Sustainability Due Diligence and Amending Directive (EU) 2019/1937,"[100] the European Union is founded, literally, on the respect of human dignity, democracy, equality and human rights: all these principles shall also be implemented in all businesses. Ultimately, it is clear that sustainability encompasses protection of the environment, with its broader ecosystem, but also the rights and values of the human being whilst carrying out business activities.

From this perspective, the possibility of using drones shall be deemed applicable to different entrepreneurial areas – not only to the agricultural sector, but also to those areas with a potential high level of risk for human beings. In keeping on this trajectory, reference shall be made, first and foremost, to remotely piloted aeroplanes, but also to autonomous vehicles in a broad sense. The thesis which shall be put forward in this part of the work is that an entrepreneur might have an interest in setting up a securitisation transaction in order to effectively achieve safety conditions in their workplace. Through the lenses of this possible

an immediate need for change in food production, distribution and consumption in the country. Research conducted by Tropp (D. Tropp, Why Local Food Matters: The Rising Importance of Locally-Grown Food in the US Food System (No. 160752); United States Department of Agriculture, Agricultural Marketing Service, Transportation and Marketing Program: Washington, DC, USA, 2019) shows that demand for fresh, locally grown food was almost $12 billion in 2014, and was projected to reach $20 billion by 2019. Commercial GHs are the major sources of fresh, locally grown food for cities. For this reason, the annual growth rate of these businesses reached 8.8% in 2016, and the market's growth forecast is expected to exceed $29.64 billion by 2020. GH production is the oldest form of controlled farming, where plants can be cultivated in an isolated environment, which is partly independent of the outdoor weather conditions. GH production is an intensive cultivation method that uses air management techniques as well as cooling and heating processes to produce high crop yields. In recent years, GH growers have started to install artificial lighting and hydroponic cultivation methods that can further increase the yield of crops and reduce their water footprint. There are no detailed literature studies linking the need for indoor urban vertical farming (IUVF) facilities in areas with a lack of solar energy, which is vital for food production (40% average sunshine percentage from April to September and around 20% the rest of the year (weather-and-climate.com)). In 2017, the import value of vegetables and fruits to Denmark amounted to roughly DKK 11.2 billion, which equals a rise of 22.81% over the last 10 years Statista Denmark: Import of Goods from 2007 to 2017. Available online: https://www.statista.com/statistics/318299/import-of-goods-to-denmark/ (accessed on 15 November 2019). In other words, Denmark imports between 24,450 and 27,850 tons of fresh fruits and vegetables annually. The country has some of the highest electricity prices in Europe, but at the same time, a very high level of renewable energy (mainly wind energy) connected to the main grid. The combination of IUVF with renewable energy and batteries can lead to a radical decrease of system energy costs.

99 S.A. Kaiser, 'UAV's: Their Integration into Non-Segregated Airspace' (2011) *Air and Space Law* 2, 161–172; U. Volovelsky, 'Civilian Uses of Unmanned Aerial Vehicles and the Threat to the Right of Privacy – An Israeli Case Study' (2014) *Computer Law & Security Review* 3, 306–420; W. Elder, 'Preparing for the Swarm: Ensuring Our Airwaves and Airspace can Accommodate Transformational Commercial Drone Technology' (2014) *Computer and Telecommunications Law Review* 5, 123–126.

100 2022/0051 (COD).

interpretation, unmanned vehicles would be instrumental in minimising the possible occurrence of risks in the workplace. The potential of this new technology may also reduce death rates as well as the injuries that can result from work accidents: falls in construction sites; exposure to chemical and toxic substances; accidents resulting from the use of dangerous machinery.

If this interpretation is correct, it should be taken for granted that there are UAVs which, if implemented under certain conditions, may ensure that working conditions are less burdensome for human beings.[101] Although this is correct, it should not be forgotten that the use of the AVs, *per se*, also means incurring risks.[102]

These risks relate to the total absence of human control, the use of algorithms and the design of evolving software that may adversely impact on the proper use of autonomous or semi-autonomous machines. Notwithstanding this, admittedly, the greatest and most obvious risk affects the protection of the privacy and personal data of workers. The latter conundrum becomes even more serious given the fact that technology used to control a drone[103] could result in capturing confidential information, such as images, conversations, sounds. Ultimately, the right of confidentiality of the filmed individuals could be in jeopardy.

Furthermore, this issue reaches out to an even wider scope, in circumstances where remotely piloted aerial systems are guided by artificial intelligence technology. In this scenario, there would be, on the one hand, a gigantic amount of data – this is due to the enhanced storage capacity of the technologies – and on the other, these pieces of information would be processed by "big data analytics" systems. A further major problem stems from the use of algorithms which can give rise to unpredictable situations, particularly in circumstances where the acquired data can be reshuffled.[104]

The incessant technological evolution and the possible combinations that can be achieved in the intertwined and interchangeable liaison between technology, digitalisation and economy may even lead to "drones" being qualified as "destructive technology."[105] This terminology, strong indeed, would be disruptive, as it would forge, thanks to the most advanced technologies of the contemporary

101 J. Howard, V. Murashov, C.M. Branche, 'Unmanned Aerial Vehicles in Construction and Worker Safety' (2018) *American Journal of Industrial Medicine* 61, 3–10.

102 K. Paroha, 'Automated Vehicles: Liability, Intangibles & Satellite Litigation' (2019) *New Law Journal* 169, 20 ff.; N. Bevan, 'Driverless Vehicles: Future Perfect? Part 2' (2018) *New Law Journal* 168, 10–12; Insurance Law Monthly (editorial), 'Motor Vehicle Insurance: Autonomous Vehicle' (2017) *Insurance Law Monthly*, Apr, 1–2; C. Darling, 'Autonomous Vehicle Consultation: Are We in the Right Lane?' (2021) *Computer Law & Security Review*, 41.

103 Usually, the technology controlling the drone is also the one owning it.

104 D. Sella-Villa, 'Drones and Data: A Limited Impact on Privacy' (2021) *University of Richmond Law Review* 55, 991–1069; L. Zhu, R. Yu, Y. Wang, B. Ning, T. Tang, 'Big Data Analytics in Intelligent Transportation System Survey' (2019) *IEEE Transactions on Intelligent Transportation Systems* 20, 383 ff.

105 J.L. Bower, C.M. Christensen, 'Disruptive Technologies: Catching the Wave' (1995) *Harvard Business Review* 73(1), ss. 43–53.

economy, a new definition of entrepreneur. As Schumpeter pointed out, such an entrepreneur is not an individual "who carries out economic operations, intending to make a profit, but [...] one who introduces innovative acts."[106] A purposive, evolutionary interpretation of destructive technologies, potentially associated with destructive innovation, comes from authors[107] who pointed out that few technologies can be defined as effectively disruptive. The crucial aspect, on the contrary, relates to the type of business that these technologies make it possible to implement.

Adding in the concept of surveillance[108] makes the link between securitisation and autonomous vehicles even more evident. Obviously, this outcome should be fitted into a much broader school of thought according to which personal data are endowed with an economic and financial value, thus engendering the postulation that they can become the subject matter of a securitisation transaction.

This further evolution of financial transactions, as depicted in this chapter, may well run a risk: a dangerous drift of the evolution of video surveillance systems, especially in relation to the fundamental rights of private individuals.[109] The connection just highlighted accentuates, in an even greater way, the potential "reification" of the individual in front of the progressive expansion of technological means.

A new scenario could unfold thanks to the role played by either Uber or, more generally, any other owners of platforms of semi-autonomous vehicles or autonomous vehicles. This generates not only a potential labour law problem, but also a privacy issue that concerns the users of such services. Specifically, if we are to admit that personal data can become the subject matter of securitisations, the funding of the platform economy could originate from personal data securitisations. This new and different variety of securitisation may well become instrumental to the purchase of autonomous vehicles. Ultimately, this would turn out to be the sustainable "car," i.e. a "green" form of transportation. Nevertheless, these optimistic conclusions beg some burning questions. The first is whether and

106 J. Schumpeter, *Capitalism, Socialism and Democracy*, Harper, New York, 1942.

107 J.L. Bower, C.M. Christensen, 'Disruptive Technologies: Catching the Wave' (1995) *Harvard Business Review*, online.

108 In essence, because personal data are valuable, the relevant surveillance may become a business model. R.C. Picker, *Online Advertising, Identity and Privacy*, Working Paper n. 475/2009, University of Chicago Law and Economics, 2009, 6.

109 About the problem of data protection and AV, see M.C. Gaeta, 'Data Protection and Self-driving Cars: The Consent to the Processing of Personal Data in Compliance with GDPR' (2019) *Communications Law* 1, 15–23; T. Mulder, N.E. Vellinga, 'Exploring Data Protection Challenges of Automated Driving' (2021) *Computer Law & Security Review* 40(Apr), online; R.L. Finn, D. Wright, 'Unmanned Aircraft Systems: Surveillance, Ethics and Privacy in Civil Applications' (2021) *Computer Law & Security Review* 2, 184–194; B. Walker Smith, 'The Trolley and the Pinto: Cost-Benefit Analysis in Automated Driving and Other Cyber-Physical Systems' (2017) *Texas A&M Law Review* 4, 197–208.

how this new model could protect both humans and workers,[110] particularly those wearing a human "jersey."[111] Second, this model, whose potential neo-liberal ramifications may not be totally ruled out, is capable of sparking off new financial speculation. However, the usual dilemma, hyperregulation versus hyporegulation, still remains food for thought for perennial discussions, as well as being a necessary trade-off that the lawmakers need to strike.

110 Needless to say, the use of the term "work" is according to its broad sense which has been used for decades in the British legal literature, as well as in the British statute. Therefore, this would encompass the employee too. In the relevant legal literature, see N. Le Thu, 'Legal Considerations for Determination of Employment Relation and Employment Contract' (2021) *VNU Journal of Science: Legal Studies* 37(2), 42–48; S. Deakin, G.S. Morris, *Labour Law*, Hart Publishing, Oxford and Portland, 2009; Z. Adams, C. Barnard, S. Deakin, S.F. Butlin, *Deakin and Morris' Labour Law*, 7th ed., Hart Publishing, Oxford, New York, Dublin, 2021, 124–129. More generally, see D. Cabrelli, *Employment Law in Context: Text and Materials*, 4th ed., Oxford University Press, Oxford, 2021; P. de Gioia Carabellese, 'The Employee Shareholder: The Unbearable Lightness of Being… An Employee in Britain' (2015) *Maastricht Journal of European and Comparative Law* 22, 81–95; S.Y. Ching Leung, 'How Do Statutes "Speak" in Recent Technology Advancement Cases?' (2021) *Statute Law Review* 20, 1–15; E. Mcgaughey, 'Uber, the Taylor Review, Mutuality and the Duty Not to Misrepresent Employment Status' (2019) *Industrial Law Journal* 48, 180–198; P. Larkin, *Relationship between Employment Status and Scope of Social Security Protection: The United Kingdom Example*, in U. Becker, O. Chesalina (eds.) *Social Law 4.0: New Approaches for Ensuring and Financing Social Security in the Digital Age*, Nomos, Baden, 2021; G. Davidov, 'The Goals of Regulating Work: Between Universalism and Selectivity' (2014) *University of Toronto Law Journal* 64(1), 1–35; S. Fredam, 'One Small Step Towards Decent Work: Uber v. Aslam in the Court of Appeal' (2019) *Industrial Law Journal* 48(2), 274; A. Rosenblat, L. Stark 'Algorithmic Labor and Information Asymmetries: A Case Study of Uber's Drivers' (2016) *International Journal of Communication* 10, online; R. Upex, 'Workers and the Gig Economy: An Appraisal of the Supreme Court's Decision in the Uber Case' (2021) *Coventry Law Journal* 26(1), 25–38; A. Lambert, P. Summerfield, 'UK Supreme Court Delivers Verdict in Uber Case' (2021) *Compliance and Risk* 10, 8–10; M. Ford QC, 'The Death of Contract in Determining Employment Status' (2021) *Law Quarterly Review* 137, 392–399; Z. Adams, 'One Step Forwards for Employment Status, Still Some Way to Go: The Supreme Court's Decision in Uber v Aslam under Scrutiny' (2021) *Cambridge Law Journal* 80(2), 221–225; D. Brodie, 'Confronting the Gig Economy' (2021) *Judicial Review* 2, 103–108; S. Yee, C. Leung, 'How Do Statutes "Speak" in Recent Technology Advancement Cases?' (2021) *Statute Law Review* 20, 1 ff.

111 See in this chapter above.

5 From fintech to agritech

5.1 Securitisations and *lex argentaria*

Emphasis has been placed, particularly in the first chapter, on the fact that securitisations originate from, and to a certain extent still belong to, the realm of specific legal systems that are quite different from those existing on the "Continent." These are the common law systems, where a civil code is commonly missing, and the legislation, particularly in contract law, is sparse.

From this perspective, it is even simplistic to note that securitisations are economic transactions, rather than contracts: as such, it is arduous to characterise them as belonging to a specific category. It is well known that civil law jurists have a penchant for the characterisation of any kind of agreement, and this effort of qualification of the transaction may result in being totally unhelpful, or misleading, for contracts imported from a common law perspective.

Both the USA and the UK, not coincidentally common law jurisdictions, are countries where these transactions have been blossoming for decades. It happens quite frequently that the passive import of transactions, via a "copy-and-paste" mechanism, may have dramatic consequences.[1] Although it is difficult to establish the causal link existing between structured finance transactions and financial cri-

1 The literature on this is vast: among others, see P. Legrand, 'Comparative Legal Studies and the Matter of Authenticity', Legal Studies Research Paper, Series Research Paper No. 08-071 (September 2008), *Journal of Comparative Law*, 367. It is emphasised as follows: "As long as it remains driven by the entrenched urge to confine its analytical framework to the identification of 'sameness' in the formulation of statutes or the outcome of judicial decisions across jurisdictions, comparative legal studies have little to offer legal theory other than the pseudoscientific respectability connected with institutional fetishism. In fact, this brand of comparative research is positively misleading in the way it propounds the presence of commonalities across legal 'systems' which can exist solely at the most superficial level and are therefore devoid of epistemological value. For example, the matrix of associative context that energises usage in any given law can be replicated into another law only partly, and only by virtue of periphrastic and metaphrastic manoeuvres which, not unlike the translation of a poem, downgrade the intensity, the evocative means, the formal autonomy of the original. This is why any purportedly 'universal' grammar of law is fatally, and damagingly, reductionist. This is why every uniformising ideology intent on sweeping away undesirable elements can legitimately appear terrifying, no matter how chaste it sounds" (*ibidem*).

DOI: 10.4324/9780429293436-5

sis, nonetheless the cultural gap with Continental Europe concerning agreements manufactured elsewhere may cause two issues. On the one hand, the legal system where the organ has been transplanted may suffer from clinical rejection and, on the other hand, given the lack of understanding of the contracts and/or economic transactions within the importing system, there might be financial distress on the players of the legal system where these economic transactions are going to take place.[2]

The contractual safeguards that traditionally have been envisaged for securitisations are hinged upon corrective "tools," although, paradoxically, they come from the opposite jurisdictions and/or legal systems. The legal opinions as well as the role of the credit rating agency have not proved effective, because these antidotes were, and to a certain extent still are, extraneous and opaque to the parties which theoretically they should protect. Upon closer reflection, these tools are knee jerk reactions of the "body"; they do not reflect what is sociologically a different environment.[3]

Connected with the first point is the observation that a stringent regulation of EU origin, such as that on the STS Securitisation, is merely an attempt to both develop and fetter – and the juxtaposition is not used coincidentally here – a

2 See again P. Legrand, 'European Legal System Are not Converging' (1996) *International and Comparative Law Quartely* 54(1), 55–56. It is observed as follows: "There are, however, serious difficulties with an approach which focuses on posited law in order to draw conclusions regarding the convergence of legal systems. In my view, neither rules nor concepts reveal as much about a legal system as appears to be assumed. Rules, for example, are largely ephemeral and inevitably contingent. They are brittle. For this reason there is relatively little in law-as-rules that has universal merit or that transcends jurisdictional boundaries. Therefore, whether they be legislative or judicial in origin, rules are pernicious to the extent that they present but a surface image of a legal system. Likewise, concepts are deficient for they are peremptory instruments used by lawyers in order to 'know' a reality which, in any respect apart from its ontological existence, is inevitably a consequence of their own representations and may not, therefore, coincide with them: a concept must of necessity be relative and, therefore, subjective because every concept, by being a concept, implies a derivation. Accordingly, rules and concepts alone actually tell one very little about a given legal system and reveal even less about whether two legal systems are converging or not. They may provide one with much information about what is apparently happening, but they indicate nothing about the deep structures of legal systems. Specifically, rules and concepts do little to disclose that legal systems are but the surface manifestation of legal cultures and, indeed, of culture tout court. In other words, they limit the observer to a 'thin description' and foreclose the possibility of the 'thick description' that the analyst ought to regard as desirable."

3 P. Legrand, 'Comparative Legal Studies and Commitment to Theory' (1995) *Modern Law Review* 58(2), 265–266. Namely: "The law derives from historical experience. So do the forms that the law embraces. Legal practices are not simple acts of accumulation and acquisition that would have taken place over the years or centuries. It would be absurdly reductionist to see legal practices as the mere formulation of rules. What accretion of elements one sees is supported by impressive ideological formations. The law in its many manifestations is an incorporative cultural form. Just as culture is a source of identity, legal practices are a source of identity. They encode experiences. To my mind, legal practices are very much a reflection of a given culture and of a given legal mentality (in the sense of the interiorised culture). They reveal an implicit structure of attitude and reference, or a way of experiencing legal order."

phenomenon which does not belong to the European economic culture, hence the distortions that may be observed on some occasions, all highlighted in this work. What the 2007–2008 financial crisis, and the following responses to them, show in the legislation on securitisations in Europe is the dearth of sociological and economic amalgamation and integration among legal systems.

The need for an integrated *lex argentaria* – a communal and global set of rules in the area of banks, investment firms and financial markets, which does not affect the different legal systems but rather stands above them – is probably what still makes the transactions at stake unfulfilled and potentially detrimental not only to financial markets, but also to societies.

In this respect, the answer provided by the EU legislature may be regarded as too harsh and disproportionate. The recent Securitisation Regulation has simply subjected a market – the securitisation market – belonging to a completely different economic and socio-legal culture to a watchdog. The animals used to run free in the past, whereas now, simply because a threat is felt, they should be observant and obedient all of a sudden.

Whether or not the beasts have really changed their temperament, while seeming to turn into mild characters, does not appear to be a question the EU legislature has asked itself. More generally, the socio-legal differences existing in different countries and their relevant legal systems[4] may certainly mislead the legislature of a country where a new legal concept is expected to be shaped and implemented.

The practical and in-field experience of green securitisations,[5] such as in the finalisation of project financing for solar, wind and bio-energy plants conceived and managed by a major bank,[6] shows that the implementation of this kind of transaction is possible even without "strong" regulation. Thus, regulation does not result in always being necessary in order to implement a "genuine" structured finance transaction, whereas leaving a certain degree of autonomy to the parties

4 Some observations from the literature are worthy of a brief summary: "No form of words purporting to be a 'rule' can be completely devoid of a semantic content, for no rule can be without meaning. The meaning of the rule is an essential component of the rule; it partakes in the ruleness of the rule. The meaning of a rule, however, is not entirely supplied by the rules itself; a rule is never totally self-explanatory. To be sure, meaning emerges from the rule so that it must be assumed to exist, if virtually, within the rule itself even before the interpreter's interpretive apparatus is engaged. To this extent, the meaning of a rule is acontextual. But meaning is also – and perhaps mostly – a function of the application of the rule by its interpreter, of the concretisation or instantiations in the events the rule is meant to govern. This ascription of meaning is predisposed by the way the interpreter understands the context within which the rule arises and by the manner in which she frames her questions, the process being largely determined by who and where the interpreter is and, therefore, to an extent at least, by what she, in advance, wants and expects (unwittingly?) the answer to be. Hence, the meaning of the rule is a function of the interpreter's epistemological assumptions which are themselves historically and culturally conditioned." P. Legrande, *What "Legal Transpants?"* in D. Nelken, J. Feest (eds), *Adapting Legal Cultures*, Hart Publishing, Oxford, 2001, 57–58.

5 See Chapter 4 above.

6 Again, the case study of Intesa Sanpaolo.

and, more generally, to the "securitisers" may even boost the effectiveness, from a non-legal point of view, of a green securitisation.

From a different perspective, it is also possible to observe that the term securitisation is becoming a word of a multifarious nature. In some EU countries, the term is conceived to refer to any transaction whereby assets, usually non-performing loans, are transferred from an owner, coincidentally a public body, to a vehicle, to ensure that the former may turn around. From this perspective, the securitisation, otherwise the quintessential private law transaction, loses its original character to become a public conduit used to solve financial issues of public bodies.

Although all these pieces of legislation make the term fashionable, they are also prejudicial to the *ratio essendi* of the legal concept. If questioned on the nature of these transactions, a jurist would answer in very different ways, according to where they operate and are specialised. The proliferation of the genera of securitisations may ultimately mark the end of these transactions, at least in the way they were originally conceived.

The EU legislature has come up with the idea of a niche STS market of securitisations; however, because this market does not benefit from the exclusivity clause, dangerous "beasts" are still roaring elsewhere. In still keeping with the metaphor, the STS securitisation may be like a zoo of few animals both on the verge of extinction and with chains, whereas the serious beasts are causing trouble in the real world. The lack of a *fil-rouge* of a securitisation contractual framework is the real gap that the EU Securitisation Regulation has not yet filled (and which perhaps the EU legislature will never fill).

From a more optimistic perspective, the concept of the smart city[7] could be helpful in order to ensure that the last rites do not need to be given to a piece of legislation which is comparatively new, insofar as it is associated with a more innovative use of international structured finance transactions. Sustainability – a concept that, more recently, seems to have become both the mantra and the panacea of global issues – may well become a more optimal way to rejuvenate securitisations. Thus, a portfolio of receivables of a sustainable nature, pertaining to properties belonging to those who reside in a "smart city," would be a more credible target for the whole market of these transactions.

5.2 Heterodox securitisations: automated machines and vertical farming

Emphasis has been placed, in various parts of this work, on the fact that the "nucleus" of a securitisation is the risk segmentation. If this is correct, there has been a transition, thanks to the structured finance transactions, from a traditional conception of a bank to a new, digitalised conception. In this process, securitisations may be interpreted as *ante litteram* digitalised transactions. Thus, given

7 Dissected and analysed in Chapter 4 above.

the digital dimension of securitisations, financial advisors and, more generally, securitisers may also become, in the near future, entities of a completely different nature. In fact, according to this line of reasoning, the digitalisation form may take over both the *modus operandi* and the very nature of corporate bodies, as least in the way they are conceived.

Once securitisers are perceived in a pure digital form, their synthetic nature may pose further questions, as to how both their responsibilities and their certification roles, particularly those made compulsory by the EU Securitisation Regulation, will be interpreted and re-assessed. Securitisations where human beings are replaced with artificial "lives" may evoke the setting of a film, perhaps a horror film, in which – also in the light of the EU Securitisation Regulation – on the one hand, the relevant "actors" are formally recognised and therefore "act" and perform on the stage, but on the other hand, their liability for the damages that they potentially cause may become unclear.

Maybe, in contemplating a future litigation arising out of this, the liability will be on the "producer" (beyond the metaphor the arranger) to ensure that a mere robot does not turn out to be the "scape-goat," *de facto* totally irresponsible vis-à-vis a Court.

Based on the above, two unorthodox typologies of securitisations – the 4.0 and 5.0 structured finance transactions – can be traced in a forward-looking economic scenario, as well as pursuant to an evolutionary exegesis of this niche area of research.

Tentatively, the first type (the 4.0) will be the personal data transaction, whereas the second (the 5.0) is the one managed, in its entirety, by synthetic players. The latter will exclusively rely on the transfer of personal data, where the ultimate purpose is the completion of a smart city or smart society. Accordingly, "smart-securitisation" may be the right way to "baptise" this second type of new structured finance transaction.

As far as the technological way to achieve this potential new transaction is concerned, this may be identified in the QR code. This system is hinged upon the management, in a synthetic way, of personal data which are transferred to ensure that a smart city, or in fact a smart society, can be implemented. In this "mosaic," the piece of personal data becomes a loan to be assigned to a third party, the SPV. The way the personal data will be transferred, in a more heterodox model of securitisation, is via a QR code.[8] The "*green caveat*" of this techno-oriented securitisa-

8 It is not too speculative to affirm that in the future the QR code will be to securitisation what the smart card was initially to the payment of commercial transactions. In the latest literature on the smart card, from its legal point of observation, see P. Nelson, 'Smart Cards – The Time Is Nigh' (1996) *Mortgage Finance Gazette* 128(1559), 28–29; I. Giannopoulou, 'The Evolution of Smart Cards: The Moneo Test' (2004) *Hertfordshire Law Journal* 2(1), 55–61; R. Farbrother, 'Profiting from Smart Cards' (1994) *Mortgage Finance Gazette* 126(1543), 42, 44–45; S. Marek, 'Smart Cards: Has Their Time Come at Last?' (1993) *Scottish Banker*, Feb, 2–5; S. Geiregat, 'Cryptocurrencies Are (Smart) Contracts' (2018) *Computer Law & Security Review* 34(5), 1144–1149; D. Hodgkinson, 'Smart Money versus Cash' (2006) *Electronic Business Law* 8(11), online; N. Yeo,

tion is the "green nature" of the underlying purpose of the loan, that is to say the fact that the loan has an environmental purpose. Admittedly, this ultra-synthetic securitisation seems to be partly reminiscent of a peer-to-peer mechanism of lending. In fact, although these kinds of transactions are still potential rather than actual, their characterisation as mixed transactions is the likely outcome of their legal perusal as things currently stand.

To sketch out the contours of this heterodox securitisation, a few points are worthy of further analysis.

In the last ten years, peer-to-peer business has interfered with banking activity, particularly that of lending money. This has unleashed a *de facto* competition of individuals, and entities too, both outside the supervisory perimeter of the regulator, against traditional banks. The strength of these centrifugal forces has been so great as to shake the foundations of the traditional banking sector.

Likewise, heterodox securitisation, as an unconventional form of structured finance transaction, in cases where it related to personal data to be assigned with a high degree of velocity via a QR code, could be regarded as a new financial phenomenon, namely a peer-to-peer securitisation.

Upon reflection, not only is there a risk of control and supervision of the securitisation – which is fundamentally the goal of the EU Securitisation Regulation – but also the prospective securitisation may lead to a bubble. Such a bubble is of a speculative nature (the financial loss that the seller of the peculiar receivables, the personal data, may incur), but also includes the damages that she/he, as a human being, may suffer from.[9] To elaborate, since the seller is transferring not simply money, there are a number of bubbles that can result.

'The Legal Statement on Cryptoassets and Smart Contracts: An Extremely Useful Baseline from Which to further Develop the Law and Regulation' (2020) *Butterworths Journal of International Banking & Financial Law* 35(3), 147–151; J. Moules, 'Smart Issuers Rival Banks' (1998) *Banker* 148(872), 100–102. While smart cards are now taken for granted, this was not the case nearly three decades ago, when there was still an oligopoly of credit institutions in this area. See P.W. Lobl, J. Wolff, 'Smart Cards – Why Their Use Should Be Regulated' (1997) *Journal of International Banking Law* 12, 263–265. It is expressly emphasised:

"Governments should at least consider regulating the issuance of smart cards by non-bank institutions. Before such institutions are authorised to issue smart cards, they will need to convince the applicable government agencies that the business of selling smart cards does not constitute a banking activity. Assuming these institutions posit an ultimately convincing argument therefore, government agencies will need to address consequent consumer protection issues. If non-bank institutions may issue smart cards, the value stored on these cards may be no more secure than the financial position of the issuing company. Suppose a customer were to purchase a smart card from an issuer who later becomes insolvent and goes bankrupt. No merchant is thereafter likely to accept for payment any smart card issued by this bankrupt issuer. The smart card holder may possess a claim against the issuer but has potentially lost the entire value stored on his card. In order to address the above identified issues, governments should: (1) establish solvency-related criteria for smart card issuers to meet; (2) require the insurance of the value stored on smart cards; and (3) establish a common regulatory framework for the use of such cards" (*ibidem*, 264).

9 The comparatively fast pace at which an individual may have access to the financial markets' borrowing, via a sale and securitisation of personal data, may inadvertently induce individuals to engage

The first bubble results, on the part of the same seller, from a penchant for over-selling, in need of money, these pieces of data. The second is on the part of investors, those purchasing bonds. Just as before 2007–2008 investors were confident that they had invested in securities backed by quality assets (whereas this was not true, because of a gigantic market failure), similarly the new bubble may be concerned with investors' induced misunderstanding: investors may believe they have purchased true personal data, whereas in reality the data are not genuine.

---

in practices of dubious ethical compliance. In other words, the possibility to easily get money, via a techno-synthetic system of creation of money, may engender practices where the real nature of the individuals results in being overwhelmed by a synthetic system. This, for instance, already happens in human cryo-conservation, more specifically in neuro-preservation. The ultimate purpose of the latter is to assure the passage from the human to the non-human, via mind-uploading. In doing so, through this wireless process, the entire "universe" encompassing recollections and feelings is copied into a synthetic and/or artificial being. This may show that a dearth of legislation may spark off a speculation on the speculation. The sad side of the matter, though, is that the subject of the speculation is, in this case, the human being. It is also worth mentioning that the practices are very expensive. In the vast literature, see R. Huxtable, 'Cryonics in the Courtroom: Which Interests? Whose Interests?' (2018) *Medical Law Review* 26(3), 476–499; A. Benn, 'Children: Orders with Respect to Children – Arrangements after Death' (2017) *Oxford Law Journal and Religion* 6(2), 413–415; D. Pocklington, F. Cranmer, 'JS (Disposal of Body), Re: Terminally-Ill Child – Wish to Have Her Body Cryonically Preserved after Death' (2017) *Law & Justice* 178, 147–149; R. George, 'Making Determinations during Life about the Disposal of a Body after Death' (2017) *Journal of Social Welfare and Family Law* 39(1), 109–111; M. Beard, Z. Fleetwood, 'Put to Rest?' (2017) *Trusts and Estates Law and Tax Journal* 184, 24–28; J. Moore, 'Stop Right Now' (2017) *Family Law Journal* 167, 22–24; S. Weil, 'Succession Law: Re JS' (2017) *Family Law* 47, 1254–1255. F. Minerva, *The Ethics of Cryonics: Is It Immoral to Be Immortal?*, Palgrave MacMillan, 2018; G. Shoffstall, 'Freeze, Wait, Reanimate: Cryonic Suspension and Science Fiction' (2010) *Bulletin of Science, Technology & Society* 30(4), 285–297; E. Weiss-Krejci, *The Unburied Dead*, in L.N. Stutz, S. Tarlow, *The Oxford Handbook for the Archaeology of Death and Burialm*, Oxford University Press, 2013; A. Taillander, *From Boundless Expansion to Existential Threat: Transhumanists and Posthuman Imaginaries*, in S. Kemp, J. Andersson (eds), *Future*, Oxford University Press, Oxford, 2021; R.W. Pommer, 'Donaldson v. Van de Kamp: Cryonics, Assisted Suicide, and the Challenges of Medical Science' (1993) *Journal of Contemporary Health Law and Policy* 9, 589–603; A.A. Perlin, 'To Die in Order to Live: The Need for Legislation Governing Post-Mortem Cryonic Suspension' (2007) *Southwestern University Law Review* 36(1), 35–58; D.M. Baker, 'Cryonic Preservation of Human Bodies – A Call for Legislative Action' (1994) *Dickinson Law Review* 98(4), 677–721; H. Conway, 'Frozen Corpses and Feuding Parents: Re JS (Disposal of Body)' (2018) *Modern Law Review* 81(1), 123–153; M. Swan, *Worldwide Cryonics Attitudes about the Body, Cryopreservation, and Revival: Personal Identity Malleability and a Theory of Cryonic Life Extension*, Springer, Sophia, 2019, 699–735; J. Lilley, *Transhumanism and Society: The Social Debate over Human Enhancement*, Springer, New York, 2008; P. Moore, *Enhancing Me: The Hope and Hype of Human Enhancement*, Mixed Sources, Hong Kong, 2008; D.R. Spector, 'Legal Implications of Cryonics' (1969) *Cleveland-Marshall Law Review* 18(2), 341–357; M.J. Sandel, *The Case Against Perfection. Ethics in the Age of Genetic Engineering*, Harvard University Press, Harvard, 2007; F. Minerva, A. Sandberg, 'Euthanasia and Cryothanasia' (2017) *Bioethics* 31(7), 526–533; R. Ilnicki, 'Cryonics: Technological Fictionalization of Death' (2018) *Journal for Philosophy of Culture* 4(6), 36–46; J.P. Labouffe, '"He Wants to Do What?" Cryonics: Issues in Questionable Medicine and Self-Determination' (1992) *Santa Clara Computer and High-Technology Law Journal* 8(2), 469–498.

If a securitisation relies on the role played by gatekeepers, such as the credit rating agencies, the dilemma is to assess the new and additional tasks that the gatekeeper will be required to comply with in this new heterodox securitisation; given the nature of the "assets" transferred, it is likely that the expertise required will be not only techno-financial, but also "human," or more generally not belonging to the traditional realm of finance. If the trend is towards a techno-securitisation, likewise a more technological gatekeeper will be needed.

Similar observations should be made as far as supervisors are concerned. If the *laisser-faire* is not suggested, nor is the same encouraged in this work, the latter does not purport to rekindle the prohibitionist eras, since this does not appear to be the right approach to the matter either. The right balance should be the one where the regulator, duly endowed with technological skills, is in a position to forecast the market, ultimately ensuring that action can be taken promptly.[10]

Although very few can doubt that the activity of the vehicle is that of an intermediation between lending and collection (whose combination is by definition entrepreneurial), it is more subtle to converge on the statement that the real entrepreneur of the universe of each securitisation, in actual fact, is the arranger, although, admittedly, the latter is surrounded by a myriad of satellites, as different companies such as the servicer – which is the same as the originator – the corporate services provider and others should be regarded.

Without an arranger, the *de facto supremo*, and all the actresses and actors of the securitisation that the former directs, the transferee company in itself does not seem able to operate at all. Thus, its qualification as an entrepreneur appears not so straightforward.

Therefore, in analysing the matter from the Continental point of view, it is possible to refer to the SPV, as well as for all the other vehicles or conduits used for structured finance purposes, as "derivative businesses" or "derivative enterprises." Their derivative nature is due to the fact that another entity, or even a complex of entities, is in charge of exercising the relevant business, where the vehicle is merely a formal body to which the contractual documents (or part of them) are referred. So are the activities of the business: the formal party is the vehicle, but the actual party is a different entity.

However, taking into account that in some jurisdictions scholars have developed the theory of the "hidden" entrepreneur, this sui generis business seems to be different from the one carried out by an SPV within a securitisations. While in the hidden entrepreneur there is a *supremo* which is remote from a legal perspective, but very close (if not merged and integrated) from a practical perspective, insomuch as to influence the juristical acts of the company, in the case of the SPV a different theory could be put forward, of the "remote entrepreneur" or "remote business" in relation to an opaque entity, indeed perhaps a "remote and opaque enterprise."

10 B. Batchelor, C. Janssens, 'Big Data: Understanding and Analysing Its Competitive Effects' (2020) *European Competition & Regulation Law Review* 4, X.

The *dominus* in the SPV acting at the heart of the securitisation is not hidden, unlike the one dear to some Continental scholars. Nevertheless, it handles and manages the activity of the vehicle, from the entrepreneurial point of view, via a complex and ultra-active mechanism: the securitisation transaction and the complex of activities entailed to it; documentation especially – articulated contracts – is the outcome of this invisible yet persistent mechanism.

The SPV seems to work as if it was driven by a "self-pilot," with a remote control, where everything is established *ex ante*, on the basis of contracts: unpredictable events, if any, are managed, depending on the relevance, by the servicer, the representatives of note-holders or, for the relevant cases, by the same investors.

The postulations of this theory are that on the one hand there is a "remote enterprise," which manages a business, but without really falling within the conceptual perimeter of a stereotypical entrepreneur. On the other hand, there is such a thing as an "opaque" enterprise, which is managed. As to the latter, this opacity depends on the nature of the vehicle that, as a non-bank subject, fully realises the bank disintermediation.

Such an enterprise acts as the vehicle *supremo*, whereas the same SPV seems to be the tip of a gigantic iceberg that floats, alongside others, in the cold and icy oceans of finance. The "piloted" SPV is distant, albeit formally independent, whereas the *supremo* appears to be the director and the screen-writer of the film. From an objective perspective, documents, as well as articulated contractual and negotiating relationships, are to be *de facto* referred to the *supremo*.

The new EU Securitisation Regulation, whilst aiming to create a "sun city" of simple, transparent and standardised securitised securities, which should benefit, at least theoretically, investors otherwise exposed, may not have achieved the true goal of virtuous regulation. Moreover, it still must be demonstrated whether such a new scheme, with its associated costs, can be considered justified.

Beyond the utopian purpose, distressing questions, rather than certainties, stem from securitisations and the relevant "statute" that comes from Brussels: a) who is the real entrepreneur in the context of an operation of this type; and b) can this series of contracts and documentations behind the self-piloted vehicle be considered an undertaking and, if so, whether this is a new advanced, but also burdensome, form of "car-driven" business.

The new regulation in this sense could be window-dressing, which on the one hand titillates investors, who now bask in the illusory certainty that their investments in securitised products are "safe." On the other hand, it lowers an iron curtain obscuring a complex corporate and business reality, which is not governed by individual entities (physical and corporate persons), as has traditionally been taught until now in corporate law, but rather by mathematical functions, algorithms. However, not only are the relevant contracts and parties shadow and opaque, but they are also impossible to dissect, so nebulous and caliginous is the relevant corporate structure. Despite the unfettered challenges, the new concept of the entrepreneur as a machine may potentially be a new model totally diverging from the traditional model.

Such a new structure could also be instrumental in a more complex structure of exchange of interests: the investor is guaranteed compensation should the SPV default, and this indemnity would be paid for by a safety net. In this scenario, the level of responsibility of the players – mainly the remote entrepreneur behind the vehicle – would not be clear either.

The distressing themes of market transparency,[11] in connection with the information given to investors, remain unaffected. From shadow banking to techno banking, we could be close to a new dimension of corporate law. Securitisation and its transfer of risk for investment purposes can simply confirm a phenomenon already in existence: the enterprise as both a machine and ultra-technological tool, compared to a traditional model of individual traders and business entities.

11 M. Imeson, 'Transparency Directive Is Clearly a Dogs Dinner' (2007) *Banker*, 157, 272; F. Maguire, 'Lourder Calls for Transparency' (2003) *Banker*, 153, 77–78; P.G. Dunne, 'Transparency Proposals for European Sovereign Bond Markets' (2007) *Journal of Financial Regulation and Compliance* 15(2), 186–189; I. H-Y., Chiu, 'Three Challenges Ahead for the New EU Securities' (2006) *European Business Law Review* 17(1), 121–134; F. Mausen, P. Peporte, 'Challenges under the Transparency Directive for Issuers of Debt Securities' (2011) *Capital Markets Law Journal* 6(4), 482–496; R. Graham, 'Transparency Directive Changes' (2011) *Company Secretary's Review* 35(17), 129–130; R. Veil, 'The Reform of the Transparency Regime in European Capital Markets Laws' (2013) *European Company and Financial Law Review* 10(1), 18–44; M. Eifert, A. Metzger, H. Schweitzer, G. Wagner, 'Taming the Giants: The DMA/DSA Package' (2021) *Common Market Law Review* 58(4), 987–1028; T. Murphy, 'Securities Financial Transaction Regulation – ESMA Public Statement' (2020) *Commercial Law Practitioner* 27(4), 85; J. Gould, 'Comparing the Market' (2018) *New Law Journal* 168(7817), 15–16.

Index

Printed in the USA
CPSIA information can be obtained
at www.ICGtesting.com
CBHW070020081224
18507CB00059B/803

9 781032 450810